Mentalizing in Psychodyna and Psychoanalytic Psychc

Mentalizing in Psychodynamic and Psychoanalytic Psychotherapy explains how mentalization-based therapy (MBT) can be used within the framework of psychodynamic and psychoanalytic psychotherapies.

Josef Brockmann, Holger Kirsch, and Svenja Taubner explain the outstanding importance of mentalizing for contemporary psychoanalysis and assess the essential conceptual innovations of mentalizing, focusing on outpatient individual therapies for patients with personality disorders. The book demonstrates the high connectivity of mentalizing to psychoanalysis and considers the further development of the concept of mentalizing. A practical and research-oriented work, the book documents numerous case studies, and detailed transcripts of treatment dialogs supplemented by extensive commentary to illustrate the practical application of mentalizing.

Mentalizing in Psychodynamic and Psychoanalytic Psychotherapy will be of great interest to psychoanalysts and psychoanalytic psychotherapists in training and in practice who are looking to integrate mentalizing into their work.

Josef Brockmann is a psychoanalyst and training analyst based in Frankfurt, Germany. He received advanced training in MBT with Bateman and Fonagy and has been an accredited MBT Practitioner at the Anna Freud Centre in London. He has accumulated many years of experience in psychotherapy research.

Holger Kirsch is a specialist in psychosomatic medicine and psychotherapy, psychoanalysis, and social medicine as well as a teaching analyst (DGPT/DGIP). He is a Professor at the University of Applied Sciences Darmstadt (EHD) and has his own private practice.

Svenja Taubner is a psychoanalyst, supervisor, and MBT trainer (Anna Freud Centre). She is Director of the Institute for Psychosocial Prevention at the University Hospital of Heidelberg University, full professor for psychosocial prevention, and the president of the MBT association for German-speaking countries (MBT-D-A-CH).

Mentalizing in Psychodynamic and Psychoanalytic Psychotherapy

Basics, Applications, Case Studies

Josef Brockmann, Holger Kirsch, and Svenja Taubner

LONDON AND NEW YORK

Designed cover image: Getty | patronestaff

First published in English 2025
by Routledge
4 Park Square, Milton Park, Abingdon, Oxon OX14 4RN

and by Routledge
605 Third Avenue, New York, NY 10158

Routledge is an imprint of the Taylor & Francis Group, an informa business

Published in German as *Mentalisieren in der psychodynamischen
und psychoanalytischen Psychotherapie* © 2022 Klett-Cotta – J.G.
Cotta'sche Buchhandlung Nachfolger GmbH, Stuttgart

British Library Cataloguing-in-Publication Data
A catalogue record for this book is available from the British Library

ISBN: 9781032674032 (hbk)
ISBN: 9781032673974 (pbk)
ISBN: 9781032674117 (ebk)

DOI: 10.4324/9781032674117

Typeset in Times New Roman
by codeMantra

Contents

About the Authors

Josef Brockmann, Dr. phil., is a psychoanalyst and training analyst. He is a psychotherapist and psychoanalyst in private practice in Frankfurt. He received advanced training in MBT with Bateman and Fonagy, and is an accredited MBT Practitioner (Anna Freud Centre). He has accumulated many years of experience in psychotherapy research.

Holger Kirsch, Prof. Dr. med., is a specialist in psychosomatic medicine and psychotherapy, psychoanalysis, and social medicine as well as a teaching analyst (DGPT/DGIP). He is a professor at the University of Applied Sciences Darmstadt (EHD) and has his own private practice as well.

Svenja Taubner, Univ.-Prof. Dr. phil., is a psychoanalyst, supervisor, and MBT trainer (Anna Freud Centre). She is Director of the Institute for Psychosocial Prevention at the University Hospital of Heidelberg University, full professor for psychosocial prevention, and the president of the MBT association for German-speaking countries (MBT-D-A-CH).

Foreword by Peter Fonagy

This book has my applause and welcome! As is often the case when things are still in the making, the new, needing to establish its identity and autonomy, may find itself separated from its origins; possibly, intoxicated by its newness, it may not want to acknowledge the connection with its roots and antecedents, thus depriving itself of a constant source of inspiration. As mentalization-based therapy (MBT) reached its chronological and arguably psychological adolescence, it, like its adolescent counterpart, the adolescent, turned away from the family of origin and increasingly came under the influence of its new friends in the world of psychosocial therapies—developmental psychology, evidence-based practice, third-wave cognitive behavioral therapy, neuroscience, "philosophy of mind," anthropology, social psychology, and so on. And yet, historically and intellectually, the origins of MBT lie in psychoanalysis and psychodynamic psychotherapy (Fonagy, 1991). Over the past 15 years, MBT has evolved into an integrative model that emphasizes social understanding and its many components, i.e., social referencing, social attention, empathy, imitation, tapping into desires and cognitions, and developing self-awareness (Bateman & Fonagy, 2019). What was unique about the MBT approach, however, was what psychoanalytic thinking contributed to it.

MBT arrived in the world on the wave of success of the theory of mind. Theory of mind served decades ago as the first label to describe the ability to explain a behavior based on the mental processes of the person in question. The concept underwent a dressing up in the story of a doll and her no longer accurate view of where a piece of chocolate was kept (the chocolate had been moved elsewhere in her absence), and drew literally thousands of experimental investigations (Devine & Hughes, 2018; Imuta et al., 2016; Wellman et al., 2001). As the theory of mind topic gained momentum, a plethora of experimental designs and philosophical conceptualizations were stuffed into the narrow suitcase of "one theory of mind possession" (recall, for example, Daniel C. Dennett's concept of "intentional attitude"; Dennett, 1987). Because the term theory of mind did not allow a clean separation between the concept and an experimental design, and because using the noun risked reifying an activity or process, the same alternative term—"mentalizing"— was brought into play in each case independently by two psychologists who represented completely different traditions: Uta Frith introduced it in her cognitive psychological description of autism (Frith, 1989), while George Moran, then director of the Anna Freud Centre, and I (Fonagy, 1989) addressed it from a psychoanalytic perspective and under the influence of both attachment theory and an important French tradition in psychosomatics (Lebovici, 1967). Although it is now 35 years ago, I remember clearly when I first presented the idea at UCL, whose psychology faculty at the time was almost invariably cognitivist in orientation. Opposition came from those who believed autism was the paradigmatic example of a failure to mentalize and that individuals with this diagnosis were as likely to be securely attached as children who were developing normally. Mentalizing was considered by these listeners to be an ability that unfolds independently of social experiences, and corresponding deficits reflected, in their eyes, biological—presumably genetic—vulnerabilities. On this point, even the most ardent advocates of the cognitivist position have since relented somewhat (e.g., Brink et al., 2015).

Where MBT sought to forge a new and distinct path was in placing the ability to perceive and interpret human behavior regarding intentional mental states in a dynamic context. Even in its original formulation, MBT went beyond the then-common definition of an evolutionarily selected ability that enabled optimal decision-making for the best of the person and the community and learning from others, while at the same time promoting competition, allowing evaluation of others, and predicting their behavior. MBT theory affirmed that mentalizing does all this and more. But mentalizing also entails imagining detached from reality; it entails myriad contextual factors, it entails skewed assumptions and distortions of understanding, behind which in turn lie irrelevant information, inaccurate beliefs, biased values, and overt prejudices, prompted by the identity and group status of individuals in interaction (see also Park et al., 2021). In a series of papers, Mary Target and I have attempted to address this complexity (Fonagy & Target, 1996a, 2000, 2007a; Target & Fonagy, 1996). We linked mentalizing to Freud's concept of psychic reality and proposed a number of heuristics that contributed to a more sophisticated use of the term "symbolization" in psychoanalysis. We also tried to reconcile our thinking with both Wilfred Bion (alpha function) and Donald Winnicott (mirroring and containment). Not that we succeeded—but we did make a conscious and voluntary attempt not to insist on originality where it did not exist. The psychoanalytic community, at least in the United Kingdom, did not embrace the concept of mentalizing. Notwithstanding our persistent efforts to publish in psychoanalytic journals (e.g., Fonagy & Allison 2016; Fonagy & Target, 1995, 2007b), mentalizing was not a topic that appeared on the agenda of the British Psychoanalytic Society.

This, as I now realize with some delay on reading this outstanding book, was not an indication of narrow-mindedness on the part of our psychoanalytic colleagues (not that they were not guilty of narrow-mindedness in other cases, for example). It was our lack of concern with the question of how key psychoanalytic ideas could be rendered in terms or in the language of the mentalization concept. What key ideas are we talking about? There are an overwhelming number of psychoanalytic theories, and Freud himself published much more on the theory than on the practice of psychoanalysis (Fonagy, 1999b). Where is the unconscious in MBT?

Where are the defense mechanisms? Where are the agents of human unhappiness-aggressiveness, envy, perversion, narcissism, and the mainstay of psychoanalytic thought, sexuality? We have made modest efforts to approach the latter construct (Fonagy, 2008), but by and large MBT has omitted the major conceptual drivers of object relations thinking such as the defense organization, the paranoid-schizoid position, and, more fundamentally, psychological conflict. Without drawing a grand analogy here, I do think that John Bowlby found himself in a similar situation when he tried to introduce ideas from the neighboring discipline of ethology into psychoanalytic thinking (e.g., Bowlby, 1981, 1984). He saw it as a challenging task to make the connections necessary to make attachment theory applicable to clinicians whose ideas had developed under the influence of the complex matrix of transference and countertransference. To a much lesser extent, mentalization theory, also an orphan among disciplines adjacent to psychoanalysis, is rejected by both cognitive neuroscientists and serious psychoanalytic thinkers. The former consider the implementation of neuroscientific constructs and research in our theories to be both simplistic and potentially naïve, as recent advances such as the default mode network (DMN) are inadequately addressed in mentalization theory (Gilead & Ochsner, 2021). The latter find little new in MBT and lament the disappearance of complexity and subtlety when subjectivity is reduced to mental equivalence, "pretend mode," and teleological function (Hoffman, 2004, 2009).

So now, by bringing the psychodynamic back into mentalizing, I very much hope that the authors are taking a real step toward reconciling MBT and psychoanalysis. I have frequent occasion to reflect on Joseph Sandler's contribution to psychoanalytic thought (Sandler, 1987), which I have long admired and still find illuminating and important. In introducing a distinctly cognitivist model, which Sandler called the "basic model of psychoanalysis" (Sandler & Joffe, 1969), he simultaneously introduced the concept of the representational world (Sandler & Rosenblatt, 1962). In doing so, he brought psychoanalysis into line with the dominant theoretical frame of reference of the 1950s and 1960s: structuralism and schema theory. Although he did not receive credit for this from many quarters, the quiet revolution that he and his colleagues at the Hampstead Clinic brought to psychoanalysis and psychoanalytic thinking became the plausible platform for object relations theory, which reconnected psychoanalytic thinking with the social scientific thinking of the late 20th century (Fonagy & Cooper, 1999).

How did he accomplish this? He focused his attention on the so-called Hampstead Index—the case reports of children and adolescents from the Hampstead Child Therapy Clinic that he found at the Anna Freud Centre—and incorporated a substantial number of the ideas it contained into his mental schema of self and object representations and the emotional responses that governed them (Sandler, 1962). The model was robust enough to support Otto Kernberg's extraordinarily creative theories and continued to hold even in the face of the relational turn in psychoanalytic thought. Sandler's reflections formed a bridge between ego psychology and object relations theory as conceived by the proponents of interpersonal psychoanalysis as well as by the Klein–Bion model and by the independent so-called British tradition. And here is the gap that the present book seeks to close. We made a mistake; MBT did not make the connection. We needed a bridge to look at clinical cases, therapies of real people, simultaneously from the traditional perspective and from the new theoretical perspective, and that is precisely what this book does so eloquently. We cannot integrate mentalizing into psychodynamic thinking unless we come to an understanding by focusing on the shared reality of clinical encounters.

But let us pause for a moment! Isn't this precisely what is meant by mentalizing? Isn't mentalizing, for instance, about creating a two-level structure, or about a common object being examined by two mental systems that coordinate their respective perspectives? Isn't it about a common focus that allows different perspectives to be acknowledged? After all, isn't our theory about coordinating one's perspective with the perspective and mental state of another individual when the focus is on an objective, actual physical reality "out there"? Have we not come to understand that by mentalizing we are matching our own subjectivity with the perceived subjectivity of another person whose physical reality is being referred to? If we look at things this way, our inability to develop a shared model with our psychodynamically oriented colleagues clearly amounts to a failure of mentalizing. Regarding the polarities of mentalizing heuristics, Patrick Luyten and I (Fonagy & Luyten, 2009; Luyten et al., 2019) have been guilty of unbalanced mentalizing. This refers less to the overemphasis of the cognitive over the affective, which many see as a major weakness of the MBT approach, than to the lack of balance between self and object. In our efforts to reduce the influence of the object on the self, to defend our perhaps fragile, rudimentary model against the far more sophisticated and advanced psychodynamic thought, we have repeatedly emphasized our own position with vigor, without seriously questioning the perspective of our psychodynamically oriented colleagues on the same clinical world.

And, as MBT teaches us, if we find that mentalizing is not succeeding—where there is no way around the complexity of the tasks our mental system faces—then we have no choice but to be humble and perhaps offer an apology. The apology includes taking responsibility for an error committed—or rather, in this case, an error of omission. I hope and wish that this book will help to close what I see as a very deplorable gap indeed. MBT could not have emerged without the psychoanalytic background of its founders George Moran, Anthony Bateman, George Gergely, Mary Target, and many others. In individual cases, members of the mentalization family have attempted to develop a dual structure. The present book, however, is the first to aim seriously and directly at tackling this task. For the sake of the mentalization family as a whole, but far more for my own, I would like to thank these remarkable authors for the most comprehensive account to date that allows us to think together mentalization theory as it has developed and its original frame of reference within the psychoanalytic corpus. Not only is this a unique book, it is also a highly creative contribution to the literature that I urgently hope will draw many more initiatives and thus bring psychoanalysis back into fruitful conversation with mentalization theory. It is late, but by no means too late.

Introduction

Using a mentalization-oriented approach changes psychotherapeutic practice and makes it easier to work with "difficult patients." This stems from the attitude that assumes that "difficult" patients are primarily people who are just difficult to reach. Likewise, the rule is that adopting a mentalization-based stance and using it to structure the treatment of difficult patients makes such treatments more successful. The participant in one of our training courses put it this way in a feedback: "I am very pleased with how much my work is improving. I have much less stress and pressure to perform, which leads to experiencing more from people. I can attend to the patient more, which increases the quality of my work." Of course, our personal experience is one thing; empirical evidence is another. Yet, empirical evidence obtained from the results of psychotherapy research supports this approach: Mentalization-based therapy (MBT) is one of the recognized evidence-based treatments, e.g., for borderline personality disorder (BPD) (see Chapter 3).

Another Book on the Mentalization Concept?

More decidedly than others, this book attempts to relate the mentalization concept to long-term psychodynamic and psychoanalytic psychotherapy, focusing on structural disorders, though not exclusively. This book addresses the interface between MBT, psychoanalysis, and psychodynamic and psychoanalytic psychotherapy from both theoretical and practical perspectives. In doing so, we boldly claim that the mentalization approach contributes to expanding the corpus of psychoanalytic models—and we do our best to prove it. It is our hope that the times now lie behind us when psychoanalytic colleagues brand something new (e.g., results oriented toward psychotherapy research) as "not belonging to psychoanalysis," as an "act of dilution," or—to put it mildly—as part of the "ecumenical umbrella"—as something tolerated even if one ultimately knows that one's opponent is wrong. Nevertheless, the danger remains that what is deemed "development"—in the sense of adaptation to research findings and newer insights—is experienced as undermining psychoanalysis (Lemma & Johnson, 2010).

The crucial weakness of the mentalization approach is simultaneously its strength: It moves away from some traditional psychoanalytic concepts, taking

DOI: 10.4324/9781032674117-1

up the results gained in neighboring sciences for the past 20 years (Fonagy et al., 2002). At the same time, in its theoretical assumptions, the mentalization concept is closely related to the very foundations of psychoanalysis, e.g., in self-development, the importance of representations or object relations, and attachment theory. In this respect, it can also be understood as an enrichment of psychoanalysis.

However, the differences between MBT and classical psychoanalysis are greatest when it comes to treatment techniques. The book defends its own vantage point because the setting, forms of intervention, and therapeutic stance of MBT differ from those of traditional psychoanalytic treatment. Whereas MBT originally referred to a partial inpatient treatment program comprising individual and group therapy, traditional psychoanalytic treatment with its three to four sessions per week in the supine position is practically no longer found in psychotherapeutic care—and indeed is increasingly being questioned even by psychoanalysts for the treatment of severely impaired patients (Yeomans et al., 2015).

This book attempts to bridge the contrast between psychoanalytic and mentalization-based models. Yet, our attempt at integration demands further discussion. From our long-term experience with both models, we believe that new common perspectives may emerge, taking evolving psychotherapy research and its findings into account.

Mentalization as a General Model for Psychotherapy

We derive our claims of the mentalization concept as a bridge from our conviction that promoting mentalization is the central, common impact factor among all therapeutic "techniques." Currently, we know of about 400 therapeutic techniques, and the number increases every year. So, should therapists expect that—finally—the longed-for innovative and effective procedure has been developed that delivers the desired success? The results of therapy research are clear: No! Evidence-based treatment methods are about equally as effective in a systematic comparison. But the fact remains that some therapists are more effective than others.

We also know that psychotherapy works mainly through common factors, the most important of which is the therapeutic relationship. Further, diagnostic research suggests we can best explain personality disorders by referencing a common so-called P-factor (which stands for general psychopathology). Therefore, a transdiagnostic and person-specific therapeutic approach is more useful in severely impaired patients than a disorder-specific one. These findings on the personality disorder dimension (P-factor) indirectly support the common-factor conception.

However, the common-factor model raises as many questions in the scientific discussion as it explains (see Chapter 1). On the one hand, the general factors need to be more specific; on the other hand, in addition to the general impact factors, specific interventions can affect specific disorders. Yet their share in treatment success remains unclear, because specific treatment techniques and interventions equally realize the general impact factors.

Directly or indirectly, all *effective* psychotherapies promote mentalizing ability and epistemic trust. They enable the patient's access to social learning within and outside the therapeutic relationship and point the way to new, "healthier" relational contexts (salutogenesis). The mentalization concept understands a personality disorder as a failure of communication and a complication in social learning—not as a failure of the individual. Therefore, from this point of view, therapy always aims to change communication systems.

When we teach the mentalization concept to experienced clinicians, they rarely experience the mentalization concept and practical approach as incompatible with their previous, familiar concepts. Rather, mentalization is considered a bridging concept that focuses on processes already implicitly or explicitly present in various therapeutic models. We are therefore convinced that the mentalization approach passes the reality test as a bridge concept. Nevertheless, two obstacles block the path of the bridge concept which do not stem immediately from the concept but from its mediation. Today, all therapeutic concepts include mentalization and the mentalization concept, only to then explicitly or implicitly conclude: "That's what we (already) do." This is effectively a defensive stance, perhaps coupled with a basic misunderstanding. It is certainly not integration. The second obstacle lies in mentalization being misunderstood as cognitive empathy or affective cognition. This absolves one from truly dealing with the mentalization concept and its associated treatment technique. The mentalization approach, together with its intervention techniques, manifests great clarity: It is easily teachable and easily learnable. On the other hand, a great danger lies in learning the techniques only schematically, neglecting the necessary creativity and therapeutic attitude that lie in the background and determine the success of the technique as well as an understanding of the therapeutic relationship, determined by unconscious processes and reenactments. The mentalization approach *needs* psychoanalysis, just as modern psychoanalysis *needs* the mentalization approach.

The Inclusion of Recent Developments

The book considers recent developments in the mentalization approach. These include:

- The further elaboration of the concept of epistemic trust in theoretical and practical aspects and regarding the therapeutic relationship (see Chapter 2.4, Chapter 6.2).
- The concept of mentalized affectivity and its implementation in psychotherapy (see Chapter 5.1). This approach extends the scope of MBT to patients with more mature structures, i.e., patients in whom the mentalizing capacity is more likely to break down because of conflict and situation. It views the processing of conflicts (content) and the recovery of mentalization ability (process) as a change in priority—a change of perspective regarding a foreground (conflict)

and a background (mentalizing ability), where working on the background is a prerequisite for working on the foreground in structural disorders.

- The incorporation of recent findings in psychotherapy research using the model of general effects (Wampold, 2015; Wampold & Imel 2015) and recent findings on the general P-factor (Caspi et al., 2014; Sharp et al., 2015), which suggests a "transdiagnostic view" and eliminates the need to differentiate between self- and interpersonal functioning deficit and the conflict model. Both findings provide evidence for the mentalization concept as a bridging concept in psychotherapy (see Chapter 1).

- In recent years, Fonagy and colleagues have contributed further theoretical considerations to the mentalization approach, considered here. How do unconscious processes and consciousness relate to each other? What is the role of libidinal impulses such as sexuality and aggression within this model (see Chapter 4)? These considerations not only have theoretical relevance, they can also influence the mentalizing attitude and treatment.

The Treatment Technique

Not only is the theory of mentalization attractive for therapists, but especially the presence of a treatment technique experienced as congruent and convincing makes it inviting. Further, it is based on developmental psychological (disturbance) models and has a high degree of transparency, both in the therapeutic process and in the actions and attitudes of the psychotherapist.

The mentalization-based treatment technique (see Chapter 3) mediates this transparency and includes an attitude oriented toward cooperation and a shared understanding. For example, the therapeutic stance of "not-knowing" is linked to the view that there are no right and wrong interventions, only different perspectives (and mistakes) that lend themselves to correction. It is an open approach toward mistakes and misunderstandings. Indeed, mistakes are valuable; they allow reflection on the therapeutic process, and they allow us to improve our ability to apply mentalization to deal with misunderstandings—or just to apologize for a mistake. Anyone who tries too hard not to make mistakes becomes rigid and inauthentic. The participants in our training sessions often discovered this attitude toward mistakes.

Two Parallel Developments

The mentalization concept has evolved over the course of two decades, spawning many differentiations.

First, MBT became a trademark, characterized by a manualized form of treatment backed by research. Today, MBT has fixed treatment components and treatment times to meet research criteria (see Chapter 3). The authors emphasize the opportunities of applying an evidence-based treatment form as a "best practice" for various disturbance patterns. Currently, this is valid for the treatment of borderline patients. MBT is characterized by a clear indication for treating structural disorders or severe personality disorders. It is considered a new treatment technique, not a new treatment procedure.

Second, the mentalization approach developed as a building block in psychodynamic and psychoanalytic psychotherapy: "MBT is a focus for therapy rather than a specific therapy in itself" (Bateman & Fonagy, 2016, p. 159). In this respect, MBT has transformed psychoanalytically based forms of treatment and their treatment techniques, while also providing new perspectives on psychoanalytic models. Several publications by renowned psychoanalysts in Germany support the link between psychoanalysis and mentalization (e.g., Altmeyer & Thomä, 2016; Mertens, 2012; Schultz-Venrath & Döring, 2011).

An Integrative Model

The therapy guidelines valid in Germany allow for long-term outpatient therapies, whereas these possibilities are considerably limited in the Anglo-American countries. Because the restoration (or development) of mentalization in severe personality disorders takes considerable time, opportunities arise in practice to combine the mentalization concept with psychodynamic and psychoanalytic long-term psychotherapy and to further justify the need for long-term therapies through an integrative model (see Chapter 5.7). We believe that the mentalization concept, particularly because of its process orientation, therapeutic stance, and mentalization-enhancing interventions, is useful for psychodynamic and psychoanalytic psychotherapies—not just in treating severe personality disorders with general impairments of self- and interpersonal functioning but also affective disorders. The integrative model has two foci: the *process focus* (promoting mentalizing) and the *content focus* (interpreting conscious and unconscious interpersonal patterns). Proposals by Lemma, Target, and Fonagy have guided its development (Lemma et al., 2011).

The mentalization approach fundamentally changes psychodynamic and psychoanalytic therapy, primarily through the process focus, the targeted promotion of mentalization with typical MBT interventions, and the broad consideration of findings from psychotherapy research. Specifically, the regulation of emotional arousals, the emphasis on affect in social interactions, and ongoing reflection on the therapeutic relationship with attention to epistemic trust as a central aspect of the therapeutic relationship stand out. To be sure, the central focus lies in promoting mentalization, but it is not an end in itself. Rather, the goal is to promote social-learning processes within and outside of therapy sessions, which is also served by including interpretations of conscious and unconscious patterns based on object-relations theories.

Chapter 6 contains detailed case examples, presenting and commenting on several episodes from psychotherapies that attempt to implement the mentalization-oriented approach, from both mentalization-oriented and traditional psychoanalytic perspectives. The book concludes with an outlook on possible consequences for education and training: the mentalization skills of therapists.

1

Characteristics of a Modern Psychotherapy

Psychotherapy research is not particularly popular or widely received among psychotherapists. Practitioners tend to base their expertise more on their training, experience, colleagues, and supervision and less on research findings (Castonguay et al., 2015). Psychotherapists level their criticism at research methods, the small-scale findings, the lack of connection to everyday practice, and sometimes the poor replicability of some results. Nonetheless, there is some pressure for legitimacy on the part of healthcare systems, which demand evidence-based practice—and various ideas about evidence-based practice do exist. However, acceptance of psychotherapy research among psychotherapists does seem to be on the rise (Taubner et al., 2014), perhaps because researchers and practitioners recently became more concerned with the other party and have formed research-practice networks to narrow the gap between practice and research. New therapeutic methods such as MBT emerged from these research-practice networks. We consider MBT a method that meets the demands of both practitioners and researchers for a modern psychotherapeutic method. To this end, we want to highlight the demands of psychotherapy research, evidence-based practice, and ideas about effective mechanisms of action and apply them to MBT.

This chapter begins by presenting the current state of affairs regarding the effectiveness of MBT with various disorders. We then introduce current findings on common and specific factors in psychotherapy. Further, we present the assumed common and specific mechanisms of change in MBT. The most important aspect is the stabilization or enhancement of mentalization as the central mechanism of change in MBT and the establishment of epistemic trust. The chapter ends with a summary of the current evidence on change mechanisms in mentalization through MBT or psychotherapy in general.

Allen, Fonagy, and Bateman identified change in mentalization as a mechanism of change (Allen et al., 2008) significant to all psychotherapies; they thus classify mentalization as a general mechanism of change, albeit one that lies in the focus of diagnosis and intervention of MBT. Indeed, in the recent conceptualization of MBT, improving mentalization could be understood as a mediator; that is, a measurable, modifiable variable that acts as a catalyst of the central mechanism of change, reestablishing social learning through functional epistemic trust (Fonagy et al., 2017a).

DOI: 10.4324/9781032674117-2

1.1   The Effectiveness of Psychotherapy and MBT

Empirical psychotherapy research can look back on a nearly 70-year history. After initially focusing on the general effectiveness of psychotherapy ("legitimation phase"), researchers later took up comparative studies to investigate the differential efficacy of various therapeutic approaches. This so-called "competitive phase" continues to this day and is sustained by the demands of evidence-based medicine. To be considered effective within the framework of evidence-based medicine, specific interventions or methods must prove that the measured effects do not occur without their expressed use, and that they cannot be attributed to any other influencing factors. To this end, the current guidelines rely almost exclusively on randomized controlled trials (RCTs) that randomly assign patients to the treatments to be compared, examine homogeneous, monosymptomatic disorders, and use standardized treatments, whereby therapist adherence is ensured via adherence testing. According to Chambless and Hollon (1998), one distinguishes different levels of evidence based on the available evidence. Methods are considered effective if proven more effective than a comparison group in meta-analyses of several RCTs (evidence level 1a) or if at least two RCTs of independent groups are available (evidence level 1b).

Meta-analyses and meta-meta-analyses show medium to large effects (Lambert, 2013) regarding the effectiveness of psychotherapy compared with no treatment (spontaneous remission) as well as with placebo (e.g., support groups, bibliotherapy, treatment-as-usual, structured clinical management). Today, there can be no doubt that psychotherapy is an effective treatment for mental disorders, and in many guidelines, it is indeed recommended as the treatment of first choice, either before pharmacotherapy or complementary to pharmacotherapy.

There are many efficacy studies of MBT in patients with borderline personality disorder (BPD), for whom MBT treatment was initially developed. This includes many RCTs contained in the meta-analyses and systematic reviews to assess the efficacy of MBT for BPD. MBT proved more effective than other treatments in adults with BPD and adolescents with self-injurious behavior. MBT also had greater effects in treating self-injury, suicidality, rehospitalization, overall symptom burden, and the severity of BPD than nonpsychological therapy, such as structured clinical management. In addition, studies revealed positive effects on social functioning levels and vocational reintegration. Like other disorder-specific psychological therapies for BPD, with its medium effect sizes, MBT reveals its superiority over nonspecialized psychological therapies (Oud et al., 2018). In light of such evidence, MBT can be considered effective and evidence-based for treating BPD and in many guidelines is subsequently recommended as a first-line treatment for BPD, along with other BPD-specific therapies (Simonsen et al., 2019).

In recent years, efficacy studies of MBT have been scrutinized regarding their translation into clinical practice. This means analyzing more complex diagnoses and different treatment settings, such as the difference between its application in day hospitals and outpatient settings. Efficacy studies have shown promising results for comorbid disorders, enabling the successful treatment of more complex disorders (BPD with addiction, eating disorders, antisocial personality) with MBT (Volkert et al., 2019). However, we need further studies to overcome the methodological problems and uncertainties that affect the entire field of evidence-based, disorder-specific BPD therapies (Storebø et al., 2020). A Danish study among adolescents with BPD (Jørgensen et al., 2021) furthermore showed that a pure MBT group offer is not well suited for adolescents with low mentalizing skills, whereas individual therapy does seem to be indicated.

To date, there have been two studies on MBT in the German-speaking countries. A randomized study (Brand et al., 2016) investigated psychodynamic group therapy with MBT group therapy in the context of day-hospital treatment; the patient group included a variety of disturbance patterns. Using a large sample ($N = 211$), the authors found no differences between the MBT group and the psychodynamic group, with both therapies showing high pre-post changes. This raises the question of whether MBT is more effective than other psychological therapy only when dealing with BPD patients, or whether the other therapy components of the day-hospital setting explain much of the results. Since group therapy-only studies of MBT have so far been effective overall—but not more effective than comparison group therapies—one might conclude that its superiority stems solely from the combination of individual and group settings. (In its original form, MBT was a partial hospitalization treatment with a combination of individual and group therapy.) On the other hand, the results could also be subject to the equivalence paradox in psychotherapy research (see below).

A study in the German-speaking countries, part of a pilot and feasibility design (Taubner et al., 2020), investigated whether MBT is feasible for adolescents with conduct disorder. Because of the small sample, however, it is not yet possible to draw generalizable conclusions about its effectiveness. Nevertheless, it did show a significant reduction in empathy pathology as well as a reduction in diagnoses. The study clearly showed that modifications are necessary to the MBT setting and the MBT interventions for these patients (family therapy instead of group therapy, motivational interviewing to build up a motivation to change, even stronger relationship building with emphasis on a rewarding attitude), and that only limited accompanying research can take place. In light of the adaptations of the core model, MBT seems promising for adolescent conduct disorder.

In summary, as a modern form of psychotherapy, MBT meets the requirements of evidence-based medicine, and various research groups have initiated efficacy research in randomized controlled trials. Regarding BPD-specific therapies, MBT is the most studied method after dialectical behavioral therapy.

1.2   Change Mechanism Models

Despite the evident efficacy of psychotherapy in general over other treatments for mental illness, many psychotherapy studies comparing psychological therapies showed little to no differences between different methods (e.g., interpersonal therapy vs. cognitive behavioral therapy for depression, Cuijpers et al., 2011; or the studies on the efficacy of MBT group therapy, see above). In psychotherapy research, this is called the "equivalence paradox" or the so-called "Dodo Bird verdict" after the story of *Alice in Wonderland* by Lewis Carroll (1865). In *Alice in Wonderland*, following a race, the Dodo Bird declares that all participants have won, and therefore all deserve a prize. In the story, however, the race has no common starting point and no common finishing point, which is also emblematic of the situation of psychotherapy research: Different therapeutic methods have different ideas of change and target the parameters of psychotherapy; it is an ongoing process to agree on universally valid standards. Some have attributed the general effectiveness of all therapy methods to common change factors (against the background of the Dodo Bird verdict). Indeed, these proved empirically to be robust explanatory variables that account for differences in outcome (Wampold & Imel, 2015). However, other studies of specific disorders, such as those applying exposure methods with response prevention for phobias or obsessive-compulsive disorders, revealed that specific treatment approaches were superior (DeRubeis et al., 2005). This, in turn, was interpreted regarding specific change mechanisms, which, like a specific drug, are thought to work only for specific problems. However, meta-analyses examining the relationship between therapist adherence (i.e., consistency of the therapist's interventions with those of the agreed-upon therapy method) and therapy outcome regarding the use of procedure- or method-specific interventions have so far shown no or only small associations (Collyer et al., 2020; Webb et al., 2010).

Therefore, we can summarize the current state of psychotherapy research as follows: Psychotherapy is effective, but disagreement remains about whether and which procedures are more effective as well as ambiguity about exactly how psychotherapy works, i.e., what mechanisms of change underlie therapeutic success.

1.3   Common Change Mechanisms and MBT

The common factors model, also referred to as the contextual model, attributes the effects of psychotherapy to therapeutic factors that are (implicitly) present in all psychotherapy procedures. Common change factors produce therapeutic change, are not explicitly embodied in a psychotherapy model, are not specific to a particular form of psychotherapy, and are not specifically effective for a particular mental disorder. However, common factors are not nonspecific, as they are sometimes erroneously called, since some have been theoretically specified, such as Bordin's therapeutic alliance. According to Bordin (1979), a therapeutic alliance consists of three different components: 1) a positive emotional, trusting relationship ("bond") between patient and therapist; 2) an agreement between patient and therapist regarding "tasks"; and 3) an agreement regarding "goals." The STA-R Questionnaire (Brockmann et al., 2011) added a further component, the "self-opening of the patient." Furthermore, common factors are not the same as the placebo effect. Although a placebo effect is based primarily on an expectation of improvement, building the patient's expectations of improvement is not an accidental by-product of therapy but rather depends on the quality of the therapy, e.g., providing a credible model of the mental problem. Therefore, although we can classify the successful establishment of ameliorative expectations as a common factor (therapy- and disorder-unspecific), it does not explain how other common factors work.

Empirical findings reveal that the following components of the therapeutic relationship are particularly related to a positive therapy outcome: quality of the general therapeutic alliance, empathy, appreciation and affirmation, goal consensus, cohesion of group therapies, and systematic patient feedback. Therapist congruence and authenticity, working in real relationships, fostering the emotional expression of patients, promoting positive expectations, managing countertransference, repairing alliance ruptures ("rupture and repair"), and an appreciation for patient cooperation (also mediated by transparency about the process) are also likely to be effective. Other promising, but understudied, aspects include controlled self-disclosure and therapist immediacy (Norcross & Lambert, 2019).

MBT promotes general impact factors through various elements present in the therapeutic relationship, the therapeutic stance, and the therapy components. MBT relies heavily on an appreciative, empathic, and validating therapeutic stance and focuses on misunderstandings in the relationship and working through them entirely in the spirit of rupture/repair. Since it uses the therapist–patient relationship as the object of mentalization training, it focuses on working within the real relationship and in controlled self-disclosures. MBT training, the therapy itself, and the supervision thereof all focus on explicitly elaborating the therapist's feelings to support the constructive use of countertransference patterns. Based on their presumed psychoeducation and use of explanatory therapeutic behavior, therapists should establish transparency and actively involve the patient in the therapy. A written formulation of the therapeutic focus also contributes to maintaining transparency about how one understands the disorder and the further MBT procedure; further, it should promote an expectation of improvement. Consequently, MBT builds strongly on the common factors.

1.4   Specific Change Factors in MBT

Specific techniques are the applied assumed specific factors depending on the therapeutic school or disorder, such as Socratic dialog or free association. The goal of MBT is to maintain the patient's ability to mentalize where it has already succeeded—and to improve it where impaired mentalization has triggered symptoms and interpersonal problems. MBT's specific theory of change can be expressed simply as follows: Improved mentalization creates a mental buffer between feelings and actions, allowing reflection on conflicting interpersonal experiences and complex affects. Patients learn to think before they act—to reflect before they act. Improving mentalization in the therapeutic relationship depends on strengthening trust in socially mediated information, the so-called epistemic trust.

One achieves the general therapeutic goal of MBT by using MBT-specific techniques, such as applying functional mentalization analysis regarding symptom behavior, addressing nonmentalizing modes, or discussing the affect focus between patient and therapist. Various studies have addressed change in mentalization as a mediator or mechanism of change in different therapy methods (cf. Katznelson, 2014). They established a correlation between increasing mentalization and decreasing symptoms in the treatment of depression in CBT (Ekeblad et al., 2016), for patients with BPD in a psychodynamic inpatient long-term treatment (Meulemeester et al., 2018), and for patients with eating disorders in a day-hospital setting (Kuipers et al., 2017). An RCT study with eating-disordered patients discovered a relationship between change in mentalization and outcome only in psychodynamic treatment, not in CBT treatment (Katznelson et al., 2020). Another RCT study on the treatment of self-injuring adolescents also found this correlation only in the MBT and not in the control condition (Rossouw & Fonagy, 2012).

Two RCTs with BPD patients (Kivity et al., 2019; Möller et al., 2017) studied the ability of therapeutic interventions to increase mentalization. They showed that mentalization-enhancing interventions produced higher mentalization ability in subsequent patient responses in both MBT and transference-focused therapy (TFP). This effect was stronger in TFP than in both schema therapy and dialectical behavioral therapy (Kivity et al., 2019).

Findings from single-case research and process-outcome studies thus far support the notion that increasing mentalization indeed represents a significant change mechanism of psychotherapy. However, that improvement in mentalization is related to improved outcome has been reported not only for treating BPD but also for depression, eating disorders, and anxiety disorders. Moreover, this relationship is not specific to MBT; it is equally operative in other psychodynamic and behavioral therapy methods. For example, under specific conditions, psychoanalytic treatment techniques such as containing and interpreting can promote mentalization, and behavioral therapy skills training can indirectly serve this function as well. In contrast, other studies found evidence that the change mechanism is specific to MBT or psychodynamic therapy. If mentalization change were a general impact factor, it could be implemented in other therapy approaches and used transdiagnostically when mentalization difficulties are present. But few studies have examined the effect experimentally, e.g., through a controlled variation of mentalization-enhancing interventions.

1.5   Integrative Change Models and MBT as an Integrative Psychotherapy Method

In the past, general and specific change factors were often presented as mutually exclusive, leading to the division of psychotherapy researchers into different "camps." One branch of psychotherapy research pursues the hypothesis that therapeutic efficacy is grounded primarily in general impact factors, whereas another branch of psychotherapy research puts the effect of specific impact factors at the center of its efficacy models. Cuijpers et al. (2019) attest that neither side has a firm empirical basis for deciding the conflict between the contextual and specific efficacy models. This led to the proposal of an integrative change model that combines common and specific factors rather than pitting them against each other. The dichotomous juxtaposition of specific and common change models contradicts the evidence; it is based on conceptual inconsistencies, as both common and specific impact factors can be related to a positive therapeutic outcome. While common factors refer to the various levels of the therapeutic process, specific factors (or techniques), on the other hand, address only the process level of therapeutic action (Orlinsky et al., 2004). Common factors address, for example, the relational level (therapist–patient relationship), the intrapersonal level (patient variables), and the level of therapeutic change (changes brought about by therapy) (Castonguay & Beutler, 2005). Common factors are realized through specific techniques, and the therapeutic alliance is the primary vehicle for determining whether specific techniques can be successfully realized (Goldfried & Davila, 2005). Thus, aspects of common and specific change factors are not independent of each other but interact in conjunction with other conditions, such as disease-related aspects and other patient characteristics. To optimize psychotherapy, we should pay particular attention to both aspects of the therapeutic process and implement them systematically.

According to the integrative approach, a successful therapy should comprise the following aspects:

a) a strong working alliance between therapist and patient;
b) a therapeutic setting pursuant to trust;
c) a psychologically grounded model of disturbance;
d) an adaptive model of change;
e) a set of specific techniques or rituals that initiate a positive process on the part of the patient.

Integrative approaches thrive on conceptualizing their technical approach by strategically aligning with general impact factors while flexibly adapting to each patient's condition.

As a modern therapeutic method, MBT combines various techniques from other successful therapies (e.g., psychodynamic, systemic, client-centered, cognitive behavioral approaches) to promote mentalization. This core goal lies in a psychological understanding of disorders that defines personality disorders, in particular as disorders of interpersonal communication. Such disorders stem from an interpersonal sensitivity that results from early aversive experiences, especially in attachment relationships, negatively affects the developing mentalizing ability, and destroys epistemic trust in others. Thus, one can view mentalization theory as a metatheory that connects different psychotherapeutic procedures through a common language regarding transtheoretical integration.

2
Central Aspects of the Mentalizing Concept

2.1   Mentalization

Mentalization is an imaginative mental activity that enables us to perceive and interpret human behavior regarding mental states. It refers to intentional mental states such as desires, needs, feelings, beliefs, and goals.

But what does it really mean? Mentalization can also be defined as:

- having "mind in mind," i.e., grasping in one's own mind the mind of another person and also grasping one's own mind using one's own mind;
- developing a coherent picture of oneself and others;
- seeing others from the inside and oneself from the outside;
- understanding misunderstandings. To clarify misunderstandings, we need to see the world through the eyes of the other, acknowledge another point of view, and distance ourselves observationally from our own point of view.

Another definition, somewhat more foreign to empirical science but nevertheless a good description of mentalization, is as follows:

Mentalization is an interpersonal behavior characterized by the expectations that a person's mind can be influenced, surprised, changed, and illuminated by learning about another person's mind.

(Bateman, oral communication)

Two features characterize successful mentalization: accuracy and resourcefulness. Accurate mentalization means seeing others as they are and seeing oneself as one is. We need to put ourselves in the other person's shoes and see the world through their eyes—which demands imagination, a precarious thing. For example, if I am overly self-critical, I may mistakenly assume that the other person thinks the same of me. Mentalization functions best when one's imagination remains connected to reality. The benefit of mentalization develops through the recognition and elaboration of different perspectives. If someone makes a statement with utter conviction, such as, "This patient is narcissistic," mentalization is usually absent. Mentalization

DOI: 10.4324/9781032674117-3

is present when we reflect on misunderstandings. The moment we realize we are not mentalizing, we are again mentalizing. Mentalizing is not static; it is a process.

Mentalization plays an important role in affect control. Successful mentalization is a good mediator and buffer between violent affects and the urge to act. Affect regulation is a common problem in mental problems (see Chapter 5.1).

We can describe mentalization by regarding four different dimensions, each with two opposing poles. Successful mentalization is characterized by flexible switching between the two poles—though that is particularly difficult when we are under high stress or subject to great affect (e.g., anger). Even during intense attachment experiences, our mentalizing ability is limited, for example, when we fall violently in love. In such situations, mentalization would often be especially helpful—and sometimes bitterly necessary.

Automatic/Implicit vs. Controlled/Explicit

In everyday life, we mainly mentalize implicitly (automatically/quickly) when things are running smoothly. Implicit mentalization allows us to automatically interpret the behavior of ourselves and others. It conveniently switches into explicit (slow) mentalization when things get rough. For example, we mentalize explicitly when we take the time and make an effort to become aware of and express what might be going on in ourselves or in another person. Today, we know that automatic and controlled mentalizing occur in two different brain regions, and that stress promotes automatic mentalization and hinders controlled mentalization.

Internal Focus vs. External Focus

We can focus on our own inner world and the inner world of others. We can do the same thing regarding our external world and that of others, albeit with a different intensity.

Self-Oriented vs. Other-Oriented

For example, someone may perceive the inner and outer world of the other very well but fails to perceive and understand their own world, meaning this person is strongly oriented toward the other. On the other hand, we also know people who are strongly centered on themselves and pay little attention to others. This is the case, for example, when we suffer from severe pain.

Cognitive Mentalization vs. Affective Mentalization

On the one hand, we often experience people with high cognitive access to mental processes—who are equally good at blocking out their own and others' affects. On the other hand, we know people who are overwhelmed by automatic, highly affect-driven mentalization and, because of the great intensity, seem unable to connect their affective experience with their cognitive knowledge. In contrast, successful mentalization integrates cognitions and affects.

One should not overuse the four dimensions for diagnostic purposes. Nevertheless, the dimensions can be very helpful to therapists during psychotherapy to orient themselves. For example, if the patient becomes too attached to one pole, it is advisable to bring the other pole into the conversation to promote mentalization. Chapter 5.4 discusses the different dimensions of therapeutic interventions.

2.2   Attachment Relationships as the Basis of Mentalization

The developmental psychological foundations of the mentalization concept of Fonagy and colleagues are closely related to those of Bowlby (Bowlby 1969, 1973), who explored attachments and their importance in the further development of the child.

Different attachment styles develop depending on the interaction experiences with primary caregivers. Attachment theory assumes that attachment develops appropriately only under favorable conditions. A secure attachment pattern ensues if the caregiver's behavior is predictable and appropriate. Insecure attachments can be further differentiated into insecure-avoidant attachment patterns, insecure-ambivalent attachment patterns, and disoriented/disorganized attachments. The latter displays no consistent pattern in dealing with attachment anxiety (Ainsworth et al., 1978; Main, 1991). An insecure-avoidant attachment pattern often occurs when the attachment figure responds predictably but with little empathy or nurturing; an insecure-ambivalent attachment pattern occurs when the attachment figure fluctuates unpredictably in affect and behavior; a disoriented/disorganized attachment occurs, for example, when the caregiver triggers massive threats in the child while at the same time activating the attachment system because the child needs protection from the caregiver. This paradoxical situation prevents the development of a stable attachment strategy.

Mothers who had better access to their inner world on the Adult Attachment Interview (AAI; Main & Goldwyn, 1996) are more likely to have securely attached children (Fonagy et al., 1991).

Criticism has been levied on the attachment concept because of its cultural dependence. Research on the attachment concept tends to refer to WEIRD individuals (Western, educated, industrialized, rich, democratic). These objections are valid, making the relevance of the concept in this form limited to the Western world. Admittedly, many questions remain unanswered (for example, Keller, 2022).

A revision of attachment theory, which Fonagy and Target et al. undertook, led to more complex assumptions about the development of the self and internal representations. It explicitly included fantasies, motives, and emotions and thus encompassed clinical psychoanalytic concepts.

From the perspective of the mentalization concept, attachment is considered not just an innate behavioral system but serves as a framework for the development of an internal representational system, which is essential for the development of the self, for the regulation of affects, and for the success of social relationships. The attachment behavior system is considered the most important foundation for close social relationships, the development of mentalization, and epistemic trust.

People with insecure attachment patterns differ in how they cope with an activation of the attachment system. When stressed, people with insecure-avoidant attachment patterns more likely display disabling strategies with distancing and emphasizing autonomy; people with insecure-ambivalent patterns often show hyperactivating strategies, i.e., a more clinging pattern in relationships with demanding behavior and the risk of self-other confusion.

2.3   Marked Affect Mirroring as Social Feedback

Interpersonal interactions with their significant caregivers significantly shape an infant's affect development; there is widespread agreement on this in infant research. Strong affects, such as intense fear, are ideally modulated empathetically in the interaction between infant and caregiver. Fonagy & Target (2002) describe the caregivers' response to the infant's expression of affect and the ensuing processes in more detail. The caregiver's affective response is expressed in a consciously or unconsciously "marked" affect, for example, by softening the child's affect or by attaching a comment to it, such as a friendly smile. The infant feels noticed and recognizes that the original affect is not being reflected. For example, if the infant is very fearful, the caregiver does not experience this as threatening and modulates it, thus defusing the infant's anxiety. The child gradually internalizes this cognitive and affective interaction and later ideally learns to regulate their own affects. The primary emotion and the significant other's responses are mentally stored and become secondary representations. However, if the caregiver were to react to the child's fear "one-to-one," i.e., with the same affect expression, the mirroring can trigger fear, because the symbolic content enabled by the marking is lost. An anxious mother who responds by expressing her own anxiety can profoundly and negatively "modulate" the child's affect regulation. Should the caregiver respond with a completely different affect, the child may misunderstand it. Failure to "repair" these ruptures can impair the child's development of affect regulation. This is a danger, for example, if the child's caregiver is seriously mentally ill.

Affect mirroring contributes significantly to self-development. As Figure 2.1 shows, the development of the self originally proceeds from primary representations to the construction of secondary representations through, among other things, symbolization and affect mirroring in primary attachment relationships. The emphasis on affect development for the constitution of the self is closely related to the basic assumptions of Freud and psychoanalysis, which likewise place affects at the center of their concepts (see Chapter 5.1).

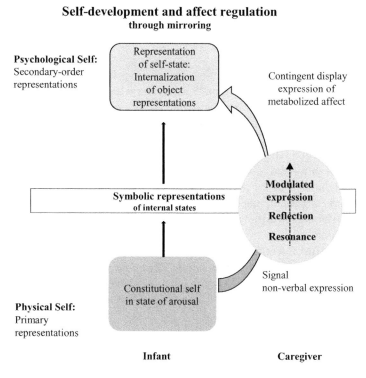

Figure 2.1 Self-development and affect regulation through mirroring.
Adapted from Bateman (2020).

2.4   Epistemic Trust

Epistemic confidence has come center stage in the recent development of the mentalization concept (Fonagy & Allison, 2014; Fonagy et al., 2015). For Fonagy, it enables the progression of psychoanalysis from drive theory to attachment theory to communication theory (Fonagy et al., 2017b).

> Epistemic trust is the basal confidence in a person as a secure source of information. (Sperber et al., 2010; Wilson & Sperber, 2012).

Here are two examples:

• We do not know our date of birth from own experience. Nevertheless, we are fairly certain about it. Why? Persons we trust have told us, and we have never felt the need to check it seriously.

- We don't really know how WLAN works exactly. Rather, someone told us how to connect our notebook to it, for example. Because of further cultural knowledge we have acquired unchecked over time, we can use it for our purposes.

Epistemic trust is trust in information derived from interpersonal communication and has two parts: First, the information must be relevant to the recipient; second, the information must come from a communicator who takes the recipient's perspective into account (Fonagy & Allison, 2014). This view is related to Sperber and Wilson's "Relevance Theory," which posits a cognitive and a communicative relevance principle. The former states that the information conveyed is relevant to the recipient (informative information); the latter states that the information conveyed is significant to the recipient from the sender's perspective; that is, it has an "ostensive appeal" (perspective intention) (Sperber & Wilson, 1995). Persons interpret information differently in this process, depending on their trust in the communicator.

Epistemic trust refers to the social and emotional meaning of trust. On the one hand, our basic trust in information from other people results from the trust we have acquired in other people. On the other hand, we achieve trust in the importance of a message when the person signals to us that the information is personally and originally relevant to us.

Epistemic Trust

- Humans are innately designed to teach others new and culturally generated information (e.g., mother to young child) and to learn from others. To this end, they need epistemic trust.
- Early attachments to persons with whom we develop sensitive relationships provide a sound basis for establishing epistemic trust.
- Communication that is "marked," i.e., that clearly reveals that the recipient is perceived as an independent and intentional being, increases epistemic trust.
- "Marked" communication increases the likelihood that the communication will be

  - encoded as relevant to the recipient,
  - generalizable beyond the specific situation, and
  - stored in memory as relevant.

Our world is full of complex demands. Our surroundings are not self-explanatory. Therefore, we depend on people as reliable sources of information. In this regard, "door-openers" (so-called "ostensive" signs/cues) act as triggers for epistemic trust. From birth, eye contact, joint attention, and "baby talk" (e.g., the higher tone we typically use to speak to a baby) open up communication channels that direct attention and foster infant confidence in the importance and generalizability of information (Csibra & Gergerly, 2009, 2011).

Epistemic trust refers to the source of the information and the context of the information (Sperber et al., 2010). It therefore also depends on the relationship to the context (Wilson & Sperber, 2012; Sperber & Wilson, 1995). New information is more likely to be credible if we judge the context to be credible. This is particularly relevant when neither the information nor the context alone is credible. The outcome is uncertain if the new information contradicts the context and both are significant.

Epistemic trust and epistemic vigilance enable social learning and the transmission of cultural knowledge. We acquire epistemic trust particularly well as children growing up in a secure and predictable environment. Secure attachment and affective resonance from significant attachment figures facilitate the acquisition of epistemic trust. It forms the basis for developing a self that experiences itself as self-efficacious. And it forms the basis for developing mentalization (see Figure 2.2a) and social intelligence. Mentalization means "holding mind in mind." This means of taking perspective leads to the other person feeling perceived, which promotes epistemic trust. It creates the basis for successful behavior in the social world.

Mentalization, however, is not an end in itself; rather, it significantly expands the possibilities of social learning. In turn, mentalization skills positively affect the acquisition and stabilization of epistemic trust and the regulation of epistemic vigilance.

Unfavorable development (see Figure 2.2b) comprises, among other things, neglect, violence, or sexual abuse at the beginning of life. Significant others on whom the child depends and without whose support the child would be lost are experienced as unpredictable, threatening, or hostile.

Such experiences constrict the development of epistemic trust, leading to hypervigilance. The contradictory experiential components within the self impede the construction of coherent structures. Parts of an "alien self" (see Section 2.6) may form and hamper the development of mentalization ability, again leading to hypervigilance. Epistemic distrust is often associated with the rapid development of heightened credulity (Kosugi & Yamagishi, 1998; Yamagishi et al., 1999). Individuals with a high level of distrust cannot draw on their own exploratory experiences and the results thereof (Yamagishi, 2001, 2011). Together with the limitation of mentalization ability, this makes social learning more difficult.

These theoretical connections have very practical consequences in therapy: For example, if a patient in therapy is continuously distrustful and thus often appears unwilling to receive treatment, therapists should first consider limiting epistemic trust. The assumption that the patient's "good will" lies behind this behavior is an interpretation that provides some relief for the therapist but may be misleading. According to another, mentalization-based approach, the patient is not difficult, just difficult for the therapist to reach.

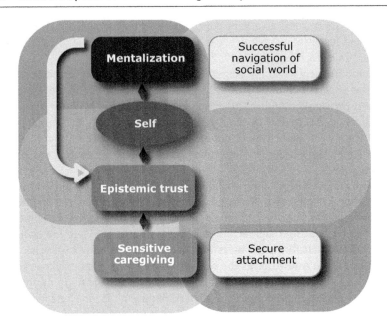

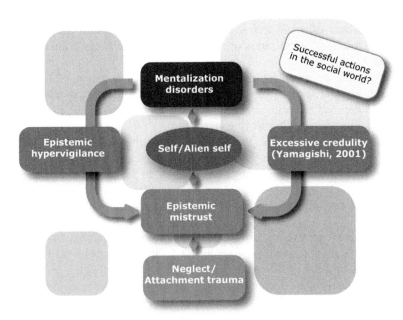

Figure 2.2a/2.2b Successful actions in the social world/Successful actions in the social world?

Adapted from Fonagy (2015).

Development of Mentalization

Figure 2.3 The development of mentalization.

On the topic of "epistemic trust," see also "Epistemic Fit" (Chapter 5.2) and a case presentation (Chapter 6.2).

2.5   Development of Mentalization

Toward the end of their first year of life, children begin to understand human action in the goal-directed, "teleological mode" (see Figure 2.3). This is where the self begins to spawn, where children experience themselves as goal-directed origina-tors. Children can distinguish actions according to their outcome and perceive their origins. They can choose from several possibilities the best means to close in on a goal (Csibra & Gergely, 1998). At the same time, they cannot yet regulate their own internal states; they still need caregivers for that purpose.

Around the beginning of the second year of life, when the child's radius of ac-tion expands, they experience reality, thoughts, and feelings in two ways: in the "equivalence mode" and the "pretend mode." The child oscillates between these two parallel modes until reaching integration at about age four—in the "reflective mode." Fonagy and Target (2003) argue that infants and toddlers initially equate the internal world with the external world (thus "mental equivalence"). Children perceive thoughts as reality rather than representations or perspectives at this age. Thoughts affect them similarly to real events. We all know the classic game of hide-and-seek: A child who covers their eyes is convinced others cannot see them.

How caregivers deal with the child's thoughts promotes or hinders the develop-ment of symbolization and representation. The empathetic experience of affect-regulating play helps the child learn that feelings do not automatically spread to the external world. Mental equivalence, a mode of perceiving the inner world, can also give rise to painful experiences because projected fantasies can cause great anxiety, and self–object boundaries have not yet been securely established. Advancing to the pretend mode therefore represents a crucial step forward.

In the pretend mode, as in play, the inner state of mind becomes separated from reality. Play re-enacts everyday life, modifying and decoupling it. The pretend mode excludes reality. It is assumed that the child has an inkling of the fictional character of the game from the beginning: Intuitively, the child distinguishes between reality and play (a stick is like/unlike a gun). The adult's reaction helps the child to create an external representation of inner states. In the pretend mode, the play figure—not the parental face—becomes the external representation of the child's feelings and thoughts. If the parents respond appropriately and playfully to offers of play in the pretend mode, the child receives the signal that their own impulses and desires are separate from reality and have no effect. In play, thoughts and feelings are disconnected from reality and are therefore unreal. In the equivalence mode, they are "superreal." The playful attitude of the parents is significant to integrating the equivalence mode and the pretend mode, as is the ability to "contain" negative affects to enable the reflexive mode.

In the reflexive mode (from the fourth to the fifth year of life), the equivalence and pretend modes become integrated; this enables reflection on one's self and on the presumed inner lives of others. The child acknowledges different perspectives and recognizes false beliefs both in themselves and others.

These early modes may resurface as a mentalizing disorder in adulthood. When we fail to develop a reflective mode (= mentalization), we revert to one or more of the earlier modes:

- In the teleological mode, for example, the focus lies on trying to manipulate the other person for one's own goals. Marriage swindlers, for example, often have a high "aptitude" regarding the teleological mode.
- In the equivalence mode, persons equate their inner world with the outer world: "Because I feel that way, that is how it really is!" This is often characteristic of someone who strings facts together without our learning anything truly relevant about the person.
- In the pretend mode, the inner world is separated from the outer world, often emerging later in pseudomentalizing. The person talks in psychojargon, for example, without really being affected by anything they say. When queried more intensely, they only repeat cliches. "Psychobabble" is typical pseudomentalizing. ("Sorry, but I have an Oedipus complex.")

For more on modes as mentalizing disorders in adulthood, see Chapter 5.4.

2.6   The Alien Self

The "alien self" is that part of our self that is not coherent with our true self. It is foreign to us and, like the self, partly conscious and partly unconscious. Every human being is home to such an alien part of their selves, though people differ in the extent or intensity of these parts. Because of their strangeness, their incompatibility with the other parts of the self, and the resulting tension—but also their threatening nature—they sometimes generate unbearable feelings when revived.

For example, an alien self can arise through early traumatic experiences, especially if the person subsequently remains misunderstood and unprotected. Prolonged neglect can also lead to the emergence of a strange self. During threatening or disorganized attachment experiences, a child may attempt to maintain proximity to the attachment figure at the expense of reflective capacity: The child adapts to the world of the attachment figure and adopts alien parts into their selves.

The basis for the development of alien parts is repeated and prolonged "faulty" affective feedback from significant others. The affects and perceptions reported back to the child fail to fit the other contents of the self—they are incoherent. A child cannot simultaneously feel and understand the experience (1) that a significant other loves them and provides for their security while (2) simultaneously feeling massively threatened. That is unbearable.

For example, if affect mirroring is inappropriately marked, the child's experience (primary representation) and the mirroring (secondary representation of the experience) become incorrectly linked. The child's self assumes (represents) the attitude and messages of the caregiver and not their own perceptions, giving rise to a strange self (Figure 2.4).

Patients with a strange self report, for example, having the impression that attacks against their self are coming from within. They experience their ideas and feelings as parts that do not belong to the self. Feelings of emptiness and unbearable malaise occur. Experiences from the outer world are not clearly separated from their experiences of the inner world because they are unmarked or inaccurately marked and cannot be distinguished. In this unbearable state of confusion, in times

Birth of the "Alien" Self

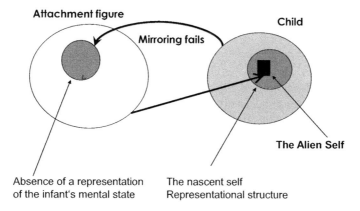

Figure 2.4 Development of the alien self.
Modified from Bateman & Fonagy (2004).

of distress, they project their feelings onto the external world, not just to get rid of feelings of guilt and unbearable inner tensions, but also to maintain congruence in self-experience.

Thus, we can understand mentalization disorders as difficulties in correctly identifying one's own and others' inner states. The heightened tendency toward projection is born of such mentalization problems. The content of such projections may stem, for example, from internalized experiences of abuse, resulting in the distorted perception of others, especially in close, emotionally significant relationships.

The concept of the "false self" from self-psychology (Kohut 1971, 1984) and the concept of strange self bear a certain resemblance, whereby the former goes back to Winnicott (1962). The differences between the two result from different conceptions regarding their development. According to self-psychology, the false self forms from the child's experiences with the expectations and behavior of caregivers; they become false parts because they arise from the child's need to conform and are experienced as coherent with one's person. On the other hand, the parts of the strange self belong to the person but arise through the distorted communication processes described above and are not coherent with the other parts of the self.

2.7   Psychotherapy as a Threefold Communication System

Fonagy and Allison's considerations start from the therapeutic relationship (Fonagy & Allison, 2014). The results of therapy research show the therapeutic relationship to be a central mediator of therapeutic success (Laska et al., 2014; Wampold, 2015). According to the mentalization concept, the therapeutic relationship induces a social learning process patients benefit from even between treatment sessions. Mentalization promotes the patient's standpoint as an independent person with their own valid experiences. We can thus understand psychotherapy as a threefold communication system (Fonagy et al., 2019).

1. The Therapist's Theory of Therapy

All evidence-based forms of psychotherapy provide patients with an understanding of themselves, their mind, and their soul. They convey to patients an understanding of their disorders and changes that occur during therapy. These sometimes implicit, sometimes explicit explanations by the therapist are important, personally relevant messages that serve to establish epistemic confidence, reduce epistemic stress, and thus prepare the way for new experiences and learning.

2. Regaining Robust Mentalization: Mentalizing as a "Common Factor"

Successful mentalization promotes epistemic trust in others as well as social learning. In this regard, mentalization closely resembles enabling and fostering a good therapeutic relationship, which is a crucial common factor of psychotherapy (Wampold, 2015): Fostering mentalization is considered a common factor in all successful therapies. According to Jurist (2018, p. 120), patients who experience successful therapy usually improve their abilities to affectively mentalize.

Fostering mentalization is based on two main aspects: presenting an attitude conducive to mentalization (see Chapter 3.6) and prompting specific interventions (see Chapter 5.4).

Fostering mentalization in therapy is not a therapeutic goal in itself but rather a way to better modulate affects as we improve the patient's self-control and sense of self-coherence.

3. Restoring Social Learning

Enhancing mentalization skills goes hand in hand with building epistemic confidence. It enables learning new and different things about one's social world and challenging old beliefs. Restoring mentalization capacity brings the patient out of the isolation caused by epistemic mistrust, since epistemic stress narrows the patient's view of their experiences. Patients need new experiences to change, and these important changes occur between sessions, in social life outside therapy. Therapy research supports this approach (Bohart & Wade, 2013, p. 243).

We can visualize every therapeutic process as a threefold communication system and put it to a stress test based on these three aspects. The third system focuses on analyzing and evaluating treatment outcomes in the social context.

3

Mentalization-Based Therapy (MBT)

MBT is a manualized therapy developed by Bateman and Fonagy (2016). Along with other disorder-specific therapies, MBT is considered one of the most effective methods for treating individuals with borderline personality disorder (BPD) (Storebø et al., 2020), and it can also be used transdiagnostically in the presence of other personality disorders. To date, the basic principles of MBT have also been applied to treating patients with eating disorders, addictive disorders, anxiety disorders, and depression; further, in children and adolescents with specialized approaches to treating attention deficit hyperactive disorder (ADHD), conduct disorder, and those at risk for psychosis. In addition, the mentalization approach has spawned therapeutic programs for mentally ill parents and prevention programs (Bateman & Fonagy, 2019).

3.1　Mentalization as a Personality Function

Instead of maintaining different categories, the new classification systems for recording mental disorders in the DSM-5 (American Psychiatric Association, 2013) and ICD-11 (World Health Organization, 2020) now assume dimensional phenomena regarding personality disorders, set along a continuum from healthy to dysfunctional. This dimensional approach addresses the criticism of categorical diagnostic systems, whose various categories of personality disorders are difficult to delineate in practice. The dimensional system operationalizes personality disorders as impairments in personality functioning. The ICD-11 adds a pathology criterion to the assessment of impairments in personality functioning; that is, whether the impairments result in substantial distress or suffering in the individual or their social relationships (Tyrer et al., 2019). The alternative DSM-5 model classifies the overall level on the domains "Self" and "Interpersonal Relationships," which in turn are subdivided into the domains "Identity/Self-Direction" and "Empathy/ Closeness," respectively.

To operationalize the level of personality functioning, researchers combined various psychodynamic diagnostic instruments to simplify them for transdiagnostic and school-independent use (Bender et al., 2011). These diagnostic instruments included the Reflective Functioning Scale (RF Scale), which has been referred to as

DOI: 10.4324/9781032674117-4

the gold standard of operationalizing mentalization and captures ability through a rater-based assessment of adult attachment interviews (Taubner et al., 2013). Thus, mentalization represented a significant element in the operationalization of personality functioning levels (Bender et al., 2011). Recently, a study of 110 individuals empirically demonstrated the conceptual overlap of the personality functioning level and mentalization, revealing that mentalization is related to all domains of the personality functioning level (Zettl et al., 2020). However, DSM-5 abandoned the use of the term mentalization in favor of a personality diagnostic that could be applied across schools (Bender et al., 2011). The discovery of a high correlation of mentalization ability with all domains of personality functioning suggests that promoting mentalization in MBT may also change overall personality functioning levels, a central idea of this treatment approach. Focusing on a central mechanism of action also strengthens other areas of personality, such as relationship skills, affect regulation, and impulsivity.

3.2 Mentalization as a Multidimensional Construct

Mentalization refers to a multidimensional construct that has conceptual overlap with other significant clinical concepts such as mindfulness, affect awareness, empathy, introspection, and psychological sensitivity. We can distinguish mentalization from other clinically related concepts as follows: Mentalization encompasses awareness of both self (mindfulness, introspection) and others (empathy); it integrates cognition and affect (affect awareness, psychological sensitivity); and it includes a dimension of explicit and implicit interpretation (Choi-Kain & Gunderson, 2008). Implicit mentalization involves a rapid, automatic understanding of self and others—which is functional in itself (and ensures survival) but can also be systematically error-prone, especially when early aversive experiences have established negative expectations of self and others.

According to neuroscientific research, we currently distinguish four domains/eight facets of mentalization:

- automatic (implicit) vs. controlled (explicit);
- internally focused vs. externally focused;
- self-oriented (self) vs. other-oriented (other);
- cognitive vs. affective.

For all domains described, one can assume that the optimal state would likely be a balance between the different facets and a balance of psychosocial demands. Mentalization as a process oscillates on a constantly shifting continuum of the various facets, depending on the affective salience of the situation. Mayes (2006) applied the results of cognitive psychology research on automated information processing to mentalization and linked them to the respective emotional arousal. The stress-dependent switching model of mentalization she posited is based on the phenomenon that, when emotional tension increases, controlled and explicit brain processes in the prefrontal cortex switch to automatic and implicit processes in the posterior cortex as well as subcortical areas to regulate personal stress arousal. Thus, on the one hand, these systems protect the cortex from overstimulation, while, on the other hand, enabling coordination between attentional, executive, and sensory cortical systems for survival. The stress-dependent switch model of mentalization assumes that the level of explicit mentalization switches over to automatic mentalization at a certain stress level. This switching process is accompanied by the deactivation of explicit mentalization and a tendency toward evolutionarily earlier protective functions such as fight, flight, or freeze responses. Yet, automatic mentalization occurs not only in stressful situations; it is the default mentalization case. However, switching to explicit and thus reflective mentalization is no longer possible in stressful situations.

In the context of MBT, three clinical concepts ("modes"), characterized by generalizing and labeling, describe ineffective automatic mentalizing: the teleological mode, the psychic equivalence mode, and the pretend mode. In teleological thinking, only observable behavior represents evidence of inner experience (e.g., a bouquet of flowers as evidence of love); in psychic equivalence, we equate our own experience with external reality (the greater my fear that the plane I am sitting in is going to crash, the more likely it is that it will indeed soon crash); in pseudomentalizing (pretend mode), an individual's mental states have no relation to their behavior or experience, which are decoupled from each other both internally and externally—"empty psychologizing," so to speak (see the case study in Chapter 3.8).

MBT aims to stabilize mentalization in interpersonally sensitive areas (e.g., regarding fear of abandonment). It creates a mental buffer that enables explicit reflection. Mental distancing and the reevaluation of such significant situations occur more easily; affect regulation and impulse control improve. The long-term goal is for patients to have supportive and fulfilling relationships through more effective mentalization.

3.3   The Transdiagnostic and Transtheoretical Disorder Model of MBT Using Borderline Personality Disorder as an Example

The multidimensional model of mentalization allows us to conceptualize the mentalization problems of individual patients transtheoretically and transdiagnostically, thereby deriving a treatment approach. We illustrate that here using the example of a prototypical BPD patient.

In addition to the criteria for BPD diagnosis, clinical psychiatric research describes three core problems in personality dysfunction typical of BPD: emotion dysregulation, impulsivity, and dysfunctional social relationships. The mentalization approach associates these three core problems with disorders of mentalization, thus creating the disorder model for BPD in MBT. Empirical studies show that individuals with BPD potentially have difficulty mentalizing emotionally significant others as well as themselves. Regarding the mentalization facets, they reflect too automatically (implicitly) and too affectively and are overly oriented toward external features and toward others. This points to an overactivation of the domains implicit-automatic, external, and affective (among others), accompanied by an underactivation of the domains explicit-controlled, internal, cognitive, and self (see also Chapter 5.4). From this, we derive a mentalization profile that forms the transdiagnostic and transtheoretical disorder model and serves as a basis for treatment planning. Based on the mentalization profile, the chronically underactivated areas are therapeutically promoted, particularly by employing so-called "contrasting movements" in the therapist's intervention technique. Thus, MBT with prototypical BPD patients generally focuses strongly on activating mentalization in the areas of self, cognition, slow and explicit reflection, and enriching internal images of self and others, as patients are less likely to address these areas on their own since they are particularly error-prone. However, it is essential that clinicians accurately assess any overactivation and underactivation of mentalization facets, especially since these may not correspond to the prototype in individual cases.

The therapist individually summarizes the consequences of the mentalization impairments for each treatment by formulating a focus. In BPD, an interpersonal trigger often generates a cascade of ineffective mentalization, dysregulated affect, and impulsive behavior. For example, an interpersonal trigger may occur through activation of the attachment system (fear of loss, fear of shaming), accompanied by specific attempts at regulation through activating/deactivating strategies toward others. At the same time, such an activation of the attachment system often leads to a loss of effective mentalization and severely limits the patient's ability to regulate affect. When their attempts at self-regulation or the behavioral control of others fail, the patient resorts to dysfunctional interpersonal strategies and eventually impulsive behavior through a combination of strong dysregulated affect (often fear or shame) and ineffective mentalization. This individual conceptualization is communicated to patients in writing and discussed in detail at the beginning of treatment. It then represents the focus of the joint work (see also Chapter 5.6).

3.4 Therapeutic Goals and Change Mechanism of MBT

The hypothesis that mentalization can be trained exclusively in an affectively meaningful (therapeutic) relationship by restoring epistemic trust is central to MBT. It conveys to the patient that exploring their mental state helps establish successful self-regulation and improves their relationships with others. Because of the connection between the development of mentalization and early attachment experiences, we do not propose promoting mentalization purely by psychoeducation, even though psychoeducation is an essential component of therapy. Rather, psychoeducation serves to enable epistemic openness, which in turn facilitates a therapeutic alliance. The main component of therapy lies in establishing an empathic and safe working alliance that promotes the exploration of feelings, thoughts, desires, etc., including the thoughts and feelings between therapist and patient. Mentalizing the therapeutic relationship is seen as the central mechanism of change; there is no need to speculate about possible thoughts and feelings because one can communicate them directly should misunderstandings, different perceptions, or misinterpretations ensue. The goal of MBT is to maintain the patient's ability to mentalize where it is already successful and to improve it where impaired mentalization triggers symptoms and interpersonal problems.

Thus, we can describe the theory of change in MBT as follows: Improved mentalization creates a mental buffer between feelings and actions, allowing the patient to reflect on conflicting interpersonal experiences and difficult affects. Patients become able to think before acting, to reflect before enacting. Improving mentalization in the therapeutic relationship thus depends on strengthening trust in socially mediated information, which in the reconceptualization of mentalization theory is referred to as epistemic trust (Fonagy et al., 2017a).

3.5   The MBT Process and Content

MBT was initially designed as an inpatient therapy and later developed into a high-frequency outpatient program in which individual and group therapies are each conducted weekly for 12–18 months. All MBT treatments follow the following scheme, regardless of the disorder:

1. diagnostic phase (including the assessment of mentalizing skills),
2. risk assessment and creation of a crisis plan;
3. formulation of a focus;
4. psychoeducation;
5. individual and parallel group sessions for adults/family therapy for adolescents;
6. short refresher or booster sessions after the end of therapy.

Following the diagnosis, MBT involves the joint development of a focus for therapy (based on therapy goals and mentalization problems emerging from symptom behavior) and a crisis plan that helps stabilize threatening behavior and is an initial mentalizing exercise. In parallel, psychoeducation takes place concerning the central assumptions of MBT and the therapeutic interventions in case of non-mentalization, which can be referred to at any time during therapy. The crisis plan, the formulation of focus, and psychoeducation comprise the first communication system to establish epistemic trust. Thereafter, we recommend a combination of individual and group therapy, especially since the group format stimulates social learning, reflection, and mentalization. In certain indications and with adolescents, family therapy can replace group therapy.

One can describe the task of the MBT therapist in the individual and multiperson setting as follows: The patient feels reflected in the therapist's mind, whereby the therapist constantly deals explicitly with the inner mental state of all participants, including their own subjective reactions. This stimulates or restores the patient's mentalization function. The therapist pays continual attention to how the patient perceives them and to the relevant feelings in each case, which plays an important role. The therapy thus focuses on the therapeutic relationship with the therapist as an active participant who emotionally impacts the patient. Because mentalization always relates to specific issues, the treatment initially addresses the core goals agreed upon in the formulation of the initial focus. These may include behaviors and symptoms, such as suicide attempts, self-injurious behavior, substance abuse, or emotional instability. As therapy progresses, the emphasis transfers to relational mentalization in the patient's life and the therapy sessions. Relational mentalization is a key factor in the treatment of personality disorders. MBT aims to increase the patient's attention to mental states (especially affects) and interpersonal contexts, using a stepwise process to reduce rigidities in the mentalizing facets (Bateman & Fonagy 2004; Taubner et al., 2019).

In MBT, the emphasis on interpreting hard-to-reach unconscious conflicts from classical psychoanalysis recedes in favor of content that is closer to consciousness. Instead of achieving insight, the aim is to restore the patient's ability to mentalize. This means addressing simple contexts and avoiding addressing complex mental states such as conflicts, ambivalences, and unconscious acts, which are hardly comprehensible for a person with low mentalizing ability. Finally, MBT does not focus on a detailed discussion of past traumatization because of the clinical assumption that, in the worst-case scenario, in a patient in the prementalizing mode of thinking, this could lead to retraumatization. Instead, the focus lies on reflecting on current experiences and perceptions with (previously) abusive persons or on changes in psychological states associated with the trauma. As the process guardian, the therapist structures each session along this focus, assuming the regulation of affect or the general arousal management for the patient(s) and paying constant attention to the mentalization level of everyone involved. The therapist can apply skills such as breathing exercises, physical exercises, verbal calming, and visualization of mental content on a flipchart—or if need be just taking a walk. Overall, therapists are encouraged to explore creative ideas to improve mentalization.

3.6   The Therapeutic Stance in MBT

Because MBT is a process-oriented therapy that emphasizes working within the therapeutic relationship, the therapeutic stance assumes special importance. Central to MBT is that the therapist always keeps an eye on their own mentalization while showing curiosity and enthusiasm for the mental experience of the other person and their mental experience. The therapist should engage in controlled self-disclosure and authenticity to mentalize the therapeutic relationship. Furthermore, the therapist should adopt an openly empathic and appreciative attitude. This involves authentically conveying to the patient that their suffering, anger, difficulties, conflicts, etc. are emotionally understood, and that the therapist is actively trying to see things through the patient's eyes. The therapist's attitude becomes, as it were, an example of the notion that the exploration of the mental is harmless, and that one can later progress from quick assumptions and be altogether wrong in one's interpretations. Therefore, the so-called stance of "not-knowing" (see also Chapter 5.3) is particularly typical and important for the MBT therapist's approach. This refers to the modest recognition that we cannot truly know what others think and feel but indeed are often subject to errors. Therefore, everyone, including the therapist, depends on actively and repeatedly questioning the other person's mental state and making their own feelings available, especially if they contrast with how the patient is experiencing the therapist. At the same time, the not-knowing stance allows the therapist to experience different perspectives in the sense of: "I can understand how you come to this impression, but when I reflect on what I was thinking at that moment, I feel differently about the situation." This attitude enables authentic contact and promotes the patient to the position of an "expert" on their own mental state. Focusing on interpersonal misunderstandings provides an optimal opportunity to elaborate on perceptions, interpretations, and subjective experiences. Of course, it requires courage and an inclination toward self-criticism on the part of the therapist to take responsibility for and transparently represent their own misperceptions, empathic intrusions, and misinterpretations.

Not-knowing also enables the therapist to speak openly about not having understood something, and it removes any possible pressure to construct meaning from something incomprehensible. The active questioning technique ("inquisitive stance") should allow the patient to explore but should not assume the character of an interrogation. The therapist should pose questions only out of genuine curiosity and not manipulatively, i.e., where the therapist actually already knows the desired answer. Therefore, questions should be marked with specific wording that makes it clear that the answer is unknown, for example, by phrasing one's interpretation as a question, adding a "maybe" or an "I'm not sure." The therapist should consider whether the patient can report something about their inner life. Repeatedly asking about the same feelings when the patient has already made it clear that they do not know the answer can feel oppressive and insensitive.

3.7   Core Interventions of MBT

In MBT, the main mechanism of change is the validation of the patient's emotional experience as well as various techniques that stabilize or enhance mentalization (Bateman & Fonagy, 2016). As a rule of thumb, the patient's affects are always empathically validated, while the therapist also carefully questions the patient's perspectives on the self and others, including the therapist's perspective (see also Chapter 5.4).

Interventions follow the logic of "top to bottom" = "surface to depth" regarding the mentalization of the current emotional therapeutic relationship. The real relationship—"How do I feel in the here-and-now with the other person?"—is more significant than the transference relationship, i.e., the repetition of patterns from previous relationships with the therapist. Repeating relationship patterns (interpersonal vicious circles) later become the therapeutic subject, but only once mentalization has been established in the therapeutic relationship. If the patient is

very agitated, the therapist should use supportive interventions, interrupting ineffective mentalization by exploring affect, certainty of interpretation, and knee-jerk
assumptions. These techniques direct attention away from facts and toward experiences and the nature of reflection (from "what" to "how"). They allow for metacognitive reflection on one's mentalization in different situations. The supportive
techniques express respect for the patient's narratives and represent a practical implementation of the attitude of not-knowing.

Another aspect of supportive and empathic interventions lies in identifying and
exploring features of successful mentalization. If the patient demonstrates accurate
mentalization, this should be highlighted appropriately, e.g., by saying, "You've
really come to understand this in a new way, what happened between the two of
you. Has this changed anything for you?" It is a good idea to ask how the successful mentalization felt, especially when reflecting on emotionally upsetting situations. But empathic validation goes beyond structuring supportive techniques; it
signals an interest in affect and reflecting on it. Through genuine human sympathy,
empathic validation identifies and normalizes affects. Normalization means that
the affects are marked as understandable and comprehensible. Empathic validation
can succeed only if the therapist sees the world through the eyes of the patient and
comprehends it affectively—and if this is openly communicated: "When you tell
me this, I have the feeling that..." or "That sounds really terrible, it makes me very
sad to imagine that..." (see also Chapter 5.4).

The therapist uses general techniques to interrupt a nonmentalizing monologue
and slow down the process of processing the experience and move toward explicit
mentalizing ("stop and stand," "stop, rewind, and explore"). In low-affect situations,
interventions are used that allow for a mentalizing exploration of the focal issues
("What exactly did you experience?" "How did you feel later?" "What did it trigger
in you?" "How did you understand it?"). In doing so, the therapist prompts the activation of aspects of mentalization the patient makes little use of on their own (contrarian movement) to insert more flexibility into the reflection. Finally, the therapist
and the patient work on the affect focus, i.e., the affect currently active in the therapy
session, to strengthen the ability to understand interpersonal processes "live." The
purpose of the affect focus is to make implicit mentalization explicit. Thus, the focus
lies not on the affect related to a specific described event but on the affect that arises
when describing the past experience/situation in the therapeutic setting. Especially
when the affect is significant to the therapeutic relationship and "hangs in the air"
should it be explicitly spelled out. In English, we use the succinct term "elephant in
the room" to point out something that is almost impossible to avoid noticing. In this
case, it is the therapist's task to carefully inquire about the affect being shared at this
moment, while at the same time making clear that it is only one possible perspective
and not (yet) assured knowledge (see also Chapter 5.3). Further, the affect should be
connected to the current therapeutic work during the session.

In MBT, new perspectives are initiated by using a specific questioning technique
called the mentalization loop (see Figure 3.1). Comparing different levels of experience within the patient's experience stimulates new perspectives in the mentalization

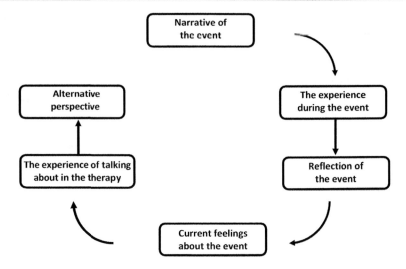

Figure 3.1 A mentalization loop for broadening the perspective, using the example of a life event (narrative) a patient brings to the therapy session.

loop, starting from a specific narrative in the patient's current experience. First, the event is studied in detail (what, who, how); then, the mental experience is explored; and a third step explores how to understand the situation and the experience in context. In the next level, the therapist asks how it feels to talk about it now in therapy (affect focus) and whether the view of the event/feelings has changed.

Below is a case example that illustrates the procedure in MBT.

3.8   MBT in a Case Study of an 18-Year-Old Man with BPD

Following an inpatient crisis intervention (suicide attempt) and failed behavioral therapy, Kilian, 18, presents for outpatient MBT with individual sessions and family therapy sessions. He reports having suffered greatly from his current partnership because his girlfriend kept seeing other boys and hated him. He could not get the thought out of his head that she might be seeing someone else. That is when he starts to hurt himself to numb the inner pain, or he fights with other boys in arranged fights. He also vomits up to ten times a day because of his agitation and has therefore been unable to attend school for two years because he is embarrassed by his incessant vomiting and cannot concentrate anyway. In the clinic and the pretherapy phase, Kilian was diagnosed with BPD. His therapy goals are to become able to separate from his girlfriend once and for all and to graduate from high school.

At the beginning of therapy, Kilian is very indignant and blames his girlfriend for the relationship's failure. However, in doing so, he entangles himself in contradictions that he fails to notice. In fact, early in the relationship, he himself had engaged in countless affairs with other girls to counteract the feeling of dependence and being at the mercy of others. And, despite the blaming and strong complaints about his girlfriend's less than affectionate way with him, he could not let go of her and indeed thought there was no other girl like her: Only with her did he know who he really was.

Diagnostics revealed an above-average intelligence but also strong psychopathic traits and a comorbid antisocial personality disorder. However, because this was limited solely to the area of violence against possible male competitors, the therapist focused the treatment on the symptoms of BPD, setting the following focus: Massive fears of abandonment trigger pseudomentalizing, so that Kilian clings to the relationship despite knowing better and tries ever more desperately to control the girlfriend or potential competitors. This was accompanied by indignation at her refusal to submit to his control, leading to violent behavior against himself or others, in an attempt to regain control of the situation and his feelings. Outside of this core conflict, identity diffusion, a sense of inner emptiness, and fear of being a "monster" were evident.

The First Contacts

Even during their first contacts, the therapist noticed that Kilian talks about himself and others almost entirely without affect and behaved with enormous politeness. At the same time, this polite manner and the constant friendly smile often failed to chime with the content of the conversation. He described himself contradictorily as a very friendly and polite person who, on other days, can be highly controlling of others and even physically abuse them without remorse. Further, he described himself as a devoted, faithful partner who then repeatedly cheated on his partner with other girls. He failed to address these different (contradictory) aspects of his person. He had few ideas regarding his talents or desires outside the relationship and his future (except to accomplish "something great"). He also fluctuated in his values between highly moral and dissocial (e.g., the fist as a means of conflict resolution). He clung to an idealized notion of a relationship and was obsessed with fulfilling his desire for unconditional love—even though the actual relationship contained nothing of this ideal. In the conflicts with his girlfriend regarding her contact with male friends, he regularly lost control of himself and had to be restrained by his friends.

Working through the conflicts revealed an apparent empathy deficit: He always saw himself as being in the right and thought others deserved no better. The therapist developed the hypothesis that the splitting of content and affect (called pseudomentalizing in MBT) was standing in the way of his reflecting on his behavior to effect change. His thought process was "stuck," much like his clinging to wishful thinking regarding relationships.

The Course of Therapy

As therapy progressed, it became apparent to Kilian that his parents had probably been limited early on in their ability to empathize with their son's needs and feelings. The therapist developed the idea that the parents had been limited in their parental mentalizing ability. The mother had been severely traumatized because of an early childhood abduction and described herself as a very young mother who had often been overwhelmed by her lively child. In the family therapy sessions, she reported locking two-year-old Kilian in his room for hours at a time when she was at wits' end. After the mother mentioned this in the family sessions, Kilian also began to talk in the individual sessions about the parenting practices he had experienced, which the therapist classified as physical abuse. The father's lack of ability to mentalize the needs of a young child was demonstrated, for example, by the fact that Kilian regularly watched horror movies with his father when he was only three years old and credibly maintained that he had been unable to feel fear ever since. The developmental psychopathological understanding of mentalization theory posits that the inhibition of Kilian's attachment-related mentalization was established early in life, since as a thinking and feeling child he had received insufficient affective consideration by his parents, e.g., by being left alone, shamed, and beaten.

The therapist determined his mentalizing profile to be an overactivation of automatic, cognitive, external, and other-related mentalization. Automatic mentalization (or the breakdown of mentalization) manifested itself in Kilian, for example, when he immediately went into "fight mode" at the sight of his girlfriend in the company of other young men; he no longer had mental control over his behavior and was convinced she was cheating on him, and that others were making fun of him. Later, he pseudomentalized the justifications for his behavior in an affect-free manner, so the therapist focused on the affective and self-experiencing in the subsequent interventions. It became apparent that Kilian had great difficulty accepting some of his feelings, such as helplessness, sadness, and fear. Many of his other- or self-injurious behaviors as well as his strongly pronounced, purely cognitive view of his feelings served to avoid or regulate these affects, which were particularly difficult for him and which he found disgusting. He had to constantly keep in touch with his girlfriend (e.g., by chat) to avoid being flooded by inner emptiness and anxiety, which he justified with cultural norms ("That's the way it should be"). He also had very stereotypical images of male and female roles in society and forms of conflict resolution. Therapy here concentrated on making his views more flexible and broad as well as strengthening his means to reflect on behavioral alternatives.

Even though the focus of noneffective mentalizing in Kilian's case lay on pseudomentalizing, other forms were also possible, such as the teleological mode ("If some boy meets with my ex-girlfriend despite my prohibition, then clearly he does not respect me and wants to harm me. If words are not enough, then actions must speak") and psychological equivalence ("If I can't be with her, I never want to be with another girl. She's the only one—all the others are boring and disgusting. Without her, my life is worth nothing. I can only ever love her. I don't know how to go on living without her").

The crisis plan established at the beginning of therapy foresaw which of Kilian's own behaviors and which behaviors of others could escalate his symptom behavior to the point of prompting a suicide attempt (e.g., drinking alcohol)—and which behaviors could prove helpful instead (e.g., talking to his friends or mother). For (emotional) emergencies, the therapist provided a service cell-phone number Kilian could use except at night.

The therapist repeatedly challenged Kilian's pseudomentalizing during therapy (e.g., by using humor or authenticity), while maintaining an empathic attitude toward his feelings. For example, the therapist sometimes felt almost tormented when the young man talked about his perceived superiority to others (others would underestimate him, and then he would gain their respect using violence). The therapist did not communicate such inner reactions unfiltered but first attempted to understand what it was about Kilian that was so tormenting. Only then could the therapist report back, for example, about wondering whether Kilian had noticed the inconsistencies in his interpretations. At another point, at the beginning of therapy, the therapist recognized a lack of curiosity about mental things and introduced this into the relationship when Kilian asked why the therapist had not inquired why the other boy "deserved" the beatings.

The following text excerpt illustrates the specific procedure. The patient describes a beating that sent the other boy to the hospital:

Therapist: How do you see it today? *(Mentalization-stimulating question)*
Patient: The other person deserved it 100%! *(Pseudomentalizing)*
Silence
Patient: You didn't even ask me what he did. *(Curiosity about the therapist's mental state)*
Therapist: I don't really care. *(Challenge)*
Patient: But he lied to me!
Therapist: Honestly, I can't follow you there. I would never say that he deserved it. *(Authentic self-revelation)*
Patient: Well, for me, he did.
Therapist: Yes, but that's probably why I didn't ask. I do care, but I suddenly didn't care just now because I found your reaction so drastic. *(Authentic self-revelation and the reflection of own ambivalence)*
Patient: He wouldn't listen to me! And he lied to me, even that day, and met up with my ex-girlfriend. *(Teleological)*
Therapist: I understand your need, but I also find it difficult to believe you *must* exert such strong control over someone else. *(Validating the urge but marking a different perspective)*
Patient: Yes, that could be true. My ex-girlfriend was afraid of me, too, even though I never hit her. *(Mentalizing)*
Therapist: And I'm quite torn about this, because I also find your sudden physical strength in those moments impressive. Reminds me of Rocky Bilboa from the movie, going from inferiority to victory. *(Authentic self-revelation and reflection of own ambivalence)*
Patient: I go through everything in my mind beforehand and prepare myself for everything. That's why I'm so confident of victory. *(Pseudomentalizing a fantasy of greatness)*

Therapist: I thought you were afraid when you went to such a fight—or did I misunderstand? *(Not-knowing stance)*

Patient: I was just excited because there were so many people there, and he could have knocked me out with a single punch to the temple. *(Mentalizing)*

Therapist: And then something happened during the fight, and it got out of hand? *(Exploration)*

Patient: Yeah, I should probably see to it that nobody ends up in the hospital. *(Mentalizing, agency, sense of responsibility)*

This excerpt shows the typical procedure of the MBT therapist accompanying the process from one moment to the next, while at the same time staying in contact with their own feelings and making this inner process available to the patient. It also becomes clear that the therapist must permanently adjust to the fluctuations of mentalization and react flexibly, and that a therapist cannot stabilize mentalization in the problem areas through an intervention. Rather, it is a long process that requires patience on the part of the therapist. In Kilian's case, this led him to ask himself questions instead of giving pseudomentalizing answers. Once he had become increasingly self-exploratory in therapy and able to reflect on his behavior in a less pseudomentalizing way, his self-injuries stopped, as did his engagements in violent fights. He then focused on attending school and moved to the top of his class by mid-term. Slowly, he came to terms with the idea of relaxing his grip on his ex-girlfriend.

However, during a party, he relapsed and brought that experience to the following session. The therapist applied the technique of mentalization loop, the first question being about the facts of the event. Kilian had seen his ex-girlfriend with her best friend; from his vantage point, both looked like they were having fun. The next step was to explore the mental experience during the situation. Kilian described himself during the encounter as in shock and had only one thought: "She is happy without me!" Later on, this triggered deeper reflections. Kilian reported that the close friendship with this friend was the first crack in the previously happy relationship; the encounter with the pair painfully reminded him of his loss. Then, however, in an about-face, he began to see the other boy as responsible for his dilemma, developing feelings of hatred and the desire to punch him. This could be interpreted as the externalization of his unbearable feelings for him, described above in the concept of the alien self. The next step in the mentalization loop triggers reflection on whether the feelings have changed since the incident and how it feels to talk about them in therapy. Now, and indeed for the first time, Kilian felt remorse and anger with himself. By balancing different perspectives within himself, he enabled a new perspective to emerge. He came to understand that he was struggling with accepting sadness, and that he tended to tilt toward black-and-white thinking, punishing others for his feelings. Fortunately, the incident had no further consequences, as the other boy left before a physical altercation could occur.

Therapy ended after a year. Kilian continued to attend school and internally committed to staying in school until graduating from high school. He took a volunteer job as a tutor, and toward the end of therapy he became able to weep over the breakup with his girlfriend and imagine a new relationship again.

4

Psychoanalysis and Mentalization

When we successfully mentalize, we can understand what is going on in our minds and in the minds of others—and we realize how this affects the emotions, thoughts, and actions of ourselves and others. This understanding of our perspectives and those of others leads to more successful interactions and social relationships. In some mental health disorders, such as personality disorders, individuals are impaired in their mentalizing ability, which can lead to misunderstandings regarding emotions, thoughts, and actions and result in breakdowns in interactions and relationships. It is vital that individuals learn to successfully mentalize in order to improve mental health and social function.

The mentalization concept, as we show below, is first a modern development of psychoanalytic theory that incorporates findings from relevant neighboring sciences. Second, it is a bridging concept that connects different therapeutic approaches. Third, it is a coherent therapy model that is research-oriented, manualized, and empirically well-supported. However, to date, it has provided little information about the therapeutic relationship and epistemic trust (because both are difficult to operationalize).

A core concern when practicing long-term outpatient psychodynamic or psychoanalytic therapy lies in reflecting on the therapeutic relationship, including epistemic trust and the transference–countertransference matrix. This is another reason why the mentalization approach needs to maintain its close connection to psychoanalytic theory and vice versa. A second level of consideration (content level, e.g., conflicts) lies in regarding repetitions of relational patterns, including promoting reflexive processes ("mentalizing in process"). This is valid for both individual and group settings (Fonagy et al., 2017c). Finally, fourth, the proposed perspective aligns well with a paradigm shift developed by Fonagy and Allison (2014), who proposed understanding psychotherapy as a threefold communication system. Based on general impact factors (e.g., coherence of the therapy theory, design of the therapeutic relationship), mentalization-promoting interventions stimulate reflective processes and enable thinking as rehearsal action or as a buffer between (urgent) affect and (successful) social interaction. This creates a greater openness toward social interactions (social learning) during therapy and between therapy sessions.

DOI: 10.4324/9781032674117-5

The Intersubjective Turn in Psychoanalysis

During the more than 100 years of its existence, psychoanalysis has developed from Freud's one-person psychology to a two-person or even multiperson psychology. This proceeded through the development of object-relations theories, self-psychology, and, more recently, infant research, taking an intersubjective turn in the course. In the object-relations theories, which are associated not only with such illustrious names as Klein, Balint, Bion, Winnicott, and Kernberg, besides the drive model, relational experiences and their internalization as representations gained in importance. Along the intersubjective route psychoanalysis took, by recognizing the importance of intersubjective relational experiences, they extended the drive model to include relational experiences, leading to the development of notions of a congruent self, largely resulting from processing these experiences.

Achieving sufficient self-coherence and a stable psychological structure is impossible under unfavorable developmental conditions. In intersubjective and relational psychoanalysis, the self becomes the central organizer of the psyche: The self becomes a psychic structure that acquires coherence, continuity, a characteristic form, and a permanent organization through self-experience (Stolorow et al., 1987). The intersubjective view expands our understanding of the human psyche to include understanding and recognizing others, sharing thoughts, and cooperating.

Regarding developmental psychology and treatment goals, intersubjective, relational psychoanalysis has much in common with the mentalization concept. The primary goal is not to bring conflicts and contents to consciousness (as found in classical psychoanalysis), but to develop the self. Only this allows the processing of inner (conscious and unconscious) conflicts. According to the mentalization concept, promoting mentalization changes how we access object-relational representations. In this, the mentalization concept also draws on psychoanalytic constructs (see below). But, it also draws on research findings, particularly from developmental psychology, affect development, and attachment theory.

Early relational experiences and their impact on relational competence significantly affect self-image and self-structure. This perspective also changes our understanding of change through psychoanalytic psychotherapy. By responding to the patient's affect states in an accepting, empathetic, and differentiated way and by adopting an empathic-introspective attitude, the psychoanalyst enables new "self-object" experiences. Based on the changes that occur in the structure of self-experience, they lead to acquiring or improving functional abilities as well as self-soothing, self-consolation, and self-empathy.

The expansion of the drive model to include the intersubjective perspective also led to changes in how transference and countertransference are viewed: The psychoanalyst is now more clearly involved in producing transference and countertransference. Whereas in object-relations theory, the question of the significance of the psychoanalyst's subjectivity and individuality in psychotherapeutic interaction remains largely unanswered, relational psychoanalysis formulates this more clearly. The therapist and the patient create a shared experience in the psychoanalytic relationship; the two have no true independence. This reflects the position of the mentalization approach and dispenses with the psychoanalytic claim to objectivity. The psychoanalyst no longer has sole access to understanding the patient's mental processes (Fonagy & Target 2007a, p. 919). The observational viewpoint now lies squarely within shared cognition. Intersubjectivity means mutually recognizing and acknowledging each other—which has consequences for the treatment technique, which differs from the classical psychoanalytic treatment technique. The most significant difference lies in implementing the recognition of the inevitable subjectivity of the psychoanalyst in the treatment itself: The psychoanalyst displays their own beliefs. However, not all psychoanalytic training centers follow these innovations: In the still ever-present treatment technique taught there, the psychoanalyst continues to assert the position of an authority and be a recognized interpreter of reality.

Furthermore, the view of the therapeutic stance has changed from Freud's original stipulations. The abstinence approach of classical psychoanalysis is not "neutral"; the patient reacts to it, possibly with the anxiety and frustration it precipitates. Thus, the patient's experience results from the analyst's attitude and not necessarily the patient's psychopathology. In intersubjective and relational psychoanalysis, the basis of analyst interpretations is empathic accompaniment with alert reflection of self, patient, and interaction.

Regarding interventions, however, relational psychoanalysis remains rather general. The treatment technique has to fit the individual circumstances (e.g., Orange et al., 1997), making concrete recommendations for action largely superfluous. The mentalization approach, on the other hand, formulates extensive ideas about treatment techniques. For example, this is definitively laid down for treating borderline personality disorder (BPD) with mentalization-based therapy (MBT), which became necessary, among other things, to meet the requirements for comparative psychotherapy research. This "manualization" contains recommendations useful for both outpatient individual and group therapy, the standard of which is the promotion of mentalization (see Chapter 5, especially Chapter 5.3 "Interpretation and Insight (Content Perspective) or Standpoint of Not-Knowing (Process Perspective)."

The intersubjective turn in psychoanalysis goes back to the work of Stolorow et al. (1987), which in turn is related to self-psychology (Kohut 1971) and led to relational psychoanalysis, whose best-known representatives are Benjamin (2009) and Mitchell (2000). The mentalization concept is closely related to this intersubjective turn in psychoanalysis. The German psychoanalysts Altmeyer and Thomä formulate it as follows:

> The mentalization concept is the most interesting, comprehensive, and influential theoretical project of contemporary psychoanalysis. It works both theoretically (developmental psychology) as well as in its therapeutic application with a relational model of the psyche, which is well on its way to becoming the 'common ground' of psychoanalytic pluralism.
>
> (2016, p. 11)

Contemporary Psychoanalysis

The distinctive feature of psychoanalytic theory is its attention to unconscious psychological processes and motivational forces to explain complex and often paradoxical human behaviors. Based on Altmeyer and Thomä's approach (2016), the mentalization concept is understood as part of the psychoanalytic tradition and situated within the pluralism of models of contemporary psychoanalysis (Fonagy & Target, 2003). Fonagy and Target clearly position the mentalization approach on the foundation of psychoanalysis, especially regarding:

- the biological nature of humans, the driving force behind mental adjustment;
- complex unconscious psychological processes that are responsible for both the content of conscious thought and our behavior, whereas unconscious fantasies motivate and determine our behavior, affect regulation, and ability to navigate a complex social world;
- constitutional and early environmental and interactional experiences involved in establishing self-regulatory processes;
- the construction of representational, intrapsychic structures based on drive-affect motives and interpersonal experiences; these representations generate expectations regarding other people, determine the representations of self and objects, and give rise to the inner world;
- unconscious desires, influenced by a developmental hierarchy of defenses;
- symptoms that can have different meanings and reflect inner representations, including relational experiences;
- the therapeutic relationship, which lies at the center of therapy and provides insight into unconscious processes (modified from Fonagy & Target, 2003).

While developing the mentalization model, Fonagy and colleagues drew on and further developed important psychoanalytic concepts and authors. Mention should be made, for example, of Spitz & Wolf (1946), who early on attributed prominence to the mother–child interaction, and Bowlby and the first and second generation of attachment theory and research (Bowlby, 1969, 1973, 1982). Affect plays a special role in child development: The emotional expression of the caregiver fulfills a comforting or holding function that supports the establishment of a child's emotional balance. Winnicott (1962) is credited with formulating the importance of maternal mirroring for the development of a sense of self and self-regulation. The child's psychic self emerges when they learn to perceive themselves as a thinking and feeling being in another person's psyche.

For Loewald (1973), all mental activity is relational (interactional and intersubjective). He considered internalization, or social learning, to be the basal mental process that drives development. Sandler (1960) introduced representations and internal working models into psychoanalytic theory, before Bowlby elaborated them further. Both assume that relational representations consist essentially of expectations. Particularly Sandler sees the representational world as a frame of reference centered on the representation of feeling states and values.

For Wilfred Bion (1962), the containment function of thinking enables us to endure failure. We acquire the ability to symbolize via the alpha function, whereupon internal, concretely perceived (beta) processes are transformed into bearable experiences (Lecours & Bouchard, 1997, p. 858). In Germany Mentzos (2017, p. 61) compares Bion's concept with the model of marked affect-mirroring in the mentalization approach and concludes that both mean something similar, though the mentalization approach is more convincing and precise in its terminology and research support. Fonagy and Target (2006) also emphasize the close relationship between the mentalization approach and Bion's notion of containment. They argue that the conceptualization of sensitivity has much in common with Bion's understanding of the containment function (Bion, 1962). If marked affect mirroring is missing, no containment takes place, resulting in cumulative traumatization. The mirroring fuses with an affect expression that is incompatible with the infant's feelings. Symbolization helps postpone the satisfaction of pressing needs and modulate strong emotions, thus serving adaptation. Lecours and Bouchards (1997) describe in detail and with great differentiation how symbolization, containment (Bion), and mentalization (Fonagy et al.) relate to each other.

Mentalization as Psychic Transformation

Within the framework of psychoanalytic theorizing, French psychoanalysts were the first to work with a mentalization concept. To better grasp psychosomatic disorders and the unimaginative, concretistic way of thinking (cf. alexithymia), French psychoanalysts introduced the term "mentalization" into psychoanalysis as far back as the 1960s (Fain & David, 1963; Fain & Marty, 1964; Luquet, 1981; Marty, 1990).

Drawing on Freud (1925), Lecours and Bouchard (1997) describe how processes of bodily drive-affect excitations are transformed into symbolized mental contents; that is, how somatic and motor processes become psychic experiences. Allen and colleagues (2008, p. 8) also see the mentalization approach as present in Freud's writings, even though he did not explicitly use the term mentalization.

Lecours and Bouchard (1997) are psychoanalysts who stem from Montreal (Canada) and thus connect the English (e.g., Bion, Winnicott) with the French tradition of psychoanalysis, situating the mentalization concept in Freud's metapsychology. "mentalizing entails making something non-mental into something mental. Thus the OED [Oxford English Dictionary] definition of mentalizing as *giving a mental quality to* something or *cultivating mentally* is a fundamentally Freudian concept" (Allen et al., 2008, p. 9).

The mentalization process refers to a preconscious ego function of transforming bodily excitations into intrapsychic representations. Mental transformation is necessary to process early raw, concrete, and unmentalized experiences before repression/defense occurs. This involves binding energy and connecting ideas during the transition from the primary to the secondary process. Previously free-flowing (drive) energy is bound into psychic energy by increasing the level in the occupation process, enabling psychic processing or representation (Fonagy et al., 2004, p. 36). This implies viewing the symbolic and repressed unconscious not as preformed but as (necessarily) mentalized beforehand.

Thus, from the point of view of these authors, mentalizing denotes a continuous, never-ending process of transforming mental content by organizing representations. It allows one to construct mental structures of increasing complexity, leading to greater symbolization and abstraction.

Mentalization, Representation, and Symbolization

> We think mentalization is a concept that is both generic and more precise in its description of this transformation process.
>
> (Lecours & Bouchard, 1997, p. 857)

If one follows these two authors, mentalization is an overarching concept encompassing the processes of representation, the alpha function, and symbolization. Mentalization occurs by associating physical and sensory sensations with mental ideas and the formation of representations as well as increasingly structuring these representations. Representation, symbolization, and mentalization are often used synonymously, but Lecours and Bouchard distinguish specific functions:

- *Representation* means elaborating and using stable ideas about an object rather than the object itself. Creating representations connects basal experiences with images and words.
- *Symbolization* builds on this, linking mental representations and leading to the imaginative use of representations (e.g., by assuming motives and intentions for actions), instead of, and in contrast to, the concrete application of immediate experiences. Symbolization connects representations and is considered the second building block of mentalization (1997, p. 858).

In this regard, the authors emphasize the importance of mentalization for tolerating and regulating affect, calling it the "immune system of the psyche" (Lecours & Bouchard, 1997, p. 857). Mentalization absorbs stress from internal and external stressors through the never-ending mental processing of physical arousal and transforms it into mental content and representation.

"Mentalization is a slow and progressive process, perhaps the venture of a lifetime" (Lecours & Bouchard, 1997, 865). According to Luquet's model (1987, as cited in Lecours & Bouchard, 1997, p. 858), transformation occurs at different levels:

1. In primary-process thinking, basal sensory experiences are linked associatively to affect-charged images (e.g., in the equivalence mode inside equals outside, thing equals representation ...).
2. In preconscious thought processes, a transition occurs from primary-process thinking (creates creativity in associations) to secondary-process thinking

(metacognitions, associations are linked to form words and language), accompanied by increasing symbolization and linking symbols to representational structures.

3. Mentalization here means conscious, reflective thinking (in the sense of controlled, explicit mentalization). Inner experiences are transformed following the laws of discourse and syntax (secondary process, logic), adapted to social communication, and made intelligible to others.

Mentalization also refers to different levels of expression and organization of the representational system (Lecours & Bouchard, 1997, p. 860), which are as follows:

- *Somatic mode:* Affects are expressed viscerally via physiological sensations, e.g., functional disturbances, pain, or somatic lesions.
- *Motoric mode:* Expression through behavior (acting out), voluntary muscle activity being the main channel.
- *Figural mode:* Object representations and primary processes dominate; mental content is expressed in images, dreams, fantasies, and metaphors.
- *Verbal mode:* Expression through words and representations (secondary process).

Table 4.1 shows the levels of organization of the representational system (Lecours & Bouchard, 1997, p. 857; modified from Allen et al., 2008, p. 10). As mentalization increases, affect is better tolerated and experienced less intensely. Mentalization enables reflective activity; in this regard, current Anglo-American publications agree with the Franco-Canadian psychoanalysts. However, the complex assignment of transformation, expression, and organization levels has not gained footing in the literature. One finds individual aspects thereof in the Reflecting Functioning Scale (RF Scale; Fonagy et al., 1998), which describes levels of mentalization and overlap with the description of the general impairments of self- and interpersonal functioning (ICD-11, World Health Organization, 2020) or explains psychosomatic disorders ("body mode"; Schultz-Venrath, 2024). What current terminology deems mentalizing represents only a subset of the process the French researchers called mentalization.

Conclusion

Mentalization encompasses basal mental processes, including representation and symbolization, that transform drive-affect experiences into mental phenomena and structures. Effective and ineffective mentalizing is also related to establishing the representational system. Therefore, it seems to make sense to reconnect the mentalization concept to psychoanalytic theorizing.

Table 4.1 Organizational levels of the representational system.

Representation leves	Examples
1. **Disruptive impulse activity***, drive-affect experiences are neither tolerated nor contained; the alpha function does not process beta elements ("short-circuiting" of mental processing).	An unbearable urge to act, violent behavior, acting-out, self-injury, sudden headaches (somatization)
2. **Modulated impulse activity,** expressions of somewhat better processed and more adaptive affects.	Unexplained outbursts of crying or fantasies of hitting someone.
3. **Externalization,** the mental representation of a desire or affect state that is simultaneously partially externalized by projection or attribution (e.g., externalizing an alien self).	The justification of own anger by a provocation from another person; blanket assertion that everyone would feel the same way in a given situation
4. **Appropriation or psychological ownership,** the comprehensive recognition of one's desires and affects as subjective and tolerable experiences.	The identification and designation of specific emotional states, e.g., attributing physiological arousal to anxiety.
5. **Meaning associations,** complex, verbal representations that add depth to mental experiences (e.g., mentalized affectivity).	Insight and reflection accompany authentic emotions and open up new perspectives for the patient.

Modified after Allen et al. (2008, p. 10).

* The contents of the drive-affect impulse may be either defended (i.e., previously sym-bolized, then defended) or not yet symbolized at all, in the sense of unmentalized and unrepresented raw sensory experiences.

Affect Regulation, Representation, and Intrapsychic Conflict

Freud's assumptions about affects and their regulation changed over time. In his first phase (until about 1897), he thought affects created in traumatic situations and blocked in their dissipation were responsible for subsequent symptoms. Freud assumed that the blocked discharge of the energy contained in the affects can lead to the transformation into hysterical symptoms. In the next phase (1897–1923), he saw affects as the psychic manifestation of drives, along with ideas and fanta-sies: Affects originate in the id. Affects form if the discharge of drives is inhibited, e.g., by education, society, or culture. Eventually, Freud (1926) says affects acquire signaling and adaptive functions and are subject to a limited degree of control by the ego. Later developments in psychoanalytic theorizing assigned increasing im-portance to affect regulation (as a preconscious ego function).

The mentalization model is highly compatible with the model of a develop-mentally acquired capacity for affect regulation as an ego function. Body-based drive-affect experiences are psychically represented developmentally and through relational experiences (e.g., depending on attachment security, marked affect mirroring, or containment) and allow for increasing self-direction (Fonagy et al., 2002).

One central commonality of the psychoanalytic models with a mentalization approach is their emphasis on mental relational representations in the self, i.e., the influence the environment exerts on the individual. These representational structures preserve and mediate developmental experiences. Children transform early interactions with their primary caregivers into cognitive-affective schemas of their self and others. At the same time, drive-affect-guided motives, e.g., desires or expectations (Fonagy & Target, 2003), shape their representations. Affect processing occurs largely automatically, outside of consciousness. In this context, unconscious processing differs qualitatively from its conscious counterpart. The assumption of motivation by unconscious affect assumes various independent processing units (neural networks) that sometimes operate side by side—sometimes cooperatively, sometimes rivalrously—and influence both conscious and unconscious decisions. The fact that individual mental states are each generated by independent circuits means these states can also conflict with each other (e.g., positive and negative affects can be activated simultaneously). Thus, internal conflicts are emergent properties of the human brain. The ego must cope with demands that are both external (contextual) and internal (emotional and motivational) in nature (Fonagy & Target, 2003).

Therefore, internal working models and representations do not correspond to a consensual reality; rather, they are individual, distorted by constitution, defense mechanisms, and drives. Developing cognitive-emotional structures to cope with incompatibilities in processing emotional information is a central developmental goal in all psychotherapies.

4.1   Mentalization and Its Influence on Psychoanalytic Theory and Practice

The Beginnings: Reflection on Motives Gains Importance

Researchers have proposed several origins of the mentalization approach, yet the founding myth is still missing some parts. Mentalization was first mentioned in the *Oxford English Dictionary* (*OED*) in 1906: "first, to construct or picture in the mind, or to give a mental quality to; second, to develop or cultivate mentally, or to stimulate the mind of" (Allen et al., 2008, p. 3).

For Fonagy and Target (2003), an empirical study of early childhood attachment security in the early 1990s provided the stimulation for a more intensive examination of mentalization: Attachment security could be predicted reliably by studying the mother's ability to reflect on her own relationships as a child with her parents (Fonagy et al., 1991). Fonagy & Target (2003) tried to identify the process by which understanding of the self as a mental originator emerges from interpersonal experiences and, in particular, from primary object relations.

Allen et al. (2008, p. xvii), on the other hand, describe the development of the mentalization model in three waves: first, the description of mentalizing impairments as a core problem of autism; second, of social and trauma-related mentalizing disorders in borderline patients; and third, the extension to other disorders and various treatment procedures.

However, one can also map the development and increasing prevalence of the mentalization approach along three paradigm shifts.

First Paradigm Shift: Changing View of Childhood— Attachment Theory and Infant Research

The first publications on mentalization (1989–1997) are closely related to attachment theory and the reconstruction of child development by modern infant research (cf. Stern, 1985). The title *The Competent Infant* by the German author Martin Dornes may serve as a cue (Dornes, 1992). Dornes reviews modern infant and toddler research results and places them squarely in the context of psychoanalytic theorizing (Dornes, 1997, 2000). Until then, the infant had been considered predominantly as passive and at the mercy of their drive needs. However, from the perspective of empirical infant and toddler research, the infant is proactive, expresses various emotions, is socially competent, and actively perceives their environment. They seek environmental stimuli and can relate different sensory stimuli to each other.

The Crucial Importance of Developmental Psychology for Mentalization Theory

Observations of infants have been systematically documented since at least the founding of the Jackson Day Nursery in Vienna in 1937 by Anna Freud and Dorothy T. Burlingham (Wininger et al., 2013). This development spawned a further psychoanalytic research tradition by, among others, René Spitz and Margaret Mahler. Film documentation, ethnographic observations, the analysis of case histories, and interviews together formed a methodological canon for establishing a theory of early childhood development based on primary data. Few disciplines have produced a comparable density of publications on early child development over such a long period as psychoanalysis (Wininger et al., 2013, p. 9). The work of Fonagy and colleagues proved to fit nicely into traditional developmental psychological theory and research within psychoanalysis.

Attachment is not an end in itself but enables the development of a representational system (Fonagy et al., 2002). Fonagy and colleagues used mentalization as a hinge for synthesizing psychoanalysis and attachment theory, anchoring the treatment in developmental psychology (Allen et al., 2008, p. 73). The evolutionary function of early object relations lies in ensuring an environment for the young child in which they can safely develop an understanding of their own mental states and the internal states of others (Fonagy & Target, 2003). Bowlby (1969, 1973,

1982) emphasizes the importance of safety (sensitivity and predictability) in early relationships. The internalization of interpersonal relationships (internal working models) is compatible with object-relations theory. According to Bowlby, the child constructs expectations regarding the behavior of the attachment figure while also regarding their own behavior (Fonagy & Target, 2003).

The early publications by Peter Fonagy's research group focused on attachment and representation (Fonagy, 1991, 1995; Fonagy & Target, 1996a, 1996b; Fonagy et al., 1991, 1992, 1993, 1998). Early clinical contributions addressed the limitations of mentalization in borderline disorders (Fonagy, 1989, 1991).

Second Paradigm Shift: Mentalization and Psychotherapy Research

Based on the repeatedly replicated research findings (e.g., Wampold & Imel, 2015) that schools of therapy and their respective techniques can predict only a small portion of the variance in psychotherapy outcomes, today the therapeutic relationship and other aspects of treatment have come to the fore. Fonagy and Allison (2014) contributed to this discussion with their model of psychotherapy as a threefold communication system.

This subjected psychoanalysis to an empirical stress test to face critical questions about its effectiveness. And although it does not do so badly (e.g., by emphasizing the importance of the therapeutic relationship), it must change under the influence of neighboring sciences (see Chapter 1).

This new perspective sees the improvement of mentalizing skills as central to the therapeutic process: "We propose boldly that mentalization—attending to mental states in oneself and others—is the *most fundamental common factor* among all psychotherapeutic treatments" (Allen et al., 2008, p. xi). In this perspective, each therapy theory respectively uses coherent explanatory models to convey confidence, hope, and security. The targeted promotion of mentalization, i.e., the systematic promotion of reflection, attribution of meaning, and emphasis on affects, leads to the restoration of social learning and change outside therapy sessions (see Chapter 2.7).

Third Paradigm Shift: Mentalization as a Basic Anthropological Constant

Human thinking is an individual improvisation enmeshed in a sociocultural matrix.

(Tomasello, 2014, p. 1)

The classical psychoanalytic view emphasized the individual's intrapsychic experiences and expressed relatively little interest in the real world behind those intrapsychic experiences. It tacitly assumed that the developmental stages of drives are more important than the role of the real environment. At the same time, many more recent theories ascribe central importance to the actual behavior of caregivers and the sociocultural context. If we consider the significant role cultural factors play in the development of the self, we can assume that psychoanalysts have not realized their own roots in Western culture (Fonagy & Target, 2003). Also, the individuated self, which lies at the center of most psychoanalytic formulations, is specifically Western in its orientation, in contrast to the relational self, which is particularly represented by non-Western cultures (Keller, 2021; Otto & Keller, 2014). Characteristic of this relational self are, for example, more permeable and mobile self-object boundaries or an emphasis on social control.

In this regard, it is by no means a new phenomenon to examine the sociocultural environment within psychoanalysis. What is new is the reference of psychoanalytic theory to findings from anthropology (e.g., Tomasello, 2014) or the cognitive sciences (e.g., the theory of mind). Theory of mind questions whether chimpanzees, as our closest relatives, possess a theory of mind and whether they differ from humans in this regard (Premack & Woodruff, 1978; Schlicht, 2022). "Theory of mind is the attempt to understand what others think, know, believe, want, plan, or like. Theory of mind thus refers to the process of accessing and thinking about the mental states of others" (Böckler-Raettig, 2019, p. 11). Theory of mind deals with the question of how to see through the intentions of others, while at the same time enabling one to visualize one's own state of mind, e.g., to mentally travel in time—a specifically human ability to visualize nonpresent needs and let them influence planned actions.

The terms theory of mind and mentalization are often used synonymously in this context (Böckler-Raettig, 2019; Förstl, 2012; Schlicht, 2022). Allen and colleagues (2008) see theory of mind as the conceptual framework for the mentalization model, which, in everyday terms, attributes behavior to mental states.

However, mentalization theory represents an extension and a critique of previous theory of mind research, which scholars have criticized as mechanistic and biologically truncated. With its false belief paradigm (Wimmer & Perner, 1983), theory of mind is seen as too narrow because it fails to capture the relational and affect-regulating aspects of behavioral interpretation based on mental states. Mentalization theory, on the other hand, takes a social interactionist approach and extends this approach to include the perspective of development.

We develop an understanding of the mind when our caregivers perceive (mentalize) us as independent psychological beings with our own intentions, feelings, and motives. Thus, mentalization theory represents an integrative bridge that links theory of mind, attachment theory, and the psychoanalytic notion of symbolization (Choi-Kain & Gunderson, 2008).

Fonagy and colleagues (2002) also take up the key findings in Tomasello's research from developmental psychology, as do representatives of contemporary psychoanalysis in Germany (Altmeyer & Thomä, 2016; Buchholz, 2006). Given the thesis of shared intentionality proposed by the Critical Theory of Habermas (1984, 2009) and Honneth (2012), which, according to Tomasello, describes the starting point of human beings, the proximity to mentalization theory becomes more than obvious: Early man developed uniquely at the point in evolution when he began to want to understand the intentions of others, in other words, when he began to mentalize (Brauner, 2018).

Tomasello (2014), a representative of evolutionary anthropology, focused extensively on developments in the early period of human evolution (i.e., the period from about 400,000 years ago to about 10,000 years ago). His models of shared intentionality and the resulting developments are based on empirical and comparative studies of communication in great apes and human infants and address the question: What makes human thought so unique?

Human thought is fundamentally cooperative. The great apes, ancestors of Homo sapiens, are social beings but live individualistic and competitive lives, their thinking is directed toward the achievement of individual goals (Tomasello, 2014). The social thinking of chimpanzees, our closest relative, is roughly equivalent to that of three-year-old children in equivalence mode. For example, great apes prefer to eat alone and do not know cooperative childcare. Their social relationships are structured more by competition and hierarchies (Tomasello, 2014).

Participation of early humans in collaborative activities with others leads to shared goals (e.g., we both know we want to hunt the deer) and shared attention, which generate individual roles and individual perspectives in need coordination (e.g., through pointing, pantomime, or initial symbols). Thus, early human begins with pointing as a sign of shared intentionality. It is not war that is the father of all things (Heraclitus) but cooperation. Freud's myth of the origin of human culture through patricide in the primordial horde did not determine the development of culture but rather the fundamentally social nature of human beings (Brauner, 2018).

Another step toward collective intentionality occurred when human populations began to grow larger and compete with one another. Competition meant that group life became a communal activity, spawning a group culture. Group consciousness stemmed from the ability to build a common cultural background through cultural conventions, norms (rituals), and institutions. This group identity was spatially expanded and related temporally to ancestors and descendants.

According to Tomasello (2014), collective intentionality involves two dimensions:

1. *Synchronous social organization:* Culture (conventions, norms, and institutions) coordinates social interactions. Mutual cooperation and group dependence caused the first social evaluation to gain in importance (e.g., choosing a cheater or a dawdler meant less success in hunting or foraging). Thus, early humans were already concerned about evaluation by others, namely, how potential partners (for hunting or foraging) evaluated cooperation (public esteem, reputation).
2. *A diachronic transmission of knowledge and the results of cultural practices:* New modes of cooperative communication allow children to build new forms of

cognitive representation, reasoning, and introspection during their long developmental period. Social learning and instruction then lead to a cultural evolution that allows for much faster adaptation and development than biological-genetic evolution. The important thing in this process is determining who I can trust in a larger group and who I should tend to be wary of so as not to be led astray (epistemic vigilance).

Living together in larger populations and competing with rival groups fostered the development of social understanding, anticipation, and imaginative mental strategies. Group cooperation necessitated sophisticated communication, especially prompting, informing, and sharing (e.g., food, feelings, attitudes). Great apes can indeed sense the intentions of other apes and humans and use communicative gestures to prompt others; but because only they align intentions, only humans communicate to inform and share. "The success of one's coalition depended on competency in social cognition, the key part of which is the symbolic representation of mental states, what we call mentalizing. Competition with intelligent conspecifics requires skill in understanding and outsmarting other people" (Allen & Fonagy, 2006, p. 56). Thus, besides cooperation, competition drove the development of social cognition and cultural development (Kirsch, 2019).

Tomasello (2014) outlines a model of the phylogenetic development of humans and thus paints a picture of our very core. He identifies several criteria to distinguish modern humans from the great apes:

- our prosocial attitude;
- our cooperative thinking and collaboration (shared intentionality);
- our social cognitions (mentalization, theory of mind);
- our communication behavior (the development of languages);
- our social learning (the transmission of knowledge and culture across generations);
- our social norms and moral identity (the result of collective intentionality).

There are good reasons to believe that these criteria are primary, in the sense that they precede the individual and form a cultural matrix along which the development of the self and its relationships takes place (including attachment patterns and internal working models).

If one follows this perspective (only sketchily presented here), we recognize mentalizing capacity as an essential anthropological quantity and part of the essence of being human. The ability to cooperate, self-direct, and integrate with social groups as well as to symbolize and imagine, to form myths (e.g., including fiction), and to establish conventions and group norms result from our phylogenetic development and rely on our means of social cognition. Thus, mentalization theory is not limited to a subject theory—oriented toward the individual—but can significantly contribute to sociological, anthropological, and other social science topics.

Conclusion

The crucial weakness of the mentalization approach is simultaneously its strength: It leaves some traditional psychoanalytic concepts behind and integrates results from neighboring sciences (Fonagy & Target, 2003).

According to both psychoanalytic theory and the mentalization model, not only do internal representations depict consensual reality, they are distorted by defense mechanisms and drives.

The reference point "affects and their regulation" enabled the working group around Fonagy to build a bridge between traditional psychoanalytic (intrapsychic) models and the newer interpersonal approaches. Nevertheless, it is legitimate to ask whether this is a genuinely psychoanalytic or rather an integrative model that relates psychoanalysis to neighboring disciplines.

4.2   Theoretical Implications

In this section, we use some central concepts of psychoanalysis (sexuality, unconscious, defense mechanisms, and transference) as examples to show, on the one hand, how mentalization theory—a modern advancement within psychoanalysis—developed new perspectives on these core concepts and how, on the other hand, mentalization theory became so well advanced in the process that it now provides a coherent and comprehensive theoretical model that relates the central psychoanalytic concepts to relevant neighboring sciences.

Sexuality and Drive from the Perspective of Mentalization Theory

The Neglect of Sexuality in Psychoanalysis

The major theories of psychoanalysis today emphasize other fields of clinical work.

(Fonagy, 2008, p. 14)

The topic of sexuality has evolved not only in society but also in psychoanalysis, albeit in opposite directions. Until the 1950s, only two institutions were considered competent to issue statements about sexuality: the churches and psychoanalysis. This is different today.

Two developments are responsible for the loss of importance psychoanalysis has experienced regarding this topic. First, psychoanalysis devoted too little attention to the social aspects of sexuality and actual sexual activity. The Kinsey Reports, for example, examined the sexual behavior of men and women in American society (Kinsey et al., 1948, 1953; see Herzog, 2015). This development peaked with

Masters and Johnson's (1966) work. Subsequently, the competence of psychoanalysis on this topic was questioned. Yet, instead of taking up the development as a challenge to include sexual acts, social, and societal aspects, Anglo-American psychoanalysis—in contrast to French psychoanalysis—counterattacked. It criticized that Kinsey et al. had treated people like animals and excluded the subject of "love" (Kinsey et al., 1948, 1953), leading to the discovery of the "love doctrine" (1948–1968).

Second, in psychoanalytic theorizing, the aspects of drive and desire took a back seat in favor of the concepts of primary love and attachment needs by emphasizing self-psychology, object-relations psychology, and the intersubjective approach (Herzog, 2015).

In psychoanalytic treatments, too, libidinal (psycho)sexuality increasingly receded into the background, allowing transference and countertransference to become the significant issues. This occurred partly because of the move away from drive theory and toward object-relations theories, self-psychology, and intersubjective approaches. Fonagy (2008, p. 32) illustrated this with a language analytic study: There was a steady increase in publications on transference and countertransference in the psychoanalytic literature between 1925 and 2000, while publications on sexuality decreased steadily over the same period.

A New Developmental-Psychological Perspective on the Meaning of Sexuality

Fonagy and Target (Fonagy, 2008; Fonagy & Allison, 2014; Target, 2013, 2015) explored the topic of sexual desire from the perspective of mentalization. In their contributions, the basis for integrating drive, sexual desire, affect, and attachment experiences lies in the theory of affect mirroring, well known from the mentalization approach. The authors draw on the general seduction theory of the French psychoanalyst Laplanche, who studied the unconscious communication of erotic experiences in the early mother–child relationship (Laplanche, 1995; Laplanche & Pontalis, 1968). The mother sexualizes the child's arousal, unconsciously seducing them but then abandoning them with an unattainable and incomprehensible meaning. Laplanche assumes a sexualization of early arousal: A lost object can never be recovered, and the search for it shapes human sexuality (e.g., the breast as lost object, then charged as a phantasmatic breast) (Laplanche, 1997). Like Laplanche, Fonagy and Target explore how and why mysterious and troubling things necessarily develop in and belong to the realm of sexuality. They attribute this to the fact that sexual desire and affect do not experience adequate mirroring and containment between the attachment figure and the child.

Psychic life rests on representations of the child's physical experiences, whose sensorimotor experiences form the basis for sensations. Psychosexuality is equally rooted in sensorimotor perceptions, and sexual arousal is ubiquitous from early childhood.

Sexuality, Affect Mirroring, and the Development of the Self

The most important task of marked mirroring is to incorporate unintegrated aspects of self-states into coherent representations. Forming a symbolic representation of affect states generates the basis for affect regulation and impulse control. However, mothers and fathers usually find it difficult to accurately mirror the child's sexual arousal. The most common reactions, they say, are rejection or looking away. Fonagy describes two studies in this regard (Fonagy, 2008): In one study, mothers reported how they responded to affective cues, including sexual arousal, in their three- to six-month-old babies. All mothers indicated that they regularly responded to and mirrored joy, fear, etc., but generally ignored sexual arousal altogether (e.g., by looking away)—although the vast majority of mothers responding to the survey had in fact perceived sexual arousal in their babies. Sexual arousal is rarely paid attention to in infant and toddler observations, and positive responses were even rarer in this context.

The demand to also mirror an infant's sexual arousal and affect induces a dilemma for the attachment figure: Inasmuch as the child experiences any affect mirroring, it is done in a way Laplanche has described as "enigmatic" or "puzzling" (Laplanche, 1995), mostly in the form of unconscious seductive mirroring of the child's desires (along with the attachment figure's desires directed toward the child) and the simultaneous frustration of needs and desires.

The processing of an insufficiently (or unmarkedly) mirrored affective experience results in the affective experience going unrecognized or perceived only with great distortion. Sexual arousal remains unmirrored and never reaches a coherent, metabolized representation, precipitating a lack of coherence and integration in the child's self. The resulting diffuse sense of self remains potentially overwhelming. If mirroring fails because the caregiver mirrors unmarkedly or inaccurately, the child internalizes a "mismatch," which the child then perceives as foreign and unintegrated—and must be projected (alien self).

The child often experiences sexual arousal as foreign, as not belonging to the self and not something originally their own because the caregiver has failed to mirror it in a sufficiently marked way. The enigmatic dimension of sexuality invites elaboration, which is usually done through someone else (Target, 2015). In (later) sexual experience, the parts perceived as foreign are then projected outwardly (e.g., the arousal of the other leads to one's own arousal). Sexual arousal becomes intimately involved in a fantasized or real intersubjective experience (Fonagy, 2008, p. 32).

Conclusion: Adult Sexuality Is Incongruent with the Self

The alien self is projected and re-introjected: arousal is experienced in the other, enjoyed, experienced with them, and then re-internalized.

> "The pleasure of eroticism [...] comes from placing oneself in a state of the psyche that feels like the state of the other, and that removes the limitations of the self [...] Sexual pleasure, by momentarily exerting control over the thoughts and feelings of the other, can be considered a particular example of projective identification" (Target, 2013, p. 134, transl. Joseph Smith).
>
> The waning of sexual interest in long-term relationships is then "actually the achievement of a more integrated state of self" (Target, 2013, p. 135, transl. JS) through the emergence of a sustainable attachment relationship.

Satisfactory adult sexuality is arguably bound by provisions: The relationship must provide both unconscious and conscious opportunities to accept the projections of the other. The attachment experiences must provide sufficient security to this end. Experiencing a reliable feeling of secure boundaries of the body self are the preconditions for sacrificing boundaries in the short term without creating too serious a threat. Mutual desire and mutual arousal are the means to a full psychosexual experience. It must be possible to reuptake the projected parts once the sexual arousal and sexual experiences have subsided. Ideally, the arc of the sexual desire to merge with the other and then return to oneself should close. If that fails, the person becomes "stuck with the other" in a threatening way (Fonagy, 2008, p. 26).

Based on these considerations, Fonagy and Target move away from the assumptions of drive psychology and refer to the intersubjective genesis of drive-oriented desires (Fonagy, 2008; Target, 2013). Early affect mirroring processes, projective identification (externalizing an alien self), and insufficient mentalization once again demonstrate the importance of mentalization in transforming intense drive-affect experiences into tolerable affect states or their passive reversal.

The Unconscious and Consciousness

Psychoanalysis concerns the differences between inner perception (subjective attribution of meaning) and external reality. These differences arise from distortions (defense mechanisms) and from early experiences (e.g., internal working models and attachment patterns). The interest in object-relations theories, infant research, and intersubjective approaches demanded theoretical insights to address relationships as structure-forming elements (the psyche as a reflection of internalized relational experiences) and to focus on the here and now of current interactions.

The shift in perspective from a biologically based theory of drives and structure to a theory of object relations, socialization, and inculturation brought internalized relational experiences, the social environment, and microcommunication processes to the fore. In this context, Gödde and Buchholz as well as Fonagy and Allison (Fonagy & Allison, 2016; Gödde, 2018; Gödde & Buchholz, 2011) inspired the current discourses on consciousness and the unconscious that relate psychoanalytic concepts to neighboring sciences (e.g., neuroscience, theory of mind, attachment, and infant research) and develop new perspectives on the complexity of conscious and unconscious processes.

The Unconscious as a Resonant Space

Gödde and Buchholz (Gödde, 2018; Gödde & Buchholz, 2011) distinguish vertical and horizontal dimensions of the unconscious, which, since it is not directly observable, is most easily described by metaphors. Freud's metaphors encompassed merely a vertical model of the unconscious: bottom (primitive, libidinal) vs. top (cultured, controlled, mature), with the core aspect of displacement and repression. The vertical model differentiates between surface and depth, while the repression barrier separates the lower and upper levels. However, in actual therapeutic situations, unconscious resonances often come into play that cannot be expressed in the vertical model but are still greatly important in shaping relationships.

A lack of responsive experiences in childhood and adolescence results in pathogenic unconscious processes associated with alienation. The focus of attention has shifted to the influence of relational experiences that determine development from birth, are internalized, and find expression in internal objects and formative relational patterns (Gödde, 2018). One can best describe them using a horizontal dimension of the unconscious, a social interactive model. The horizontal model emphasizes social resonance phenomena that "value the surface and seek meaning in verbal and gestural exchanges, not what lies behind them" (Gödde & Buchholz, 2011, p. 11, transl. JS). This system of social resonances juxtaposes visible behavior with invisible motives and intentions. The psychoanalytic view of the unconscious is extended here to a communication model and supplemented by the common search for intentions, i.e., feelings, motives, memories.

Unconscious Interpersonal Processes

One finds inklings of the social-interpersonal model already in Freud, although he did not elaborate on them further. His call for free association and equal attention served to promote the possibility of perceiving the unconscious, i.e., subtle details, irritations, and changes of topic in dialog; this resembles the early, sensitive interaction between mother and infant. Such actions require great openness to avoid presuming or labeling what is primary and what is secondary, because early categorizations often obscure the view of unconscious resonance phenomena (hence, the equal attention).

Even infants are proactive in forming relationships and seeking social resonance. The latter is vital for building consciousness and the coherence of the self throughout life. The perception of others as intentional agents builds on the emotions of important caregivers, combined with the desire to initiate responses as initiator. This creates coherence and expands the complexity of self-organizing states (Gödde & Buchholz, 2011). "Such a rearrangement of its guiding differences could cause psychoanalysis to abandon the illusion that it could investigate the inner space of the soul for itself, that is, without external references" (Gödde, 2018, p. 39, transl. JS).

Conclusion

Gödde (2018, p. 40) distinguishes the following means of accessing the unconscious:

- through the interplay of free ideas and free-floating attention;
- through transference and countertransference;
- through scenic understanding;
- through the ability to perceive, co-experience, and shape the intersubjective events in the relationship, to explore motives and intentions, and thus to promote the development of the psychic interior, symbolization, and mentalization.

Consciousness as an Integrative Action of the Brain

Whereas Freud understood consciousness as merely a perception of unconscious mental activity, Bion described how one acquires consciousness through the "digestive work" of the alpha function (Bion, 1962); undigested, diffuse sensations ("beta elements") become conscious and available through communicative processes (symbolization).

Fonagy and Allison go one step further and suggest that conscious perception is an integrative action of the brain and a vulnerable developmental process (Fonagy & Allison, 2016). They argue that three aspects are necessary to perceive something consciously: First, to consciously perceive a concrete or abstract object as an object, one must assemble impressions or perceptions from the flow of events as an entity (inner horizon). Second, the subject must exhibit a wholeness called "coherence." Conscious perceptions of objects (including self-perception) involve synthesizing them into a coherent whole. Symbolization can create such coherence. Third, the consciousness of something comprises "intentionality," which describes the human capacity to relate to something, colloquially expressed as "purpose." Therefore, we can view consciousness as an intentional synthesis of perceptions into a coherent whole, the goal being to communicate that experience to others. And the intention to communicate is implicit in consciousness. Social learning—the communication of experience—distinguishes us from other species and makes social cooperation and competition a central part of our nature. To function, love, and work in social groups, our subjective experience must acquire the properties of coherence, intentionality, and an inner horizon to enable communication.

Consciousness, then, involves processing experience. However, before this processing (i.e., symbolization, e.g., through language) takes place, experiences are too diffuse to be communicated: The psyche needs a mechanism for highlighting those experiences that are useful and shareable with others, a kind of searchlight to pick out socially relevant information. Consciousness thus serves as an experiential filter (Fonagy & Allison, 2016, p. 14). The "inner horizon" separates what can be communicated from the hidden list of all possibilities. Consciousness assigns a symbolized message to the perception of an object. Intentionality—being directed toward something—is the central structure of conscious experience and essentially highlights social relevance.

This consciousness is socially mediated. The child must turn to the outside to learn how to recognize those aspects of their inner experience that form the basis of their ability to cooperate with others. By observing the reactions of others, they learn which elements of their experience other people react to as well. The elements of the baby's inner experience picked out by the mirroring reactions of other people become the building blocks of mental function that enable the child to live in a world that requires them to cooperate socially. By developing secondary representations of emotional states, the child satisfies two basic needs: an inner balance between mental forces and the desire to be integrated into the social world, where, on the one hand, we respect the separateness of other psyches while at the same time establishing close emotional relationships and working relationships with them (Fonagy et al., 2002). The child needs that proximity to another person who, through marked mirroring actions, can produce an external image matching the child's internal state (cf. Bion, 1962; Fonagy et al., 2002). The implication of the assumption that subjectivity consists of mirroring is that a child's internal states achieve adequate representation in their consciousness only when they are confirmed by marked and matched responses from caregivers. What Freud conceptualized as the dynamic unconscious—the boiling cauldron of the id—is the child's unmirrored, unreflective inner states (Fonagy & Allison, 2016).

Fonagy and Allison (2016) distinguished three forms of the unconscious:

1. *The nonconscious brain functions:* It is characteristic of brain function that certain brain activities are not associated with consciousness. Nonconscious brain functions are generally accepted in modern neuroscience to describe implicit, procedural mechanisms.

2. *The primary unconscious:* This refers to the nonconscious states of fragmentation and disorders of consciousness, e.g., after trauma or in severe depression, that lack intentionality. In normal development, these contents remain inaccessible to conscious experience.

3. *The psychoanalytic unconscious:* Intrusive, disturbing mental contents that are intentional, but, because defense mechanisms produce distorted perceptions, are differentiated from the primary unconscious (Fonagy & Allison, 2016, p. 11).

As a psychoanalyst I believe that people have nasty and horrid things in their minds. Fortunately most of the time they stay where they ought to be: in our unconscious. But if someone is traumatized or experiences things that defy representation in reality, then they have an internal experience that becomes conscious though it shouldn't be. That's really what Liz Allison and I were talking about, and it's an idea in progress.

(Interview with Peter Fonagy, in Duschinsky et al., 2019, p. 225)

To distinguish between the primary unconscious and the psychoanalytic unconscious, we need to take a closer look at marked mirroring processes.

Mental life rests on the representations of bodily experiences in the child, whose sensorimotor experiences form the basis. The most important task of marked mirroring is to incorporate unintegrated aspects of self-states into coherent representations. Forming a symbolic representation of affect states generates the basis for affect regulation and impulse control (Target, 2013). A diffuse, unmirrored sense of self remains potentially overwhelming and unintegrated. When mirroring fails because the caregiver mirrors in an unmarked and/or distorted manner, the child internalizes a mismatch (alien self), which in turn must be projected (Bateman & Fonagy, 2004).

However, even in normal development, the child's sexuality or aggression, for example, can be mirrored only partially in a marked way because they would cause too much "discomfort" to the caregiver and trigger reluctance to extend a sensitive, emotional response. Thus, when the child communicates aspects of sexuality or destructiveness to their caregiver, the caregiver only partially mirrors the experience (Fonagy, 2008). This causes sexuality and hatred to be experienced as "intentional," even though they are not fully consciously experienced. Even when such contents are consciously perceived as disruptive and intrusive, they are intentional in structure and, therefore, meaningful. Though distorted by defense processes, they express drives that are moving toward consciousness. They are expressed as desires and needs, thoughts and feelings—in other words, as mental states. A psychoanalytic understanding of unconscious processes and distortions, e.g., in transference and countertransference, can help make them conscious and change them.

But there is a second type of nonmirrored internal states which comprises the content of the primary unconscious: Traumatic environments, neglect, physical, or emotional abuse reflect states of destructiveness, isolation, and despair that prove unbearable and normally do not enter consciousness. Such destruction disrupts the formation of attachments and inevitably challenges the coherence and intentionality of conscious experience, manifested in intrusive thoughts (e.g., flashbacks) and disturbing images (e.g., intrusions). Therefore, the content of the primary unconscious manifests itself as a disturbance of consciousness, destroying the coherence and intentionality of consciousness. The intrusion of the primary unconscious undermines the implicitly purposeful nature of human experience. In extreme cases, it can replace intentionality with diffuse meaninglessness and precipitate a fragmentary quality of experience (Fonagy & Allison, 2016, p. 18f.).

Conclusion

The relationships between conscious awareness and unconscious processes are complex. Consciousness can be seen as an evolutionary achievement and a developmentally acquired ability shaped through mirroring processes with close caregivers. Thus, consciousness is not superficial as opposed to the "depth" of the unconscious. The simultaneity of conscious and unconscious shaping of relationships focuses attention on communicative (micro-)processes in the joint shaping of (professional) relationships.

Defense Mechanisms

The normal development of the regulation and integration of affects proceeds from disconnected affects and experiences to the integration and construction of specific connections between previously disconnected capacities. Mentalization understands disturbances in reflective functions primarily not as a consequence of fixation or regression but as the coexistence of different self-states. Fonagy and Target (2003; see also Chapter 5.6) assumed that various internal working models coexist, so, initially, it is not a matter of regression, fixation, or deficits.

Fonagy and Target (2003) considered affect regulation a prelude to mentalization, and mentalized affectivity forms the core of psychoanalytic treatment: the experiential understanding of one's feelings far beyond intellectual knowledge. That is where resistance and defense mechanisms arise that may not be directed solely against specific emotional experiences but against psychic functioning modes as a whole. Thus, we are dealing not merely with distortions of mental representations that oppose therapeutic progress but with inhibitions of psychic functioning per se (Fonagy & Target, 2003; Fonagy et al., 2002).

It is assumed that people with severe personality disorders or moderately to low integrated structural levels exhibit general (and not just situational) weakness in mentalizing ability. This is attributed to distorted or absent affect mirroring or trauma, which weakens the coherence of the self and results in large portions of an alien self. The patient experiences and thinks in prementalizing modes (e.g., concretistic, teleological, or hypermentalizing) and distorts different levels of reality perception (e.g., self-perception and other-perception). Yet, we also find situational mentalizing breakdowns at more integrated structural levels. Generally speaking, such breakdowns in mentalization occur during intense psychosocial stress. This approach does not specify which types of intense affect are involved but refers primarily to a more quantitative (neurobiological) view (Luyten et al., 2012; Mayes, 2000, 2006). The intensity of affective arousal runs parallel to the inhibition of activity in the prefrontal cortical regions. If we include qualitative aspects (i.e., the quality of the affect), then aggression, disgust, shame, guilt, or activation of the attachment system—for example—come on the shortlist. This chimes with the clinical experience that conflicts and intense feelings of shame or guilt can block the mentalizing ability, or that nonmentalizing modes are also used for defense purposes (see also Chapter 5.5).

Consequently, the therapeutic goal is to monitor interaction patterns as well as identify and correct maladaptive models, primarily by improving the overarching mental ability to selectively activate alternative interaction models. In terminology borrowed from cognitive science, we can refer to this ability as mentalization or reflective functioning (Fonagy et al., 2002).

The mentalization approach thus supplements psychoanalytic explanations of the phenomena of defense mechanisms and regression by adding coherence of the self and the structure of thought and experience. In addition to the dimension of content (e.g., conflicts), this lends more weight to an orientation toward process (how experiences and thoughts are expressed), which in turn leads to an expanded view of intrapersonal and interpersonal processes. This expanded view influences the treatment technique.

The widespread awareness of the mentalization approach has already subtly influenced psychoanalytic practice. Two changes are characteristic of the focus on mentalization processes (Fonagy et al., 2002): First, interventions following the mentalization approach tend to be experiential, focusing on relatively conscious (and preconscious) mental states and the here and now. The goal is not providing the patient with increased insight (in the sense of recognizing contexts) but rather improving their ability to reflect (introspection, e.g., perception and affect differentiation) and establishing a representational system and a capacity for symbolization (so-called "mental internal space"). Again, mentalization prioritizes process over content.

Transference and Countertransference

> Clinical observation confirms that each patient displays certain specific emotional "dark zones" that are less mentalised and others that are more mentally elaborated.
>
> (Lecours & Bouchard, 1997, p. 871)

Most manifestations of transference emerge, e.g., in less-structured patients, initially as disruptive or modulated impulse activity. Their gradual transformation into mentalized affectivity leads analysts and patients to encounter ever increasingly complex experiences that forgo the need for expression.

This perspective allows mentalization to occur in analyses with both neurotic and less well-structured but integrated patients, both of whom sometimes show less-elaborated drive-affect contents. These are poorly mentalized or appear in a defensive form. Analysts should adapt their interventions to the mentalization level of the analysand.

The mentalization model emphasizes how experience is transformed and how it is expressed—not its content. However, every process presupposes content, and the task of the therapist/analyst is to elicit and explore the mental contents the patient finds difficult to mentalize, especially those related to conscious and unconscious conflicts in attachment relationships (Lecours & Bouchard, 1997).

By addressing and challenging the patient's mental faculties, putting internal states into words, and differentiating between feelings, the analyst can break down overwhelming and anxiety-provoking experiences into simpler, more manageable units, thereby supporting the development of a pretend mode. With this attitude, the patient can begin to think about thoughts as ideas and not as reality, while preserving their connections to the inner world. We consider these interventions to be narrow interpretations that generally refer to aspects of the mental world that are neither unconscious nor overly complex (Fonagy et al., 2002).

> In some respects, our approach to transference work is traditional: we employ interpretive interventions only in the context of support and, as all therapists do, we aspire to tailor the interventions to the patient [...] we concentrate on the patient's mentalizing capabilities. Moreover we construe transference work as active mentalizing in the patient–therapist relationship [...] interpretive interventions have the potential to promote mentalizing in patients who are able to remain in the mentalizing mode and to hold multiple perspectives in mind in the face of strong affects.
>
> (Allen et al., 2008, p.187f.)

When interpretive work focuses on the mental representations of the transference, it exerts a stabilizing influence on mentalization. It focuses the patient's attention on distorted perceptions and interpretations of present interactions to better understand distortions. Any interpretations relate to the here and now or to the patient's past relational experiences. Thus, one hallmark of mentalization in transference lies in distinguishing and separating the present from the past, reality from fantasy.

This treatment technique also focuses on processing the therapeutic relationship in the here and now. Mentalizing the transference means stimulating the patient to think about the relationship they are engaged in at that moment. Starting points are transference markers; that is, subtle clues that suggest a transference response. Transference markers often emerge early in therapeutic work, but the more advanced the therapy, the more often the therapeutic relationship can become the focus of attention (Allen et al., 2008, p.190 f.).

Failure to mentalize can create, maintain, or even exacerbate relationship difficulties. A breakdown of context-specific mentalization occurs in stressful situations and results in a situation-specific inability to consider the thoughts and feelings of others. Such a context-specific breakdown may involve the person believing that the other person is intentionally trying to provoke them or ignoring the other person's mental state altogether (Fearon et al., 2006). The patient may perceive prolonged silence, an abstinent therapeutic stance, and settings that promote regression as threatening, triggering such stress. We discuss these relationships in more detail with regard to treatment in Chapter 5.2 "Transference and Countertransference" and Chapter 5.3 "Interpretation and Insight."

4.3   The Necessity of Psychoanalytic Understanding in the Mentalization Approach (and Vice Versa)

In addition to the more elaborated, systematized, and manualized MBT, some unsystematic and non-evidence-based clinical reports, mostly casuistics or case vignettes, describe the targeted use of mentalization in psychoanalytic treatments. They expound the explicit support for mentalization where appropriate, either in a particular phase of treatment (usually at the beginning), regarding particular topics of high emotional arousal, or in conjunction with breakdowns in mentalization.

The research group led by Vermote, Lowyck, Vandeneede, Bateman, and Luyten (Vermote et al., 2012) developed a model introducing a mentalizing focus into psychodynamically oriented treatments for patients with personality disorders, without altering the characteristic features of psychodynamic treatments. The authors assume that MBT and psychodynamic therapy are independent treatments that can be well integrated because of their many similarities. Further, they believe that mentalizing treatment can help patients control their affects and impulses, setting the stage for psychoanalytic treatment. To integrate mentalization into a psychodynamic therapy culture, they recommend considering the following dimensions (modified from Vermote et al., 2012, p. 249):

1. The *background dimension,* consisting of a sense of inner security (attachment security, working alliance, therapeutic framework). They extend the secure base model by adding the concept of "epistemic trust" (Fonagy & Allison, 2014).
2. The *mentalization dimension* (symbolization), which emphasizes process (i.e., how does the patient mentalize in certain relationships?).
3. The *object-relations dimension,* oriented either toward object-relations theory (Kernberg), self-psychology, or intersubjective theory. The level of self and object representations enables shifting from process thinking to content aspects (working through inner conflicts).

One can combine this model with the approach of psychotherapy as a threefold communication system (Fonagy & Allison, 2014), approaching these dimensions as successive or parallel phases of treatment and explicitly including the relational dimension (e.g., epistemic trust, transference, object relations). This model suggests that applying an approach focused more on the mentalization process in patients with little integrated structural level can be advantageous. If basic mentalization is possible, the focus should be oriented toward situational breakdowns of mentalization, e.g., in stressful interactions, and place a greater emphasis on content, conflict, and reflection on the relationship and transference.

Vermote et al.'s (2012) three dimensions correspond to the "process focus" and "content focus" in Lemma et al.'s (2011) Brief Dynamic Interpersonal Therapy (DIT): The process focus involves promoting mentalization with typical MBT interventions; the content focus includes the therapist's formulations and interpretations of interpersonal conscious and unconscious patterns. The authors describe the treatment concept as suitable also for patients with a more integrated structural level (see also Chapter 5.7).

Vermote et al.'s (2012) object relations and Lemma et al.'s (2011) focus on formulations and interpretations on interpersonal conscious and unconscious patterns point to an aspect that is not central to the mentalization concept and MBT. Missing is the psychoanalytic notion that the self also develops from the process of inner awareness too. In addition to affect reflection, self-awareness comprises multiple psychodynamic processes of the self-recognizing subject, an example being identification processes. Psychoanalysis has more to say about this, particularly with its object-relation theories.

Case Reports

Both Fonagy and Target describe numerous case vignettes or excerpts from their psychoanalytic treatments in which they employ a mentalizing focus (Fonagy, 2008, 2015; Target, 2016). Target describes a high-frequency psychoanalytic treatment of a then 25-year-old borderline patient. From the beginning, she distinguishes between disturbances of mental processes (symbolization, representation) and inner conflicts (defenses), each of which demands a different approach, although both can be treated with psychoanalysis. For the first two years, she initially applied a mentalization-oriented approach, mirroring feelings and marking them in these sequences. She encouraged the patient to name or reflect on her feelings together with the therapist. In the following years, when the patient had begun to symbolize and had significantly increased her tolerance of affect and its communication, Target expanded the transference work. In the presence of a structural weakness in the mentalizing ability, Target suggests, the therapist should carry out the classical analytic work of transference interpretations or interpretation of unconscious conflicts only *after* having worked with mirroring and affect containment. Applying classical psychoanalytic interpretive work without containment work causes structurally disturbed patients to react with acting out or concretistic thinking.

Target (2016) recommends this approach for patients who fail to benefit from classical psychoanalysis. This suggestion is based on the assumption that patients with severe personality disorders need a marked mirroring of their affects within the safe environment of a psychotherapeutic relationship. A high-frequency psychoanalytic setting, she argues, is optimal for expressing the raw material of concretistic or teleological, libidinal, and unprocessed affects within the safe (transitional) therapeutic space. This presumes a technical approach similar to the mirroring of a mother toward her infant child: "contingent" (timely), "congruent" (matching), and "marked" (emphasizing the difference in the mother's and the infant's affect experience) (White, 2019).

In her commentary, White critically questions whether the (theoretical) differences between classical Kleinian analysts (containment, symbolization) and mentalization-oriented approaches (marked affect mirroring and promotion of mentalization) are really that great in the actual practice of high-frequency psychoanalysis. White does see differences in the modifications of the analytic stance (White, 2019); that is, the differences between positioning oneself at the patient's side to "supportively" describe the inner and outer worlds from the patient's point of view (thus maintaining the dyad); and facing the patient directly as a separate counterpart (thus promoting triadic thinking). An analyst who maintains a separate counterpart position becomes a projection figure for the split inner world of the (structurally disturbed) patient in the transference. Target does not renounce altogether the position as a separate counterpart for the patient; rather, she describes how she works through any transference fantasies of her patient that may arise in the transference (see also Chapter 5.2).

Mary Target is one of the central founding figures of the mentalization approach. Her article from 2016 clarifies her "balancing act" between mentalization focus and classical Kleinian analysis and her attempts at integration (White 2019). The conceptualization and perspective of mentalization theory could be very helpful in describing and understanding how to deal with "difficult patients" from a developmental perspective.

Critique of the Mentalization Approach by Psychoanalysis

Britton (2000) (a Kleinian) criticizes the very need for mentalization theorists to change the psychoanalytic model and treatment technique for severely disturbed patients. He claims that changing the technique is tantamount to acting out and exposes the insufficient attempt at understanding the transference–countertransference constellation. White's critique culminates in an (analytic) interpretation of underlying motives: "My guess is that the power of scientific research and the demands of the healthcare system keep tempting analysts to change their technique, to shorten treatments, and to work in a symptom-oriented way" (White, 2009, p. 1185, transl. JS). Mentalizing this accusation, one might respond that this too is but a perspective, an attempt to fathom intentions and motives. However, the criticism here is formulated from an analytical, knowing position.

Others expressed their criticism more subliminally. Schultz-Venrath answered metaphorically:

> Nevertheless, one of the most potent means of resistance against MBT is when experienced psychotherapists claim to have *always* worked in this way. Here, we can take our cue from sailing regarding learning and teaching: As the "windforce" increases, therapists are required to not only nosological-contextual knowledge (analogous to possessing a nautical chart) but also specific skills to keep them from capsizing.
>
> (2024, p. 162)

This criticism is surprising since it is not a matter of abandoning central psychoanalytic concepts such as drive or the unconscious. The mentalization approach even emphasizes that drive conceptions are needed to move from Cartesian dualism (body and mind as separate worlds) to an integrated, embodied understanding of the psyche (Fonagy et al., 2002). At stake, therefore, are not the concepts of drive or unconscious; up for discussion is expanding the ideas about the unconscious that have emerged, partly because of advances in neurobiology and observations in individual case research. Leading psychoanalysts such as the former president of the International Psychoanalytic Association (IPV), Kernberg (2006, 2012), or the former head of the IPV Research Commission, Peter Fonagy (Fonagy et al., 2002), have been warning for decades, clearly but cautiously: "It would be quite profitable for psychoanalysis to open up to its neighboring disciplines to redefine and further develop its tenets."

Outlook

There are more psychoanalytic theories out there than we need. Despite numerous overlaps, each theoretical corpus has its distinctive features. Deciding what speaks for and against a theory is an important task of psychoanalytic research in the future.

Fonagy and Target (2003) propose the following for the future development of psychoanalysis:

- Define psychoanalytic constructs and techniques more rigorously.
- Elaborate developmental models for late childhood, adolescence, and adulthood.
- Advance comparative psychoanalytic studies that contrast alternative psychoanalytic frames of reference.
- Incorporate other disciplines and their data-collection methods to develop a standard of reporting that includes multiple perspectives (including those of patients).
- Reflect more on the interactions between the intrapsychic world and the environment, including considering stress and trauma as well as the social and cultural context by which object relations develop.
- Psychoanalytic clinicians and researchers should show greater engagement in demonstrating to society at large the relevance of psychoanalytic theory and treatment.
- Therapy can be successful only if it achieves both intrapsychic and interpersonal goals, in which mentalized affectivity plays a significant role.

It can be based on two selection criteria: coherence and consistency with the known facts (Fonagy & Target, 2003).

Thus, the mentalization model includes theoretical models of psychoanalysis and empirical findings from the relevant neighboring disciplines. This concerns particularly findings from modern developmental psychology on the development of the self and internal representations.

5

Mentalization in Psychodynamic and Psychoanalytic Psychotherapy

The chapter shows how the mentalization concept changes the perspective on psychoanalytic treatment techniques and provides new aspects. To this end, we briefly present and contrast individual elements of the psychoanalytically based psychotherapy treatment technique with the mentalization-based treatment technique. Such a juxtaposition does not intend to spark controversy but to demonstrate which parts can be complemented or combined and which parts remain incompatible. At the end of this chapter (see Chapter 5.7), we present a model that can serve integration.

Restricting the mentalization approach to the psychotherapy of structural disorders is not a very serious limitation regarding psychotherapeutic practice. For example, the German psychoanalyst Mertens reports that the famous American psychoanalyst Benedek was asked in the 1990s how many psychoneurotic patients she had treated in her long life. "Three to four," she answered (Mertens, 2015). Mertens pointedly quotes this anecdote to argue that psychoanalysts have always and mostly treated personality disorders, i.e., individuals with structural limitations, modifying the classical treatment technique to fit the patients.

5.1 Treatment Goal: Making Unconscious Conscious and Mentalized Affectivity

Making the Unconscious Conscious

Psychoanalytic therapy aims to make the unconscious conscious to express it via language. Only what we can capture in language can become conscious of unconscious conflicts, affects, and desires. Freud usually equates the unconscious with the repressed but also mentions that the unconscious has genetically transmitted contents, something he calls the "core of the unconscious." Thus, the unconscious is psychodynamic: It pushes through to the surface, is causally effective, and is demarcated from what is temporarily not remembered, the preconscious. Current views in psychoanalysis about the nature of the unconscious are by no means uniform, as psychoanalysis can look back on more than 100 years of theory development. Recent conceptions (Gödde & Buchholz, 2011) differentiate the "horizontal

DOI: 10.4324/9781032674117-6

unconscious" from the "vertical unconscious." Fonagy and Allison (2015) propose differentiating "nonconscious," "primary unconscious," and "psychoanalytic unconscious." Chapter 4.2 looks at the various views regarding the nature of the unconscious, its content and structure, and the dynamics of the unconscious from a modern perspective.

Psychoanalytic treatment focuses on making conscious repressed, unconscious conflicts, traumatic experiences in childhood, transference components in the therapeutic relationship, and defense constellations. The analyst's central mode of action for turning the unconscious into consciousness is *interpretation.*

For Fonagy and coworkers (Fonagy & Target, 2003), "mentalized affectivity" forms the core of psychoanalytic treatment. Freud also placed affect at the center of his concepts: Early on, in his *Studies on Hysteria* (Breuer & Freud, 2004, [1895]), he assumed that blocked affects in a traumatic situation produced symptoms. Later, he formulated a theory of affect derived from drive theory (libido aggression), which presumes the bodily origin of affect. By assuming that the ego mediates between the superego and the id, he further developed his approach to include affect regulation.

The development of affect regulation is also a central aspect of the mentalization concept, here in connection with attachment theory (Fonagy et al., 2002). In mentalization-based therapy (MBT), it becomes the overarching goal of promoting mentalized affectivity.

Although the mentalization concept stands on its own today, it is based on the legacy of the psychoanalytic theories that preceded it, especially ego psychology, object-relations theory, Winnicott's "holding object," and Bion's "containing." According to Jurist (2018), there is still a long way to go in understanding the relationship between mentalization and affect regulation. We can deduce this interest from increased publications related to affect regulation and mentalization (Jurist, 2018).

Mentalized Affectivity

> Emotional experience is the first step towards a thought. At the end of the road, we find thinking.
>
> (Green, 1998 in Jurist, 2018, p. 102)

> Although many of us think of ourselves as thinking creatures that feel, biologically we are feeling creatures that think.
>
> (Taylor, 2008, p. 19)

A central element in many forms of mental suffering is that we are at the mercy of our affects, be it, for example, great anxiety, strong depressive affects, or unbearable feelings of dark emptiness. The feeling of being at the mercy of one's affects is significant, especially in patients suffering from a structural disorder. For example, difficulties in controlling violent affects play a central role in many borderline patients: fear, anger, erotic desires, unbearable emptiness, fear of being alone, feelings of strangeness. Here, too, improving mentalized affectivity is central to successful longer-term therapy. However, the problem is not limited to borderline personality disorder (BPD). According to Gross and Jazaieri (2014), massive affective problems and regulation problems are present in 40–70% of all mental disorders.

We can distinguish three stages of affect regulation (Fonagy et al., 2002):

Stage 1: To ensure an organism's balance (homeostasis), we must change the affect states in an action- and body-related manner. Affects precede the cognitive— both evolutionarily and developmentally in the neurobiological development of the newborn to the adult. Thus, affects are the primary motivational system.

Stage 2: Affects can be communicated and are at least partially conscious; they become cognitively accessible and more involved in decision-making processes; they are less blind; they become capable of communication and interactional regulation through symbolization/language. Building a representational system allows for the differentiation and modulation of affects. In psychotherapy, it is important that patients find their own language for their feelings and emotional states, do not adopt the language of therapists, and that therapists do not label or interpret the feelings.

Stage 3: Mentalized affectivity enables reflection on the affective state. It allows the application of meaning to affects and the expansion of control over affects. Mentalizing thus becomes a buffer between affect and action. Mentalized affectivity is considered the most mature form of dealing with affects.

First and foremost, mentalized affectivity denotes a complex understanding of one's affect experience (Fonagy et al., 2002). In a further step, mentalized affectivity allows extensive control over one's affects, also regarding controlling actions (Stage 3). Actions are not governed by uncontrolled affects, such as fight and flight behaviors, which can be triggered in a flash. Mentalized affectivity contributes to the building of self-structures.

Often, MBT is seen as a cognitive therapy method. The origin of this view may lie in the fact that the mentalization concept refers to the theory of mind and the results of empirical research, which include elements of behavioral therapy. However, this view is refuted by the central importance therapy gives to the concept of mentalized affectivity and its implementation.

According to Jurist (2018) and Allen et al. (2008), one can divide affect elaboration into three therapeutic steps: 1) the identification of affect; 2) the modulation of affect; 3) the communication of affect. Working through these steps increases control over affect and the resulting actions. But working through affects requires sufficient time; it cannot be done mechanically or cognitively.

1.   The Identification of Emotions

Contrary to the assumption made by many therapeutic schools, we are often unaware of our emotions. We then have "aporetic affects" (from the Greek aporia meaning perplexity; Jurist, 2018). It is an everyday experience that we feel something but cannot quite pin it down. It takes time to put these feelings into symbols, i.e., descriptive words. Often, even a simple term is insufficient to describe a feeling (e.g., emptiness or "feeling weird"), and numerous words may be necessary. Having one's affects understood often demands a language that we find more in literature than in the ICD-10 or ICD-11. "Often, I become a melancholic. I don't know where it comes from. Then, I fixate everyone like an owl [...], and a darkness overtakes my soul, a darkness as impenetrable as the October fog" (Goethe 1766, in a letter to his sister; Goethe, 1985, vol. 28, p. 603, transl. Joseph Smith).

The phenomenon of our being unaware of our feelings is different from alexithymia. Alexithymia, often very inaccurately characterized as emotional blindness, indeed represents the inability to adequately perceive one's feelings; but this phenomenon is generally present in persons with alexithymia. It is a trait associated with a paucity of imagination and inadequate perception of the psychological quality of affects. Instead, the emphasis is on the physiological, physical (raw, unmentalized) aspects of affects.

Psychotherapy harbors the danger that the therapist hastily mislabels or misunderstands the emotions in question and names something out of intuition or experience. For example, the therapist may say: "You feel anger now, is that it?" Patient: "No." The therapist: "More like rage?" The patient says, "Yes." That abruptly ends the discussion, perhaps only out of a (presumed) need to explain something. Therefore, the mentalization approach suggests continuing to maintain the central attitude of "not-knowing" to encourage patients to find out on their own how to identify their affects and put them into words. The patient's own perception and experience of affect—and the subsequent identification and designation of affect— allows them to slowly regain the perception of authorship.

The model of mentalized affectivity has changed over time. Initially, it was assumed that mentalized affectivity simply meant that a person could think about their feelings; today, the process character receives greater emphasis (Jurist, 2018). Accordingly, changes in the patient occur through the process of perception and the identification of affects, including referencing autobiographical experiences and past memories in addition to the here and now.

2.   The Modulation of Affects

There are three approaches to the modulation of affect: the cognitive processing model, the mindfulness model, and the mentalized affectivity model. We briefly present them here to illustrate the differences in the concept of mentalized affectivity.

The cognitive processing model: This model is based on cognitive behavioral therapy. It follows the notion that cognitions regain control over affect and the resulting behavior. Emotional regulation here is a top-down mechanism: Cognitions regain power over affects. The differentially developed model includes Socratic dialog to achieve persuasion and education as well as behavioral and skills training. Cognitive restructuring leads to new cognitive strategies for controlling affect and behavior. Cognitive changes entail changes in affect.

A special case is the classical behavioral therapy method of exposure, which can be particularly effective because it simultaneously leads to cognitive and affective restructuring in patients with anxiety symptoms if interventions are successful.

The mindfulness model: This model originated from Asian philosophy and found its way into behavior therapy as the "third wave of behavior therapy." It contrasts with the classic cognitive model of behavior therapy, which formerly claimed generality. In contrast to attempts to change affective experiences or to seek alternatives, the principle of mindfulness goes in the opposite direction: Affects must first be perceived and accepted as they are; it is not a matter of controlling them cognitively. This approach is described as "inner self-commitment," i.e., accepting affective reactions as they occur.

The model of mentalized affectivity—attachment, mentalizing, self: Constrained mentalizing involves affects, and effective mentalizing also involves affects as well. But here, both are linked to the skills of regulation and modification. Affects are linked to the context and have a meaning reflected by the person. Thus, mentalized affectivity as an aspect of affect regulation is not just a process in the Here and Now; rather, it is influenced by, among other things, autobiographical memory, attachment experiences, and the development of the self.

People are not born with the ability to regulate affect. Children learn to regulate their affect when their brain matures and by interacting with their caretakers. Affect regulation represents a critical achievement of early childhood (Calkins & Hill, 2007). The child learns to differentiate affect through the affect mirroring experienced in the first years of life (see Chapter 2.3). In contrast, the child and the adult later accomplish affect modulation—initially required by caregivers and important to the relationship—themselves through the increasing internalization of soothing objects.

The attachment system plays a central role in the regulation of affect. In a secure attachment, affects can be calmed or modulated, which often depends on whether the adult experienced reassurance earlier as a child. When distress occurs because of great affect, we seek protection from attachment figures or attempt to soothe ourselves, according to the pattern of our attachment system. A person can thus modulate their affects, either with the help of real external relations or on their own through internalized good objects. Ideally, this helps to downregulate affect. Traumatic experiences can cause profound and persistent limitations of this regulation, both physiologically (hypervigilance) and by destroying epistemic trust (see Chapter 2.4).

3.   The Communication of Affects

After identifying and modulating affects, the next step is to express affects and their relationship to behavior. Communicating affects lays claim to their authorship; this can occur internally (i.e., toward ourselves) or externally. It often happens quite consciously as an explicit act of mentalization, e.g., when the patient perceives their feelings in the here and now and puts them into words. The outward communication of affects enables lively communication with other persons. Also, it allows affects to be expressed both directly and indirectly, e.g., through music.

The identification of affects, the modulation of affects, and the communication of affects—these three aspects are connected to our awareness of our agency over affects. Our awareness of our own agency begins with the identification of affects; the modulation of affects further actualizes the authorship; and the communication of affects manifests that authorship as something real.

Why Is Mentalized Affectivity a Central Goal of Treatment?

Mentalized affectivity is a form of emotion regulation that involves the ability to reflect on one's thoughts and feelings, whether from childhood, current events, or the present context. It is associated with a person's sense of (also) being the initiator of their feelings ("sense of agency"). Further, the fact that mentalization is impaired when affect is high plays a significant role because it favors misinterpretation: Misinterpretations weaken epistemic confidence. At the same time, conversely, epistemic distrust precipitates misinterpretations (see Chapter 2.4). Erroneous interpretations of affect, both in oneself and in the other person, especially in the social context, often present a core problem for patients.

We can also understand the development of mentalized affectivity (or its failure) in a larger framework:

- Mentalized affectivity contributes to establishing self-structures. Therefore, in psychotherapy, it is imperative that patients find their own voice for their feelings and emotional states and do not simply adopt that of the therapist. The foundations of identity develop parallel to the development of self-structure. In successful therapeutic processes, the patient experiences how affect differentiation contributes to expanding or changing their sense of identity. The globalized world causes the individual to view the search for identity as a central need—relegating the topic of sexuality to second place in importance. We see this today in how the issue of sexuality is permeated by questions of identity.
- We observe patients with symptoms of "functional somatization" and patients diagnosed with a disorder on the autism spectrum who cannot name their affects in a very differentiated way. The therapeutic approach here consists of emotional validation and joint affect regulation.
- Individuals from the radical right-wing milieu turn to the blood-and-earth ideology as well as to the meaning of flags as a symbol of their own identity. They express their affects in this manner because they are unable to use more differentiated designations and often feel drawn to this undifferentiated, raw form of perceiving their own affects and those of others.
- Some patients achieve a reduction of diffuse internal tension by splitting off parts into a strange self (i.e., parts split off from the rest of the self and experienced as such) or by somatization (i.e., shifting into the body).

Changes to Affect Processing and Behavior

The concept of mentalized affect involves the notion that mentalizing affect allows for better control of affect and results in positive feedback effects on the control of behavior. For example, improved mentalization results in control over self-injurious behavior or the modulation of the intensity of response in partner relationships. As a marker of effective mentalizing, mentalized affect involves two aspects: First, it allows perception of the affect and keeps the affect operative; second, it enables differentiated cognitively mediated attempts at problem-solving. This approach is what the Italian metacognitivists from the behavior therapy school back (Carcione et al., 2008; Semerari et al., 2003). They examined this aspect under the term "metacognitive mastery," which they understood as an operationalization of the ability to use mentalization under stress to solve problems. The patient reflects on the process and their behavior not as a fact but as a task to be mastered. This allows the patient to plausibly describe the problem. Successful "metacognitive mastery" is characterized as "adopting a rational and critical attitude to the beliefs that are behind a problematic state, using one's knowledge about others' mental states to regulate interpersonal problems and accepting in a mature way one's personal limits when trying to master oneself or influence events" (Semerari et al., 2003, p. 245). Brockmann et al. (2017) examined this aspect in a single-case study and found that the success of treatment via "metacognitive mastery" could be well demonstrated.

Conclusion

The treatment goals in psychoanalytic psychotherapy and MBT are different but similar. Although the traditional psychoanalytic technique is more content-oriented (concerned with uncovering unconscious connections and content) and MBT is more process-oriented (promoting effective mentalizing and mentalized affectivity), the goals of these two approaches culminate in creating more successful self-direction and self-availability. The latter enables patients to have more satisfying relationships since they judge their reference persons and their intentions more realistically, in turn making more closeness possible. Mentalization promotes the development of more stable object representations. Mentalized affectivity is a prerequisite for developing (positive) object relations and a characteristic of stable object representations.

Further commonalities in the two treatment approaches are that they both attach great importance to affects and affect processing, and they assume a representational system as an internal structure. In this context, affect processing occurs through conscious as well as preconscious and unconscious processes.

5.2   The Therapeutic Relationship, Transference, and Countertransference

All evidence-based therapies attempt to create an atmosphere of trust and safety in the therapeutic relationship, making it possible for the patient to reflect on and report significant experiences. This effort is crucial because one of the few undisputed findings of decades of psychotherapy research is that the therapeutic relationship is the central impact factor of psychotherapy (Laska et al., 2014; Wampold, 2015; Wampold and Imel, 2015). The results show that the common impact factors of evidence-based psychotherapies are the central impact factors of these psychotherapies—not the specific techniques of individual therapies. Yet, most therapeutic schools tend to hold on to their specific impact factors—their "trademarks"—which they attribute to their specific techniques. The therapeutic alliance described by the psychoanalyst Bordin, characterized by three components (Bordin, 1979), became the guiding principle for research into the therapeutic relationship: a bond between therapist and patient characterized by trust and positive emotional tones; an agreement regarding the respective tasks; and an agreement regarding the therapy goals.

The Psychoanalytic View

The concept of the therapeutic relationship in psychoanalysis is closely related to the concept of transference and countertransference. In general, in psychoanalysis, transference means shifting affects and ideas related to the experience of significant persons in childhood onto the psychoanalyst (Freud, 1912; Laplanche & Pontalis, 1967). This occurs regularly in the psychotherapeutic relationship. In an intense treatment relationship, the patient experiences affects, cognitions, desires, and fears toward the psychoanalyst which are understandable from previous relational experiences. Countertransference occurs because of the psychoanalyst's transference—because the psychoanalyst is also involved in the process. The theoretical assumptions behind the transference concept in psychoanalysis are manifold. Classically, they derived from the drive model, later from the object-relations theories, including self-psychology and intersubjective theory. We briefly discuss these basic assumptions here, since we want to emphasize the treatment technique.

In psychoanalysis, interpreting the analyst's transference is of great importance. From a mentalization-oriented point of view, the classical transference interpretations of the psychoanalyst were interpretations of the patient's mentalization processes. Regarding treatment, work done *in (during)* transference must be distinguished from work done *on (about)* transference.

Work done *on (about)* transference may be characterized as follows:

- In the interpretations of transference, the patient's statements are traced back to certain patterns. For example, the therapist says, "You have mentioned before how you reacted to this situation. Perhaps that triggers something in you we should explore."

- In the interpretations of transference, the therapist also uses the patient's reactions to reflect on their relationship to therapy and collaboration. For example, one uses phrases such as, "The way you're reacting, it might have something to do with me and how you perceive me."
- The therapist relates the patient's statements to early interpersonal experiences or experiences with the therapist: "Could it be that the way you reacted might have something to do with your being left alone as a child?"

We must distinguish this from work done *in (during)* transference as another classic psychoanalytic approach. Here, the analyst initially and largely abstains from interpretations and focuses on the here and now. This approach is closer to the concept of MBT than work done *on (about)* transference.

Work done *in (during)* transference may be characterized as follows:

- The therapist encourages the patient to explore the present relationship with the therapist. The therapist accepts and explores the patient's enactments as well as their own involvement and possible enmeshment.
- The therapist validates the patient's experience: "You see it this way, so there must be something to it. Can you try to explain it to me?"
- The therapist openly and appropriately applies some of their countertransference feelings. They clearly identify them as their own feelings. Only when the patient has clearly understood this does the therapist consider the patient's role in producing these feelings.
- The therapist formulates alternative perspectives: "You see this as an affront from your boss, but your boss's reactions might not be so clearly directed toward you. I mean, I don't know for sure, but that may have been the case. It was their feeling, but was it also your perception from the outside looking back on things more closely? Could you consider that?"
- The therapist offers their cooperation to facilitate a new understanding.

According to Körner (1989), who decidedly distinguishes work *on (about)* transference from work *in (during)* transference and argues for work *in (during)* transference, says the danger in working on transference lies in transference interpretation projecting that the analyst is stepping out of the perceived relationship. Moreover, there is the risk that the patient processes such an interpretation in a pseudomentalizing way (i.e., in the pretend mode). It then becomes a fantasy about understanding; contact with reality goes missing, and the patient's personal affective experience remains largely untouched: The interpretation likely becomes inconsequential for the patient.

This concept has been rightly criticized: Working during transference in the here and now neglects that the transference relationship develops along a temporal axis and along personality structures that endure over time. Psychoanalytic theories are significant to precisely understanding these aspects; they help to elucidate what is happening in the relationship. Psychoanalytic theories are also of great value as background knowledge: One can only recognize something for which one already has a concept. And recognition is a prerequisite to orienting oneself. In the ocean, a ship and its captain remain lost without land visibility and nautical knowledge. Thus, psychoanalytic theories help the psychoanalyst to orient and structure their perception and experience, to ponder what is happening in a therapy session, and to determine where the journey may be going. Psychoanalytic theories can make the psychoanalyst creative in the patient relationship and broaden the mentalizing therapist's field of vision.

Mentalizing Transference and Countertransference—The Mentalization-Oriented Perspective

The specifics of MBT are based first and foremost on the assumption that the therapist must consider the situational and structural differences in a patient's mentalization abilities. A patient may experience increased emotional arousal, limiting their mentalizing abilities; if it is foreign to the patient, it may make them feel unsafe to talk about the therapeutic relationship and their related feelings in the therapist's presence. If the patient wants to understand a transference interpretation, they must be capable of stable self–object differentiation even under heightened affective stress. The patient must be able to distinguish between their own thoughts and feelings and those of the analyst as well as between reality and their imagination. For example, the patient performs this feat when the therapist presents the following interpretation: "You are experiencing me as if I had reacted like your father." The patient must be sufficiently capable of regulating an emotionally upsetting situation while maintaining mentalizing skills. However, the impairment of regulatory abilities is often precisely one of the problems that lead patients with severe emotional distress to psychotherapy.

According to the mentalization concept, the work done during transference—mentalizing the therapeutic relationship—should be squarely in the foreground. According to the above, this is indicated only when the patient has low arousal and can already mentalize, in which case the therapist should mark the interpretation clearly as a comment. The interpretive authority remains with the patient. MBT identifies transference markers (repetitive interpersonal patterns) and sees transference less as a copy of old relationships and more as an expression of attachment patterns and interpretive errors. A special case is the alien self (see Chapter 2.6), which reflects early relational experiences associated with strong affect and where the reference back to the psychoanalytic object-relations theory is clear.

The proposed Integrative Treatment Model (see Chapter 5.7) also puts work done during transference, i.e., mentalizing the relationship, at the center. The psychoanalytic object-relations theories are part of the integrative model.

The Therapeutic Relationship and Epistemic Trust

Epistemic trust is also relevant to understanding the therapeutic relationship (see Chapter 2.4). Epistemic trust—the willingness to receive information from significant others and to learn from them—facilitates good relational experiences. Epistemic trust is closely related to previous attachment experiences. Individuals who have had prolonged poor, confusing, and aversive experiences or have been traumatized often have high epistemic distrust or high epistemic vigilance (hypervigilance) of the social environment. A person with high epistemic distrust has difficulty opening up in therapy. Severely disturbed patients are, therefore, often perceived as difficult to treat; from this understanding of epistemic mistrust, however, these patients only tend to be challenging to reach initially.

Epistemic trust grows when the addressee (the patient) feels that their counterpart (the therapist) is engaged in important communication tailored explicitly for them. These messages are especially credible when the addressee feels perceived as an independent person. Ostensive stimuli signal to the addressee that the communication is directed toward them, and that the message has meaning for them. Ostensive stimuli thus make the message more credible (Csibra & Gergerly, 2009, 2011; see Chapter 2). Another aspect of epistemic trust is responsiveness on the part of the patient. Responsiveness is the second key impact factor of therapy, according to Wampold and Norcross (Norcross & Wampold, 2019; Wampold, 2015). In the STA-R Questionnaire on the therapeutic relationship, the factor that emerges most clearly and stably is "fear of opening up." The correlations between the therapeutic alliance, as assessed by patients at the end of treatment, and symptom changes (SCL90-R) during treatment were found to be significant ($r = .43$) (Brockmann et al., 2011).

Epistemic Fit

Trust comes from a sense of feeling one's self understood by another mind.
(Interview with Peter Fonagy, in Duschinsky et al., 2019, p. 224)

Epistemic fit affects epistemic trust and consists of several aspects:

- On the patient's side, how the patient thinks about themselves (according to their personal narrative).
- On the therapist's side, how the therapist thinks about the patient's self-conception.
- On the patient's side, how the patient thinks about the therapist's ideas about them.

The patient experiences and feels the degree of agreement between how the therapist thinks about them and their own narrative about themselves (see Figure 5.1). The decisive factor here is not the actual agreement but what is experienced by the patient. This is not a matter of right or wrong, realistic or unrealistic, but of personal perspective.

Experiencing that one's narrative about oneself is recognized by the other person reinforces epistemic trust (Campagna et al., 2019; Duschinsky et al., 2019).

Figure 5.1 shows that the central thing is the agreement between the two images:

- The image the therapist Virginia has of the idea the patient Donald has about himself.
- The image the patient Donald has of the therapist Virginia's idea has about him.
- If the images match, epistemic trust emerges.
- Of particular importance here are the nonverbalized narratives the patient about themselves, which may be conscious, semiconscious, or unconscious and are perceived/recognized by the therapist.

In this example, the patient describes great successes achieved early on, but the therapist senses the patient's subliminal silent doubts and great efforts, which the patient cannot express. If the therapist intuitively senses the parts not being openly communicated by the patient in the narrative, and if the patient senses that the therapist is sympathetic to them, this strongly promotes epistemic trust in the patient. Conclusion: On a preconscious level, there is an epistemic fit here between patient and therapist.

Feedback

Several studies indicate that therapists often have a distorted image of the therapeutic process, specifically of the therapeutic alliance. This finding is independent of the therapeutic orientation of the respective therapist. Norcross, a recognized

Figure 5.1 The therapist Virginia and the patient Donald—epistemic fit.
Adapted from Bateman (2020).

expert and researcher in the field of therapeutic relationships, was asked about the bottom line of his knowledge for practitioners. He answered: Ask for feedback from patients about their experience of the therapeutic relationship!

Research and practice show that psychotherapists are relatively poor in assessing how empathic the patient experiences their therapist and how good they think the therapeutic relationship is. On the other hand therapists often believe they are fairly accurate in their assessments (Norcross 2010, p.117ff.).

The results of therapy research suggest that feedback about the ongoing therapeutic process stemming from sources other than the therapist's observations and intuition can benefit the therapeutic process. Feedback to the therapist can keep the therapeutic process from reaching an impasse and improve treatment outcomes (Laska et al., 2014), especially when the treatments are difficult, for example, with severely structurally impaired patients and those who are difficult to reach.

However, employing feedback systems using questionnaires poses a dilemma. On the one hand, it is undisputed that the patient's perspective on the therapeutic process is a significant source of information and one that has been given too little consideration in psychoanalytically based procedures. On the other hand, there are problems related to their implementation, especially to methodology. A major obstacle may be that, when questionnaires are routinely presented, a sense of banality and meaninglessness—of no longer experiencing therapeutic benefit—creeps in among patients and therapists repeatedly confronted with the same questions and answers. In long-term therapies, for example, one may have to type in the answer to the same item on a questionnaire literally hundreds of times. Researchers, on the other hand, tend to base their studies on experiences gleaned from short-term therapies. Of course, experience varies widely in this regard.

In addition, to be used routinely, the questionnaires must be short, so that the evaluations provide only very limited information and in fact may increase the dilemma of how to capture a hypercomplex event (such as a psychotherapeutic interview) with simple methods. Information from narratives, on the other hand, contains qualitative data. Therefore, it seems necessary to combine quantitative data with qualitative data if one wants to do justice to the subject matter: language and numbers, "empirical culture" and "literary culture" (Brockman, 1995).

In MBT, feedback on the therapeutic process is of great importance. This is realized mainly through supervision of therapy sequences supported by video and audio recordings and role-plays. Especially video recordings are considered indispensable in MBT: They provide an unbiased view of the process from the outside perspective—the perspective of an observer. They are also a good starting point for reflecting on transference aspects and content-related questions. Role plays of therapy sequences are also significant and almost always practicable. They have the great advantage of directly and more strongly involving the experience.

Feedback through Role-Play

We can discover more about a person in an hour of play than in a year of conversation.

Plato

The therapist describes to the group the problem or question regarding a patient or a treatment session. The therapist recalls a situation from the therapy session and assumes the patient's position, starting with the therapeutic situation in question. The therapist plays the patient in the here and now. Another group participant assumes the role of the therapist and tries to intervene in a way that promotes mentalization. After a sequence of about five minutes, the game is stopped. The group participants share their emotional reactions and observations as observers; only then do the players share their experiences. One can also have another participant play the therapist again in a second round, as they may have other ideas, especially if the therapeutic process reached a dead end the first time around. The group leader can also "double" the therapist or become an auxiliary ego and thus try to help the therapist implement new ideas in the game. Changing roles further encourages the experimental attitude already inherent to such role-play.

It is important to recall the experimental and processual nature of role-play. This form of feedback involves some danger of judgment and know-it-all toward the therapist who introduces the case. Therefore, it is significant that the therapist be aware that supervisors are always in a better position than the therapist, and that supervisors view the therapeutic situation with more composure from an external position. It is also important not to lose sight of the central goal of mentalization-oriented supervision: to let the therapist regain their mentalization skills.

Conclusion

Contrary to Bordin's (1979) formulations regarding the therapeutic alliance consisting of the three components bond, tasks, and goals, classical psychoanalysis considers the handling of transference to be quite central to interactions in the therapeutic relationship. Dealing with transference and the nature of transference interpretations are very different things: Transference interpretations can be conducive to mentalization as "work during transference," whereas, from the point of view of the mentalization concept, "working on transference" appears to be unsuitable for treating patients with severe structural impairments.

Emphasizing transference in the psychoanalytic concept often causes neglect of the other aspects formulated by Bordin regarding the therapeutic alliance. In the MBT concept, these aspects are further emphasized in treatment goals and tasks, psychoeducation as well as the relevance of epistemic trust and feedback.

5.3   Interpretation and Insight (Content Perspective) or the Not-Knowing Stance (Process Perspective)

Interpretation and Insight

Interpretations play a central role in psychoanalytic treatment techniques. They serve to enable insight on the part of the patient. On an abstract level, the description of interpretations concerns making the unconscious conscious; on a concrete level, interpretations concern the current conflict dynamic, defense mechanisms, and the transference process, for example, the genetic interpretation of the connection between childhood and the current conflict. What one understands as an interpretation varies. Sometimes it refers to a quasicausal explanation and other times to the attribution of a meaning. The central assumptions of psychoanalytic interpretations include that unconscious motives act like causes, that people never act without intention, and that their own intentions are sometimes not conscious.

In psychoanalysis, interpreting unconscious parts of a conflict has long been considered the central impact factor of treatment. The unconscious is supposed to become conscious through interpretations. While the epistemological content of empirical psychotherapy research is not the sole yardstick for psychoanalytic psychotherapy and is limited because the use of simple methods is at odds with the hypercomplex data from psychotherapy, it is nevertheless noteworthy that interpretations have so far found rather little confirmation in psychotherapy research as a significant impact factor (Wampold, 2015; Wampold and Imel, 2015). The findings caution against expecting interpretations to deliver significant therapeutic gains, even though a recent large metastudy found insight to be significant for therapeutic success and a relevant impact factor in various forms of therapy (Jennissen et al., 2018). Insight may have received insufficient attention as an impact factor in psychotherapy research up to now. Despite its central importance as a treatment ideal since the beginning of psychoanalysis, insight as an assumed therapeutic effect factor has remained very imprecisely formulated.

In classical psychoanalysis, insight refers primarily to the cognitive and affective insight a person gathers into their own unconscious or preconscious conflicts. The mentalization concept understands insightfulness as a reflective competence that relates to the self- and interpersonal functioning regarding cognitive and affective preconditions by linking it to mentalizing ability, thus complementing the psychoanalytic view. Resistances that can be explained psychodynamically can make insight difficult, as can a lack of mentalizing abilities, which can make insight processes impossible. Bram and Gabbard (2001) pointed out that psychoanalysts tend to unquestioningly interpret difficulties in gaining insight as defense mechanisms or resistance on the part of the patient. In many cases, however, analysts fail to see the clear self- and interpersonal functioning deficits that can upend a patient's ability to gain insight. Psychoanalysts remain true to the classical conflict model but the mentalization concept sees mentalization deficits as a central problem in gaining insight.

MBT relativizes the expectation of the effectiveness of interpretations. Nevertheless, the mentalization concept does involve unconscious processes, whether regarding the primary unconscious or the psychoanalytic unconscious (Fonagy & Allison, 2016) or regarding the horizontal and vertical unconscious (Gödde & Buchholz, 2011; see Chapter 4). MBT also makes interpretations in the broadest sense through the psychoeducation and transparency it provides within treatment, which also includes the therapist providing explanations and interpretations about their approach, e.g., information about the applied psychotherapy theory in the sense of "psychotherapy as a threefold communication system" (see Chapter 2.7).

What Speaks Against Interpretations from a Mentalization-Oriented Point of View

Processing interpretations can overload patients with limitations in self- and interpersonal functioning. Interpretations are helpful only if the patient can reflect on them from an affective angle; otherwise, they remain only theoretical knowledge. However, patients with self- and interpersonal functioning deficits, whether because of epistemic hypervigilance, epistemic distrust, or difficulties in controlling affect, often find it difficult to maintain the ability to mentalize in the presence of affective involvement. The patient then processes the interpretation—at best—in a pseudomentalizing or aversive manner as a fixation.

What Speaks for Interpretations from a Mentalization-Oriented Point of View

Patients search for explanations, patterns, and meaningful contexts in their often stressful interpersonal experiences. For patients, interpretations can become "statements by the therapist that open the door to new insights" (quote from a patient). Successful interpretations create meaningful contexts for the patient, which, in turn, can serve as answers to questions about the emergence of psychological suffering, the inability to love, aggression, and limitations in mentalizing abilities. This is where the mentalization concept, in conjunction with its psychoanalytic roots, can provide humane answers based on current scientific findings. Such interpretations can promote mentalization and create epistemic confidence. Patients who choose psychodynamic or psychoanalytic treatments expect the therapist to provide some clarification concerning unconscious or near-conscious connections—which is justified. Other patients expect to receive good advice or explanations that simply dissolve their difficulties into nothing. Such patients are disappointed by every psychoanalyst, something Freud (1910) described far back.

Although there is much to be said for using interpretation in MBT, classical psychoanalytic therapy and MBT differ significantly in how they deal with interpretation. Classical psychoanalysts tend to *interpret* feelings more often, whereas

MBT therapists encourage patients to *explore* them. Classical psychoanalysts interpret earlier because they ideally share with the patient the conviction that, as a psychoanalyst, their training uniquely enables them to grasp the patient's unconscious conflicts, desires, and structures better than the patient. The MBT therapist, on the other hand, approaches things more from the angle of dialog and intersubjectivity. And, more radically than the traditional psychoanalyst, the MBT therapist pursues the goal of perceiving their own affects alongside those of the patient—recognizing them, calling them out, understanding them, regulating them, and discovering how they connect to their experiences and conflicts. In doing so, the MBT therapist stays more in the here and now and establishes the reference to the past less often.

The Not-Knowing Stance

Taking the not-knowing stance is the counterpoint to interpretation. In any interpretation, the therapist empathically communicates to the patient something the patient does not yet know. From the standpoint of not-knowing, however, the therapist encourages the patient to find out something they (or both of them) do not yet know. Taking the standpoint of not-knowing means the therapist is curious about what the patient has to say about themselves and their experience, and how they see this from their inner perspective. What they do not do is provide interpretations to the patient on how they *should* understand the experience based on their presumed therapeutic competence and experience.

Taking the standpoint of not-knowing is illustrated by the questioning technique of the legendary TV detective Columbo. It is characterized by a curiosity that maintains a benevolent relationship with the counterpart in the interaction, following the intention to truly find out something. Inspector Columbo does not mind appearing to be stupid and naive (in addition to being poorly dressed). He thinks out loud, tells the other person his hypotheses if necessary, and admits to the other person that he is quite uncertain about his assumptions. He says, for example:

"Could it be that..."
"What I'm wondering is..."
"I don't understand at all how..."
"I don't know, but what do you think about the hypothesis..."
"Would you mind if I take a look around your place?"
As he leaves, Columbo always turns around and surprisingly (and naively) asks one final question, "Oh, I'd like to ask you one more question..."

The example of Detective Columbo is, of course, limited. The therapist is not a detective, nor does the therapist query the patient as someone who is only apparently ignorant. For real therapists, on the contrary, it is rather difficult sometimes to tolerate the helplessness connected with this therapeutic approach. Yet, it is precisely because of their helplessness that therapists give interpretations, enter into a Socratic dialog, or distribute well-intentioned advice.

What Characterizes the Not-Knowing Stance?

Authenticity: having a genuine interest in finding something out using exploration.

Humility and modesty: result from a stance of not-knowing and are linked to the requirement to show self-reflection.

Accepting different perspectives.

Asking for detailed descriptions of experiences: Actively asking the patient about their experiences ("how-questions") promotes the process is are more helpful than asking for explanations ("why-questions"), including asking the patient about their experiences over time in the sense of "micro-slicing" ("salami tactics").

Maintenance over time: being curious, including identifying differences in perspectives, takes patience and persistence.

Appropriate understanding: admitting that you also don't understand something, that something doesn't make sense to you, or that something is still unclear.

The not-knowing stance means the therapist focuses on emotional experience. They do not name the feelings for the patient; rather, they help the patient to perceive and name their feelings. The therapist tries to maintain this stance throughout. A therapy session in which the therapist fails to realize the not-knowing stance is, according to the model of MBT, not a true therapy session.

Example of a Poor-Quality Not-Knowing Stance

Therapist: You missed the last session.
Patient: I missed the subway.
Therapist: Honestly, I can't imagine that? Did it really take you that long? Why didn't you just come late to the session? I think what you're really telling me is that you didn't want to come.
Patient: Yes, to be honest, I didn't feel like it.
Therapist: Okay. But we have an agreement that you come regardless of your desire, right?
Patient: I know.
Therapist: You did agree to the terms of the therapy, didn't you?
Patient: Yes.
Therapist: It's okay, it can happen. So next time it will be better, right?
Patient: No, no, you are absolutely right.

Example of a Higher-Quality Not-Knowing Stance

Therapist: I waited for you here on Friday. What happened?
Patient: I missed the subway.
Therapist: Really? How so?
Patient: To be honest, I didn't feel like coming either.
Therapist: How's that?
Patient: I don't know.
Therapist: Let's find out! Did it have anything to do with the therapy setting, maybe? It's really an interesting topic.
Patient: I don't want to talk about it.
Therapist: Let's find out.
Patient: No, I really don't.
Therapist: I'm interested in it. It might be important. Could it have something to do with me?
Patient: I don't think you're the best therapist for me.
Therapist: I'm glad you said that! After all, it could be important that you don't waste your time here or that we're making it unnecessarily difficult for ourselves.
Silence.
Therapist: Can you say more about that?
Patient: I compare you with my last therapist, who also always asked questions and looked at me so skeptically.
Therapist: Do you experience my questions as controlling? Then maybe I should change something.
Patient: Yes and no. It's not that bad now...
(Adapted from the MBT Adherence and Competence Scale (ACS), 2019)

Consistently maintaining a stance of not-knowing impacts treatment:

- This approach leads to a certain equality between the therapist and the patient since neither is the "know-it-all" in the relationship. This attitude does not result in interpretations of the patient's behavior in the therapeutic relationship presented with a tone of certainty. Further, this approach largely avoids interpretations of conflicts on the edge of consciousness, because the therapist would thereby convey knowing better after all.
- The not-knowing stance provokes mentalization. When the therapist unconditionally tries to understand the patient (without denying their own expertise as a therapist), they create the basis for the development of a patient's basal trust in a reference person (therapist) as a secure source of information (i.e., epistemic trust), which forms the basis for a good therapeutic relationship.

Strictly speaking, the MBT treatment technique rejects interpretations altogether, as shown by the MBT Adherence and Competence Scale (ACS) (2019). There are good reasons for this:

- When proffering interpretations, the therapist leaves the solid ground of not-knowing. In fact, interpretations can often prevent mentalization by replacing shared reflection with a statement from the therapist.
- The therapist takes up the position of the "knower" and the patient (necessarily) the position of the "unenlightened." This is especially true when interpreting unconscious or preconscious events, since, according to the psychoanalyst's theory, the patient inherently has limited or no access to them.

There is much that is correct about this view, but in long-term psychotherapies, the conditions may not be so clear, so that a differentiated use of interpretation would seem to make sense. Interpretations can represent a helpful intervention technique in long-term therapies for structural disorders, as elaborated below.

When Interpretations Can Promote Mentalization

Interpretations formulated as an idea rather than a certainty can further mentalization, from the standpoint of not-knowing. Thus: "I don't know for sure, but what do you think of the hypothesis..."

In video demonstrations, the psychoanalyst O. Kernberg also formulated his interpretations as a questioning offer: "Do you think it is so? Or is it wrong?" Here, the therapist does not convey interpretations with paternal authority but as an idea offered to the patient for reflection: "Can it be that..." Interpretations intended (and understood) in this way and introduced experimentally into treatment can challenge the patient to mentalize.

- Psychoanalysis distinguishes between "actual-genetic interpretations" and "genetic interpretations." The former consists of clarifying the background of experience in the here and now; the latter involves the biographical roots of the respective experience. The therapist traces the content of the experience back to earlier experience and interprets the present problem as a repetition of the unresolved earlier conflict pattern. In MBT, the focus of interpretations lies on the actual-genetic, and the focus of treatment lies on the current process in here-and-now experiences. More than 20 years ago, Fonagy (1999a) expressed his skepticism about the intensive exploration of the past in therapy. Also, in Jurist's (2018, p. 121) experience, too intensively exploring the past with affects attached to memories can damage a person whose mentalizing abilities are severely impaired. His experience says this can lead to a disorganized and eruptive therapeutic process with a malignant course. However, treatment can be successful in these patients if the focus of affective mentalizing remains in the here and now.

- Interpretations that allow the patient to feel "seen" in unspeakable parts and parts they feel belong to them reveal the epistemic match (see Chapter 5.2) and promote epistemic trust in the therapeutic relationship.

For educational reasons, it is appropriate to ask seminar participants to refrain altogether from making interpretations to better show the concept. Most therapists find it rather difficult to maintain an authentic attitude of not-knowing, especially when the therapist (and the patient) get caught up in an affectively charged situation or a situation of great perplexity—or both. But especially then, the therapist must maintain the point of view of not-knowing, even though therapists of all schools tend to resort to their proven interpretation techniques. For example, the therapist may promote a certain feeling to the patient when searching for an expression or theoretical explanation of the feeling, depending on the therapy in question. Conversely, mentalization is more likely to come to the fore when the therapist challenges patients to explore their feelings themselves. That is the first step toward regaining control over themselves and the situation.

Therapists often adopt a pattern of interpretive communication: They mentalize for the patient rather than supporting the patient's efforts to more effectively mentalize themselves. This is true for MBT therapists as well. However, the goal of MBT remains to jointly initiate joint exploration of feelings and thoughts. "Interpretations are most effective when the patient finds them himself" (Mentzos, oral communication).

How Interpretation Works from a Mentalization-Based Perspective—an Example

A phenomenon that occurs again and again in therapies: The elephant is there, in the room, invisible yet perceptible, present without being mentioned. So, what is the elephant? Where is the elephant? No one sees him concretely, yet he is there in the room. No one speaks to him. Sometimes, you feel you could reach out and grab him with your hands, and sometimes he can be very powerful. This may have to do with the therapeutic relationship, some tacit topic or affect. It may be something that stands between the patient and the therapist. Sometimes the elephant remains undefined, making it difficult to put a label on him. The therapist's job is to address the elephant by encouraging the patient to work with him to first find the elephant, then name it, and finally talk about it.

The Elephant in the Room

Patient: I can't think of anything else to say about this. I haven't been able to think of anything the whole time.
Therapist: I've felt the whole time that something is wrong here today.
Patient: I don't!
Therapist: That sounds strange to me.

Silence.

Therapist:	How do you feel about it when we are silent?
Patient:	It's okay!
Therapist:	There's something different about today. Is it just me who feels this?
Patient:	I had a heart attack, was in the emergency room, my husband canceled my appointment here—and you didn't even call!
Therapist:	Okay. I understand.

Silence.

Therapist:	What do you say about that?

Silence.

Therapist:	So, I'm heartless. Is that it?
Patient:	Something like that.
Therapist:	Let's talk about it.
Patient:	We've known each other for so long, so I thought I had a bonus with you.
Therapist:	I see. Can you tell me more about that? This is important to me.

This dialog also contains some interpretations. Something is addressed that has gone unaddressed. The therapist interprets the situation: "I've felt the whole time that something is wrong here today," and insists: "That sounds strange to me." These are interpretations in an initially opaque situation. The therapist later says, "So, I'm heartless. Is that it?" The therapist is offering something here that is interpretive in nature. He could also have explored things further in a more questioning way, but that—according to the therapist's intuition—might have been perceived by the patient as inquisitorial, artificial, and distancing.

Conclusion

Interpretation as a treatment technique and applying insight as an impact factor in psychotherapy represent different treatment techniques in traditional psychoanalysis and MBT. Originally, the MBT treatment concept does not comprise interpretation: Interpretations pertain to a content perspective, whereas the attitude of not-knowing refers to the process perspective. These two perspectives can complement each other; interpretations can have various characteristics. An interpretation (or hypothesis) that stems from not-knowing and preferably refers to the here and now can indeed promote mentalization. But central and distinct from this in MBT is the standpoint of not-knowing.

5.4   Regression or Working in the Here and Now

Regression

In psychoanalytic theory, regression describes the temporary withdrawal to an earlier stage of personality development. Freud initially characterized this as resistance but later thought regression to be the breakdown of defenses for the benefit of therapy. Regression to stages of early object relations—as we would call it today—thus serves to work through early developmental inhibitions in psycho-analytic treatment.

Psychoanalysis understands regression as the changes that occur in psychic functions, both regarding ego functions and relatedness to each other as well as desires and wishes.

Behind the idea of promoting regression lies the thought that one must soften pathogenic structures to make early conflicts, desires, and affective states stem-ming from old object-relation experiences accessible to interpretation and con-sciousness. This enables profound changes in the framework of the therapeutic process, especially transference and countertransference.

The patient's regression during the therapy session is revealed in their of-fering an emotional relationship and in affective moods related to previously experienced states and relationship constellations, i.e., in transference. The pa-tient slides back into childhood while simultaneously maintaining stable ego functions. The psychoanalyst promotes regression by maintaining a rather re-served attitude, implementing little structure in the treatment apart from the setting and the advance agreements, and providing ample opportunity for free association. These conditions allow early transference components to easily unfold.

Psychoanalytic psychotherapy is characterized by work in regression. It as-sumes that there is a certain consensus about what regression in treatment means, although this is hardly the case: Regression expresses itself differently in the conflicts of functionally severely impaired patients than in those of patients with predominantly stable ego functions. While the latter may regress temporally and partially to an early stage of their development within the session, patients with severe personality disorders, such as persons with BPD, spontaneously "slip" into a regressive state. And their regression is often highly affectively charged, so that control is largely lost, situationally and temporally. This is characteristic of the dy-namics in individuals with severe functional limitations, i.e., personality disorders. These differences in regression likely prompted Bion to remark, "Winnicott says patients need to regress, Melanie Klein says they must not regress. I say they are regressed" (Bion, in Britton 1998, p.71).

Evidence-based therapeutic approaches to treating severe personality disorders and complex posttraumatic disorders do not promote regressive processes. Ap-proaches that have been well-studied and are successful structure treatment along two features: First, an active attitude of the therapist, which protects the therapeutic relationship and helps the patient regulate their affects; second, transparency within the treatment, which also serves to convey security. This also includes establishing a consensus on therapeutic goals and tasks. The scientifically evaluated treatments for BPD (Storebø et al., 2020, Cochrane Database of Systematic Reviews, 5) are counted among the evidence-based approaches, including MBT. Wampold's and collegues meta-analysis of well-studied approaches to the treatment of severely traumatized patients ("bona fide" treatments) reaches similar conclusions (Wampold's et al., 2010, p. 931).

Regression during treatment sessions is problematic in patients with severe personality disorders for two reasons: First, our experience from treating borderline patients and individuals with severe personality disorders shows that regression can limit mentalizing skills and, in particular, cognitive control functions during treatment—but these are exactly the functions and abilities these patients usually urgently need to cope with life, even outside therapy sessions. This is the case, for example, when regression causes traumatic content to surface that then triggers threatening affects and limits cognitive functions. Ego functions urgently needed to stabilize mentalizing abilities can falter. Second, ideal psychoanalytic therapy means the patient can—and should—regress during the therapy session, and that this regression is reversed at the end of the session. Yet that is often unrealistic for most patients with functional limitations, who often do not possess these control skills outside the treatment setting and therefore persist in regression at the end of the therapy session. Therapy that promotes regression runs the risk of actually reinforcing the lack of control skills outside the therapy session.

MBT treatment is structured as follows:

- an active attitude of the therapist, who assumes responsibility for the therapeutic relationship;
- an active regulation of the patient's "arousals" to regulate their affects;
- transparency in the treatment (e.g., the therapist: "I am silent because I am thinking");
- presence in the "here and now" with references to the past, inasmuch as they contribute to understanding the here and now;
- a largely team-oriented treatment setting, which demands that the therapist maintain a network and coordinate supervision if the treatment of severe personality disorders occurs in an individual therapy setting.

The therapeutic attitude aims to give the patient security and not to abandon them in earlier, often very strongly affective states, where mentalization had usually collapsed. The patient should stay in therapy—"Not too far from the fire, but not too close to it"—and thereby develop the ability to mentalize in the face of bearable affects.

Here and Now

MBT focuses on the here and now in sessions. Below, we exemplify the three key treatment techniques anchored in the here and now: empathic validation of the patient's experience and experience, recognition of nonmentalizing modes, and encouragement of contrarian movement (polarities).

Empathic Validation

Empathic validation means more than just being empathic; it also means describing things empathically and remaining open without judging. But it goes beyond that—empathic validation also means:

- letting someone know that what they are feeling, thinking, believing, and experiencing is real and comprehensible—in other words, normalizing the emotions;
- naming what the patient does not name (e.g., naming feelings when cognitions are prominent and naming thoughts when feelings are prominent);
- acknowledging that there is more than one correct way to see things and situations.

The therapist can check whether they are in fact empathically validating the patient by asking the following questions:

- Do I correctly understand the patient's present inner world? Am I communicating this to the patient?
- Can I identify the patient's affects and describe their effects?

To maintain an empathic validating stance, the therapist should be aware:

- that every point of view has right and wrong aspects;
- that two things can be contradictory and yet both be right;
- that there is something to learn from everyone.

Empathic validation puts the therapist in the patient's shoes to see the world through the patient's eyes. It expresses genuine interest in the patient's perceptions and emphasizes affect. Effective empathic validation also means maintaining eye contact with the patient. That may sound easy, but it is not, especially when the patient is not currently mentalizing effectively but is, for example, making paranoid or intensely hostile attributions. It is challenging for the therapist to maintain a nonjudgmental point of view (both internally and externally) when the patient makes extreme, judgmental, or highly affective statements. Therapists often find it difficult to validate when they disagree with what is being said and are concerned that they are confirming or promoting misperceptions or ineffective mentalizing.

Recognizing Ineffective Mentalizing and Interventions

The six domains described in Figure 5.2 (reported in this chapter and the next) characterize ineffective mentalization.

One can view the three typical forms of mentalization disorders—equivalence mode, teleological mode, and pseudomentalizing mode—in light of developmental psychology. These modes draw on typical early stages of mentalizing development:

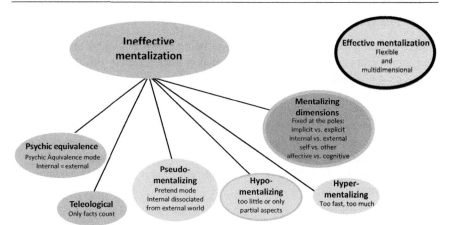

Figure 5.2 Ineffective and effective mentalization.

equivalence mode, teleological mode, and pretend mode, which later imprint as pseudomentalizing. A nonmentalizing mode may occur in a particular situation (e.g., stress, anxiety). Also, the mode may change from situation to situation. However, a nonmentalizing mode can also be characteristic of a person in the sense that they frequently use this mode in their communication with other people as well as when addressing themselves.

Pseudomentalization is characterized by:

- speaking in a psychologizing language without really addressing the connection between inner process and outer reality;
- idealizing insight for its own sake;
- a lack of connection between inner and outer reality, i.e., the two worlds are decoupled. There is usually also a lack of "grounding." The narrative can seem and indeed be dissociative.

Here are some rather unfruitful interventions on the part of the therapist:

- Taking the patient's insights at "face value."
- Continuing to talk "smart" to the patient and thereby encouraging the patient to continue this path of "research."

Here are some more fruitful interventions on the part of the therapist:

- Checking whether one has truly understood something or whether one has succumbed to pretty words.
- Adopting an attitude of not-knowing, e.g., inquiring about references to external reality.

The equivalence mode is characterized by:

- equating the inner world with the outer world: "Because I feel that way, that's the way it is!" "No sooner said than done!" "It is what it is!"
- a lack of attention to the thoughts, feelings, and desires of others;
- a tendency to make massive generalizations, prejudices, and black-and-white thinking;
- reporting on interpersonal matters using facts, facts, and more facts;
- reporting rules and responsibilities, with many "shoulds" and "should nots."

Here are some unfruitful interventions on the part of the therapist:

- continuing to ask for facts in an attempt to clarify issues;
- discussing things with the patient, including feelings.

Here are some more fruitful interventions on the part of the therapist:

- displaying empathic validation;
- proposing alternative views or introducing them ("challenging");
- seeking a less-tense topic where the real world can easily be connected with the affective world in a mentalizing way;
- projecting an attitude of not-knowing, e.g., "How are you doing with me now?"

The teleological mode (the instrumentalization of mentalization) is characterized by:

- reading the motives of others exclusively from their actions. ("If you really want to help me, then do this...");
- exerting coercion toward the therapist that something must happen;
- using mentalization to control someone else's behavior;
- attempting to induce specific thoughts and feelings in another person, e.g., when a marriage imposter tries to make a person fall in love;
- intentionally subverting another's ability to think, e.g., by causing arousal;
- deactivating one's own mentalization as protection against the harmful/malicious intentions of relational persons, e.g., the unbearable idea that a person familiar to me is threatening my life through sexual violence.

Here are some unfruitful interventions on the part of the therapist:

- giving in to urges hastily in the hope of positive change;
- becoming angry at being unable to discover or experience the distress behind manipulative behavior.

Here are some fruitful interventions on the part of the therapist:

- empathically validating distress and naming the affects that belong to this distress;
- attempting to explore affects associated with nonmentalizing.

Hypermentalization characterizes the "ability" to read too much into oneself and the other. This is often associated with speculation about motives and affects. Hypermentalization is also associated with hypervigilance, unquestioned assumptions, and uncontrolled excessive reasoning (Bateman & Fonagy, 2012). Hypermentalization often goes hand in hand with epistemic vigilance/epistemic distrust and high arousal. Hypermentalization is not simply "too much mentalizing," i.e., too much of a good thing.

Hypermentalization is characterized by (Sharp et al., 2013):

- a failure to differentiate self from others regarding attribution to a mental state;
- limitations in the ability to integrate cognitions and affect;
- difficulty switching between automatic and explicit mentalizing depending on the requirements or context.

According to Luyten et al. (2021), the lack of self–other differentiation, also referred to as self-other diffusion, is characteristic of BPD.

The therapeutic management of the hypermentalizing mode is similar to that of the pseudomentalizing mode.

GENERAL RECOMMENDATIONS

The therapist should strive to return patients from the nonmentalizing to the mentalizing mode. To do this, it is first necessary to recognize the mode of the mentalizing disorder to prevent getting into the same rut as the patient: The pull toward it is often strong. When the patient reports facts after facts, the therapist is often inclined to keep asking for facts because some things remain unclear. If the patient talks "smartly," the therapist is delighted at the "insights" and encourages the conversation to go on, failing to notice how both of them are gradually losing their grip. If the patient presses the therapist to act regarding their distress, the therapist may feel uncomfortable and even give in to the patient's need for security or react gruffly and unsympathetically. Then, it is helpful to stop the patient—to hit the "pause button"—which may be necessary if the therapist feels that they no longer understand what is happening or registers that the affects have reached a level they cannot mentalize. The therapist can then say, "Can we stop for a moment? When you talk to me so loudly and violently, I feel overwhelmed. I can't think clearly." Sometimes, it helps to ask the patient to find the point of the session at which joint mentalization was still possible and then return to that point.

Stimulation of Contrary Movements (Polarities)

One can analyze a patient's mentalization during the psychotherapy session on four dimensions (see Figure 5.3), each of which is described by two opposite poles. Effective mentalization occurs at the balance point between the two poles, i.e., when both poles are considered in the communication. Where a person is along this continuum at any given moment may depend on the situation or the patient's personality.

The poles are characterized as follows:

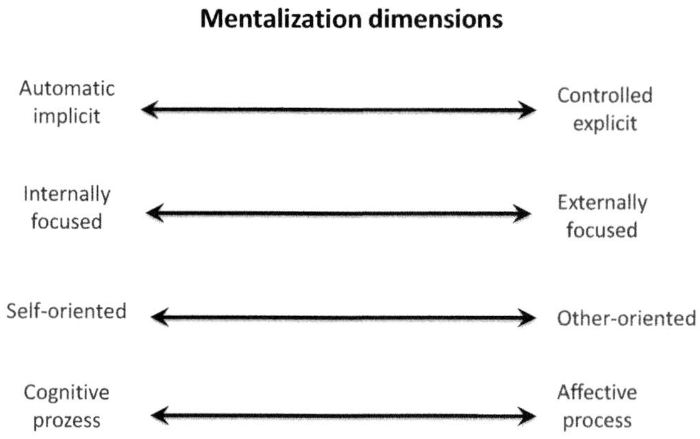

Mentalization dimensions

Figure 5.3 Mentalization dimensions (polarities).

IMPLICIT MENTALIZATION VS. EXPLICIT MENTALIZATION

Implicit: This is quick and reflexive mentalization. This is how we usually mentalize in everyday life. It is characterized by a high sensitivity to nonverbal signals, especially regarding the intentions of others. A secure attachment is a good prerequisite for successful implicit mentalizing.

Explicit: This is characterized by "slowly, one thing after another." It requires reflection, attention, effort, and is more verbally mediated. We need explicit mentalization when implicit mentalization fails and when we experience misunderstandings in coping with anxiety and uncertainty. Therapy demands explicit and slow mentalizing when discussing distressing problems, unresolved conflicts, or severely distressing issues.

INTERNALLY FOCUSED VS. EXTERNALLY FOCUSED

Internally: This is the ability to make assessments based on inner perceptions, both in oneself and others.

Externally: This includes a high sensitivity to nonverbal messages and a strong tendency to make judgments based on external characteristics and observations. The danger here lies in making rash assumptions without checking them internally.

ORIENTED TOWARD SELF VS. ORIENTED TOWARD OTHERS

Self: Overemphasis on this pole harbors the danger of fixation on one's own perceptions or limited interest in perceiving the mental state of the other. It may lead to self-dramatization and fantasies of grandeur.

Others: Overemphasis on this pole causes a high susceptibility to affective contamination, which is associated with the ability to empathize with others and the danger of losing one's grip on one's own inner world. Overemphasis on orientation to others can lead to the exploitation/abuse of oneself as well as—the other side of the coin—to an implicit exploitation/abuse of others.

COGNITIVE ORIENTATION VS. AFFECTIVE ORIENTATION

Cognitive: Overemphasis on this pole is often associated with low emotional empathy. Understanding is rooted in the intellectual, the rational, or the concrete. The danger here is that understanding becomes narrowed to a criminalistic, exaggerated, or propositional approach. People at this pole strive to speak about personal problems by emphasizing facts. We find this phenomenon in a different form in antisocial personalities: Good cognitive performance and empathy for the fellow human being are usually blocked, and affects remain artificial, fabricated, or staged.

Affective: Persons at this pole are highly sensitive to affective signals. They are highly susceptible to affective contamination and tend to be overwhelmed by affect when their own inner world or that of another becomes the focal point.

GENERAL RECOMMENDATIONS

The therapist must first determine where patients are located along the individual poles in the therapy session. One or two dimensions can be particularly illuminating if they are particularly out of balance. For example, if the patient strongly leans toward the cognitive pole in their speech, the therapist must introduce the affective pole into the conversation, because effective mentalization takes place when both poles are taken into account. The goal of moving the patient toward the affective pole is not to change the patient but to develop a neglected dimension. Development can take place, for example, by using stimuli that challenge the patient's affective reactions.

Challenging

Challenging characterizes interventions that test the patient in surprising and creative ways. Challenging should interrupt the patient's nonmentalizing, nudge them a little off the well-worn path, and encourage a change in their perspective—which should increase the chance of getting back into mentalization.

How does challenging work? For example, when the intervention lies outside the framework expected by the patient, perhaps even irritating the patient a little. At the same time, the interventions must remain nonjudgmental, playful, and include some humor. A challenging intervention is always a risk; it can go wrong, fail, or hurt the patient. Therefore, the therapist should have the character and the ability to apologize. For this risk to be successful, it presumes a certain trusting relationship between the patient and the therapist.

Here's an example: A patient who is very performance-oriented and very strict with themselves says to the therapist, "Hey, you're not trying very hard here today!" The therapist: "I know, I know. Sorry. I'm a lazy person." The patient: "And you're okay with that?" The therapist: "Yes. Are you not okay with it?"

What Therapists Should Do

- Use simple and brief interventions.
- Center on the here and now and encourage further exploration.
- Focus on affects.
- Encourage a medium level of intensity of emotional involvement that is neither too close to nor too far away from the fire—that is neither too "cold" nor too "hot."
- Provide experiences of security that facilitate the patient's exploration of internal states.
- Engage the patient to view interactions and own experiences from different perspectives.

What Therapists Should Not Do

- In MBT, it is not the therapist's job to tell the patient how to feel, what to think, and how to behave.
- It is not the task of the therapist to tell the patient what the underlying reasons are for their difficulties, whether conscious or unconscious.
- Any attitude that presumes "I know how this patient ticks" or "I know how the patient should behave and think and why the patient is the way they are" can harm patients, especially patients with structural disorders, borderline patients, and those with prolonged traumatic experiences or neglect. To avoid succumbing to these temptations, resort to the attitude of not-knowing.

Conclusion

Traditional psychoanalytic and mentalization-based procedures posit different treatment techniques for patients with severe structural impairments and personality disorders relative to "regression facilitation" vs. working in the "here and now."

There are also differences regarding how to weigh the past vs. the present. Both forms of treatment consider the perspective of the past and the present and are not mutually exclusive. Rather, they can be understood as flexible alternations of background and foreground, although the weighting of the two perspectives is different. MBT's concept and treatment technique focuses on communicative processes that occur in the here and now, whereas traditional psychoanalysis relates more to the patient's history in treatment.

5.5   Defense and Resistance

In psychoanalysis, defense and resistance refer to the psychodynamics of regulating intrapsychic and interpersonal conflicts. While resistance is usually conscious and perceptible to the observer or therapist as a manifestation, defense mechanisms can be accessed only as an unconscious pattern. Defense mechanisms develop against conscious, but mostly preconscious or unconscious contents, which are often connected with strong and threatening affects. Defense mechanisms consist of repression, splitting, or projective identification. Defenses are necessary for mental regulation and can contribute to healthy mental development, but may come at a high cost: severe psychopathological symptomatology as well as mental and psychosomatic illness.

A prerequisite for analyzing the defense mechanisms found in classical psychoanalysis and changing defense constellations through interpretations is the assumption that the person has a sufficient structural level. This presupposes, among others, sufficient abilities for affect perception, affect differentiation, and affect symbolization. If these prerequisites (which are also prerequisites of effective mentalization) are not given, obstacles to therapeutic work cannot be traced back to a defense against conflicts in the sense of the classical psychoanalytic model and thus cannot be worked on interpretatively. The obstacles can then be traced back to the prerequisites for effective mentalization. Presuming a psychoanalytically underpinned defense may lead to misunderstandings that in turn lead to strong negative affects (e.g., fear, anger, lack of understanding) unrelated to the defense. Viewing and interpreting these negative affects as part of defensiveness is problematic because, as the term suggests, the patient exhibits resistance (for unconscious reasons), whereas in reality there are deficits.

Although the concept of defense and resistance do not occur in MBT—which generally avoids using such terminology—the concept of psychodynamic defense does elucidate some aspects of MBT and allows for a broader understanding of the psychodynamics of mentalization disorders. We can illustrate this by looking at two aspects in the much-cited model for psychoanalytic focus formulated by Menninger and Holzman (1958), namely, the "triangle of conflict." This triangle condenses aspects of basic psychoanalytic theory into what is clinically essential (see Figure 5.4).

All three aspects—the anxiety, the "defended" (e.g., conflictual impulses, traumatic memories, shame or guilt), and the defense—can be unconscious, described by the familiar defense mechanisms (e.g., repression). The therapeutic procedure can be explained and described in the following: With which defense can which fear remain suppressed, and which keeps away which impulses? The interpretive

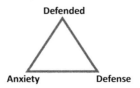

Figure 5.4 The psychodynamic focus—the triangle of conflict, after Menninger and Holzman (1958).

process begins with the defense, linking the defense to the fear when it is labilized, progressing to linking the defense to the fear, and finally to what is being devended. (Example by Klüwer 2004.)

The model describes patients who exclusively use intellectualized and detached language to speak about affectively significant relationships, as characterized by the prementalizing mode of pseudomentalizing. In this example, the defense is the defense mechanism of intellectualization. The anxiety is initially unconscious but comes alive when the defense, i.e., the inappropriately intellectual language, is addressed. Fear then points toward what is being defended against, e.g., shame over a traumatic event experienced.

Defense is the gateway to change. This is true for classical psychoanalysis as well as for MBT. In the first step, the exploration of defense mechanisms is closely connected to the patient's affects. Psychoanalysts who follow this model initially focus on intellectualization; mentalization-based therapists focus on pseudomentalizing. They differ, however, in that the mentalization-based therapist then continues to focus on the process, whereas the psychoanalytic therapist is more likely to commence interpretation, thus referring more to content-related aspects. The limits of the triangle model emerge where pseudomentalization is not a defense mechanism but results from deficits in mentalizing abilities. Both the presence of a defense and a deficit in mentalization are theoretically possible and must be considered and weighed in practical cases.

Another example of the usefulness of the concept of defense in MBT concerns interpersonal psychodynamics regarding the alien self. A psychodynamic defense may consist of a person's ability to create coherence in their self by projecting incoherent alien self parts into another person. The defense mechanism is initially projection. Here, as in the triangle of conflict, the defense mechanism serves to ward off massive, possibly diffuse fears/threats, feelings of unbearable emptiness, and inner tensions generated by the incoherence of self and other-self. However, according to clinical experience, the defense is also associated with more severe complications and can be understood through the defense mechanism of projective identification, since the defense mechanism usually leads to a strong dependence on the person on the receiving end of the negative parts.

Contrary to the assumption of classical psychoanalysis that what is being defended is a conflict, one can also assume that the patient is defending themselves against an affect experienced as threatening (e.g., a traumatic experience). The defense mechanism then refers to the awareness of an affect experienced as threatening and as a threat to the limitians of self- and interpersonal functioning. This assumption enables us to use the psychoanalytic concept of defense to understand the difficulties that occur in affect elaboration in MBT. However, the consequences for treatment remain more or less the same. The psychoanalyst should start with the defense mechanism and then connects the affects arising from labilization with the defense to arrive at what is being defended. Even in such a case, one need not see the emergence of the prementalizing mode as a deficit but as the emergence of a defense mechanism. By using the equivalence mode, the patient fends off, for example, any affects perceived as threatening by concentrating on what is factual and concrete. The MBT therapist who recognizes, for example, how the patient's inability to perceive and reflect on their affects limits their mentalization because of the equivalence mode then also focuses on the defense mechanism (the prementalizing mode) to enable more effective mentalization. In both cases, the interventions target affect elaboration. Though the two approaches are based on different assumptions (deficit vs. conflict), the interventions of the approaches initially serve affect elaboration and changing the restricted mentalizing. Another difference lies in the MBT therapists staying in the process, while classical psychoanalysts tend to prefer interpretation.

Conclusion

The MBT concept exercises great restraint regarding the terminology of defense and resistance. Nevertheless, the psychoanalytic concept of defense can explain specific aspects of the mentalization-based treatment technique and enrich the views on psychodynamics. Differences do exist, however, in the further treatment technique: The MBT therapist remains in the process, and the classical psychoanalyst elucidates aspects of content through interpretations.

5.6   Free Association or Structuring

Free Association

In classical psychoanalysis, the patient's free association and the psychotherapist's counterpart of equal attention form the methodological basis for analyzing unconscious processes. The procedure of free association is constitutive of the psychoanalytic technique (Laplanche & Pontalis, 1967). Patients express resistance to free association, which then becomes the object of processing. Although the method of free association has undergone much differentiation and limitation in the course of the history of psychoanalysis, it has always remained central to psychoanalysis and is today still considered a basic psychoanalytic method along with the request that the patient communicate to the analyst if possible everything that comes to mind and not to distinguish between what is unimportant and what is important. This allows an intensive interpersonal relationship, because the patient communicates something to the psychoanalyst and is always faced with the question of how far to trust the psychoanalyst. The patient's ideas are not random but rather related to their problems; yet, the request to also communicate unimportant things means the patient and the therapist do not overly focus on certain topics. The dissolution of structures here is intentional: It gives the unconscious space to come through to the surface. In this respect, any structures that relate to the content of the treatment are effectively obstacles, because the structures indicate where the patient and therapist have to look. In contrast, for the classical psychoanalyst, "I don't search, I find." (Klüwer, personal communication.)

Freud used free association as a significant technique to access unconscious material in his psychoanalysis, which usually took place five hours a week. Today, when one- to two-hour sessions have become the norm even for psychoanalytic treatments, the time and space for free association are significantly reduced. Significant events from everyday experience and the need to talk about experiences closer to consciousness push themselves into the low-frequency treatment time. Nevertheless, the patient's free ideas, free association, and the therapist's equally applied attention continue to be valuable agents in the treatment process of psychodynamic and psychoanalytic psychotherapy. The goal is to search not only where there is light but also where things are dark and unknown.

The importance of the concept of free association is one reason for the existing reticence regarding the structuring of treatment in the treatment forms derived from psychoanalysis. The analyst's caution in this regard sometimes implies the unspoken view that adhering to the setting and the rule of free association is more or less sufficient to enable a successful treatment process. There is a reluctance—even refusal—to focus on concepts that introduce structure into the therapeutic process. Likewise, the analyst is hesitant to provide structured patient information about the methodology used, psychoeducation, and clarification of therapy goals together with the patient.

The "myth of free association" has been criticized several times throughout history, e.g., by Fonagy and Mitchell as representatives of intersubjective psychoanalysis (Fonagy, 2001; Mitchell, 1988). These authors think the prioritization of free association as a treatment method masks the dialogic structure of psychoanalytic therapy.

While the more traditional psychoanalytic treatment prefers structuring the psychoanalytic treatment process through spontaneous free-associative flow (e.g., Bion 1970), MBT focuses on actively supporting the patient by structuring the therapeutic framework and the treatment itself.

Structuring

One finds the structuring of MBT treatment in a number of elements: the therapeutic stance, the active shaping of the working alliance, psychoeducation, creating a focus during a therapy session or a treatment phase, and the crisis plan. In Chapter 3, we provided information on the therapeutic stance, formulation of focus, and focus processing within a session (mentalization loop) in connection with the MBT core model.

Psychoeducation in Outpatient Individual Therapy

Psychoeducation promotes transparency and provides reassurance to the patient. According to the concept of psychotherapy as a threefold communication system,

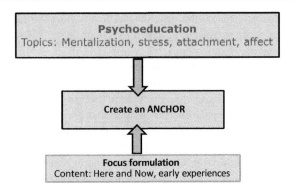

Figure 5.5 Psychoeducation—outpatient.

the patient receives information about the therapist's basic assumptions, the treatment concept, how the therapist envisions the development of the symptomatology, and which positive changes the therapist expects to occur. The patient knows what the therapist's role will be and what the patient's role will be in treatment.

In team-based facilities that work according to the MBT concept, psychoeducation usually takes place over several one-hour group seminars, each with its own topic and combining information with role-plays and exercises to engage the participants. For a detailed description of individual topics, exercises, and role-plays for education, see Allen et al. (2006, 2008) and Haslam-Hopwood et al. (2006).

In outpatient therapy in independent practices, brief written information about the mentalization concept regarding mentalizing, stress, attachment, and affect may be helpful to patients. After adapting the content and mode, information on the mentalization concept can then be communicated to the patient during treatment. The initial phase of treatment, for example, during the formulation of focus, offers many opportunities to connect the central problem reported by the patient and their therapy goals with aspects of the mentalization concept. This sets anchors to which reference can be made again during treatment (see Figure 5.5).

> Example: In a love relationship, great panic, despair, or anger can ensue when our partner does not answer a WhatsApp within a few hours. We do things we feel sorry for afterward, for example, we may threaten our partner to contact someone via Tinder. In these situations, when we also have a strong fear of losing our partner, we panic and lose our ability to reflect. We call this a "mentalizing breakdown." Strong stress, among other things, limits our mentalizing ability. Let us examine this more closely in the next therapy sessions to find out how you can better deal with such a situation.

Another possibility is to encourage the patient to have playful experiences regarding the mentalization concept, such as

- writing down experiences between sessions that affected my mentalizing ability;
- writing down an experience in which I could regulate a strong negative emotion.

The patient should focus on observing how they achieved this and then describe it meticulously.

Formulation of Focus at the Beginning of Treatment and within an Individual Session

The effectiveness of a mentalization-oriented approach depends on how the therapeutic process is structured, both within therapy and within an individual session. Structuring is the second central pillar of MBT, along with the standpoint of not-knowing. In well-structured patients, the common thread in a therapy session emerges largely on its own: The therapy session moves to where the anxiety is. Alternatively, as described above in the Triangle of Conflict from a psychoanalytic point of view, it may develop where the anxiety is seen in connection with the defense mechanism (see Chapter 5.5). However, for more low-structured patients and for patients with severe personality disorders as well as for persons who have been traumatized for a long time, the therapist must often work together with the patient to find a treatment structure.

The Focus at the Start of Treatment—the MBT Passport

The MBT therapy plan, called the MBT Passport, is a narrative framework that can guide both the patient and therapist at the start of treatment and throughout therapy. This therapy plan occurs in publications under various names, for example case formulation. It can be understood as a roadmap for therapy. The therapist develops it together with the patient during the first phase of therapy, and it serves as an aid in structuring the treatment. Examples of a therapy plan may be found in various publications (e.g., Allen et al., 2008, pp. 172ff.; Bateman, 2011; Bateman & Fonagy, 2016, pp. 157ff.). The time available for jointly developing a treatment plan is limited in psychotherapeutic practice. The points listed here and the suggested stimulating questions (in *italics*) provide a manageable revised basic framework. Grove and Smith (2022) describe this in more detail.

The MBT Passport

Past

What has happened in my life? What coping strategies have I learned?

Present

What "triggers" me? In which situations do my (interpersonal) problems become clear?

How do I see my relationships at these times?

How do I see myself←⟍   *How do I experience other people*
when I'm struggling?   *Feelings*←⟋   *when I am struggling?*

How do I cope with this?

Positive coping or negative coping. Epistemic trust?
Mentalizing difficulties (understanding social situations and how to cope with them)
For example, orientation toward polarities (cognitive process vs. affective process, automatic vs. controlled, self-oriented vs. other-oriented, internally focused vs. externally focused).

Anticipated problems in therapy?

Situations? How could we deal with them?

My Goals for Therapy

Adapted from Grove & Smith (2022)

This template provides the structure for a narrative, "What happened in the past, and what does the present look like? How does what is difficult today relate to what was difficult in the past?" It is also essential to look at present and past attempts to cope. It resembles behavioral analysis known from cognitive behavioral therapy, though the psychodynamic perspective remains a fixed component and is anchored by focusing on the internalized problematic object relationships, the associated affects and the difficulties of mentalization. Looking into the future then relates to the therapy by asking about possible therapeutic obstacles.

The Relational Passport, presented in the next section, provides a way of diving more deeply into the interpersonal issue, which is already a topic here, with a view toward attachment experiences and social anxiety.

The development of the MBT Passport is primarily a cognitive matter, although it also relates to affects that can give rise to later work. Developing the MTB Passport may also serve as a good exercise for mentalization, as one must keep emotions at a low level when approaching the task at hand. The joint effort initially serves to create a further orientation for the therapeutic treatment. Joint formulations by the patient and the therapist are important, as the personal formulation should reflect the patient's point of view.

Focus at the Start of Treatment—the Relational Passport

The therapist and the patient seek to identify an interpersonal focus that best describes the characteristically problematic interpersonal relationships. For this task to be insightful and meaningful to the patient, the patient needs knowledge about the mentalization concept; that is, about the connection between attachment and mentalization and the connection with affect regulation. Previous psychoeducation sets the stage for jointly formulating a focus. In MBT, elaborating the focus orients the patient to current relationships. A look back into childhood can help identify vulnerabilities, but the present remains central. To help with the formulation of focus, Bateman et al. (2019, p. 103) suggest using Bartholomew and Horowitz's (1991) interpersonal circle model as a guide, which captures interpersonal behavior using the two axes of attachment anxiety and attachment avoidance (see Figure 5.6).

The horizontal axis—attachment anxiety—represents the patient's self, while the vertical axis –attachment avoidance—refers more to their relationship with others. One can enter relationships with individuals into this pattern. A pattern is denoted using a dot. For example, someone may be highly aversive in a professional

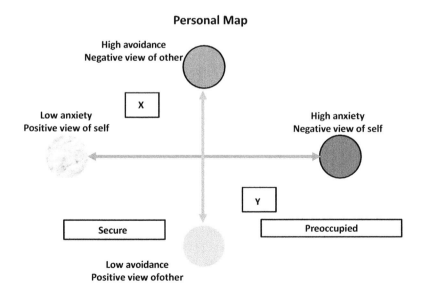

Figure 5.6 The interpersonal circle model as part of the formulation of focus. After Bateman et al. (2019, p. 107).

setting but have little anxiety in these relationships (X). On the other hand, one may greatly fear loss in love relationships and is highly ambivalent toward the relationship (Y). As the example shows, one may have a different pattern toward different people. Such a focus can also be used to look at what can be expected of patients and therapists in therapy and in the therapeutic relationship.

The therapist and the patient then proceed to formulate the focus, for example, like this:

- Educate the patient about attachment and attachment anxiety (psychoeducation).
- Explore vulnerabilities and problematic interpersonal issues with the patient, initially free from a theoretical framework.
- Situate the findings regarding the person (vertical axis) and the relationship with others (horizontal axis) within the coordinate system of the interpersonal circular model.
- Elaborate the consequences the interpersonal pattern has, e.g., loneliness in the case of strong avoidance of personal relationships (Figure 5.6, X-axis).
- Relate how the pattern is reflected in the therapeutic relationship and what common difficulties might occur in therapy.

Bartholomew and Horowitz's (1991) circle model may aid in formulating focus. Other approaches are also possible, but they should be limited to interpersonal events and aspects in the Here and Now and not include deep psychodynamic hypotheses. The point of this model for formulating focus is not to identify specific defense mechanisms used to keep anxiety at bay; that lies beyond the means of this model: The purpose of dealing with interpersonal patterns in MBT is not to identify causalities and provide insights but to structure treatment and provide a common orientation in the therapeutic process.

Elaboration of a focus is largely a cognitive matter and only marginally touches on affective experience. Therefore, it would be unrealistic to expect insight beyond the described framework. Elaboration, however, stimulates the patient to engage with their perspective and the perspective of others and thus becomes part of a facilitation of mentalization processes. The case studies with Sven (see Chapter 6.1) show how to create a focus.

Therapy Goal Formulation

In addition to formulating an interpersonal focus, formulating a therapy goal is useful for structuring the treatment. The therapy goals should be formulated as concretely as possible so that the success of the treatment can be seen and assessed by the patient and therapist. For example, the therapy goal "improve self-esteem" is not specific enough; it would be better to formulate the therapy goal as "reduce the number of self-injuries" or "increase the amount of time my boyfriend does not need to check in with me during the day."

Crisis Plan

In the case of severely distressed patients, it is advisable to work out a crisis plan together with the patient as early as the first phase of treatment. Not all treatment cases result in an emergency, but a crisis plan is useful to keep handy. Going deeper into the individual points is therapeutically valuable because the crisis plan stimulates the patient to reflect on situations and mental states that might trigger a crisis and consider what measures could contribute to their stabilization during such a crisis. This also provides the chance to practice mentalizing about these matters during a noncrisis phase, reflect on otherwise overwhelming and undifferentiated feeling states in a quieter moment, and break them down into essential aspects (Bales & Bateman, 2012). Such an approach is also helpful because patients often do not have precise ideas about their internal states and quickly feel overwhelmed by intense feelings. It is reminiscent of the appearance of a UFO and the well-known "UFO effect": The UFO suddenly appears out of nowhere.

The following box contains a suggestion for a structured crisis plan

---

Guideline: Crisis Plan

What can the patient do in a crisis?

- Things I can do myself when I am in a crisis.
- Things I should not do myself when I am in a crisis.

What can the therapist do and not do?

- Things I want the therapist to do that will help me in a crisis.
- Things the therapist has done in the past that were not helpful.

Immediate help that was effective in the past.

Additional Information

- Information for the doctor or other professionals.
- Contact addresses of those who have the emergency plan.

Focus within the Therapy Session: The Mentalization Loop

Creating a focus within a psychotherapy session is done best via a "mentalization loop." At the beginning, the therapist has the task of finding a focus for the session together with the patient. The therapist actively participates in this process, listening, giving suggestions, and structuring things, but does not impose a topic on the patient. Once an event—something the patient has experienced—has been determined, one works out the focus. In the beginning lies the narrative of the event; then, the focus turns to the experience during the event; finally, separate from this, there is the focus on the experience of what it is like to talk about the event in therapy. The endpoint is marked by the challenge of entertaining alternative perspectives. Chapter 3 describes the differentiated course of the "mentalization loop" and provides an example.

Conclusion

The patient's free association and the therapist's technique of equal attention form the methodological basis of traditional psychoanalysis for analyzing unconscious processes. This approach has profoundly influenced psychoanalysis-derived forms of treatment and continues to contribute to the rationale for the reticence and skepticism about the structuration found in modern psychoanalysis-derived forms of treatment. According to such skepticism, the constraints arising from structuration limit the analyst's openmindedness and neutrality. On the other hand, there is a need for modifying the complementary structuring of the treatments for patients with structural limitations and severe personality disorders, as revealed by the evidence-based means of treating BPD, such as TFP or MBT. This is also true for structure-based psychotherapy, which, in the meantime, plays a role in the theoretical and practical considerations of psychodynamic and psychoanalytic therapists. Such structuring is realized, among other things, by psychoeducation, joint consideration of treatment goals, and focus formulations. It is also reflected in the active attitude of the therapist, as described in the MBT core model (see Chapter 3.7).

5.7   An Integrative Treatment Model

Mentalization in psychodynamic and psychoanalytically based long-term therapy consists of two aspects: the process focus and the content focus.

- **Process focus:** the promotion of mentalization
- **Content focus:** formulations and interpretations about interpersonal conscious and unconscious patterns

---

The *process focus* refers to promoting mentalization according to the mentalization concept and the treatment technique derived from it. The *content focus*—the therapist's formulations and interpretations of the patient's interpersonal conscious and unconscious patterns—draws on psychoanalytic object-relations theories. This model goes back to the proposals of Lemma et al. (2011) regarding Brief Dynamic Interpersonal Therapy (DIT) and statements concerning the implementation of the mentalization concept in psychodynamic settings by Vermote et al. (2012). The basis for such integration is the mentalization concept, which has an advantage over older psychoanalytic concepts by not carrying as much metapsychological baggage and being more receptive to newer sources outside of psychoanalysis (Jurist, 2018, p. 90).

Regardless of the diagnosis, MBT is indicated in psychodynamic and psychoanalytic therapy according to the following model:

(a) For patients who have severe impairments of self- and interpersonal functioning (personality disorders). A low level of self- and interpersonal functioning seems to be associated with limitations in mentalizing ability (Zettl et al., 2020).
(b) For patients who have difficulties in affect regulation related to mentalizing problems and for whom, for example, an expansion of mentalized affectivity can lead to a psychological buffer between experience and action.

The Process Focus: Promoting Mentalization

Promotion of mentalization is oriented as described in the treatment technique of the MBT core model (see Chapter 3). It is also oriented toward mentalization-based treatment techniques regarding its compatibility with traditional psychoanalytic treatment concepts (see Chapter 5).

1. How to Promote Mentalization?

- The not-knowing standpoint is the central treatment technique for promoting mentalization. The therapist applies this approach by asking open-ended questions and expressing an authentic interest in the patient's feelings and experiences. The therapist asks how-questions and not why-questions and can distinguish between appropriate knowledge and not-knowing (see Chapter 3 and Chapter 5.3).
- Recognizing ineffective mentalization is central to promoting true mentalization. A therapist who interrupts ineffective mentalization and stimulates effective mentalization during the therapeutic process must be acquainted with the nonmentalizing modes, the teleological mode, the equivalence mode, the pretend mode, and hypermentalization as well as the mentalizing dimensions (see Chapter 5.4).
- The therapist can promote effective mentalization by keeping the four polarities of mentalization in mind: implicit vs. explicit mentalization, cognitively vs. affectively oriented mentalization, mentalization oriented toward the self vs. toward the other, and mentalization focused outwardly vs. inwardly. If the patient

tends to dwell too much on one pole, the therapist can stimulate a countermovement toward the neglected polarity. Effective mentalization always takes place in the balance between the poles (see Chapter 5.4).

- The central goal is mentalized affectivity. The therapist supports the patient in exploring affects related to their internal or external experiences, identifying, modulating, and expressing them (see Chapter 5.1).
- The therapist acknowledges mentalization. The therapist reports back to the patient when the patient has indeed mentalized and encourages the patient to continue on that path.
- Empathic validation means seeing the world from the patient's eyes and letting the patient know that their point of view is comprehensible (see Chapter 5.4).

2. Mentalization—the Structure of the Treatment and the Structure of the Session

To what degree the therapist should structure treatment depends on the patient's structural limitations and the severity of their personality disorder. The degree of external structuring by the therapist therefore varies from case to case. The therapist must employ structuring to promote mentalization according to the MBT model, usually to a greater extent than traditional psychodynamic and psychoanalytic treatment approaches. Nevertheless, in their textbook, Thomä and Kächele (2011) also conceptualized psychoanalytic psychotherapy as a stringing together of foci (Thomä & Kächele, 2011). Focusing on the perspectives, motives, and feelings involved as well as on the analysis of their associated preconscious and conscious processes restricts free association to the jointly chosen focus.

Treatment structuring means the therapist adopts an active attitude and transparency, providing the patient security. If necessary, the therapist regulates stress with the patient because a high stress level severely limits mentalizing abilities. A jointly developed interpersonal focus is imperative to structuring the treatment. To this end, it is helpful for the therapist to inform the patient about the mentalization concept being pursued (psychoeducation) and the crisis plan, if necessary (see Chapter 5.6). The treatment structure also includes feedback, for example, when the patient fills out questionnaires or the therapist participates in supervision using video recordings or role-plays (see Chapter 5.2).

Structuring the session means: Together with the patient, the therapist strives to identify a focus for the session, i.e., exploring the event belonging to the focus, identifying the affects, and seeking alternative ways of looking at things ("mentalization loop," see Chapter 3).

3. Mentalizing the Therapeutic Relationship

To avoid misunderstandings, the mentalization approach bypasses the transference and countertransference concepts. Nevertheless, there are clearly common roots and overlaps with the psychoanalytically based concept. Both forms of treatment attach great importance to reflecting on the therapeutic relationship or transference, whereby the patient's experience, i.e., how they experience the therapeutic relationship, is first empathically validated, and only then are the patient's experiences explored together. Much later, the countertransference marked and brought into play as the therapist's own experience (see Chapter 5.2).

The Content Focus: Interpretation of Conscious and Unconscious Patterns

Besides the process focus, realized by promoting mentalization with the typical interventions of MBT, the content focus contains the therapist's comments and interpretations of the interpersonal conscious and unconscious patterns, especially their affective parts. The content focus helps the patient better understand the connections between symptomatology, interpersonal experiences, and their history.

The interpretation of conscious and unconscious patterns adheres to the object-relations theories, the best known of which were posited by M. Klein, W. Fairbairn, and O. Kernberg (Klein, 1952; Fairbairn, 1952; Kernberg, 1980) as well as M. Balint, D. W. Winnicott, and H. Kohut (Balint, 1968; Winnicott, 1962a; Kohut, 1971). At first glance, these are very controversial, but they have several commonalities (acc. to Lemma et al., 2011). For example, according to the notions behind all object-relations theories, the development of object relations follows internal, culture-independent maturational steps that can be disrupted, among other things, by traumatic or highly affective experiences. In this process, as a person develops, the relationship patterns become more complex, and early patterns in the object relations tend to repeat themselves later in life. Ultimately, impairments in the development of object relations promote a path to possible later psychopathology.

In contrast to the Freudian conception of psychoanalysis, all object-relations theories see a preoedipal origin in connection with the described psychopathologies (e.g., severe personality disorders). One of the common features of object-relations theories is that the perception of transference patterns in psychotherapy enables us to view the patterns of early object relations. Such insights also became necessary because the existing methodology that stemmed from the old concepts could not reach many patients seeking help from psychoanalytic psychotherapy, who ended up being considered untreatable.

One cannot reduce object-relations theories to simple, unified consensus statements; rather, we must characterize them according to different dimensions (Lemma et al., 2011). While drive theory is no longer important in some object-relations theories, e.g., in intersubjective-relational psychoanalysis (Mitchel & Black, 1995), others combine drive theory with object-relations theory (Kernberg, 1980). According to Friedman (1988, as cited in Fonagy, 1988), one can distinguish "hard" and "soft" object-relations theories. "Hard" theories are those of M. Klein, W. Fairbairn, and O. Kernberg, which emphasize hatred, envy, and destruction, and use techniques that confront the patient with unconscious destructive impulses. Their model of psychosocial development views personality disorders in the context of the young child's limited abilities to process intrapsychic conflicts. This leads to defensive disintegration (development of partial objects) and early defense mechanisms (splitting, projective identification). The "soft" object-relations theories are those of Balint, Winnicott, and Kohut, which emphasize love, growth, and creativity, and employ therapeutic techniques that promote growth and apply one's resources, albeit also regression. While the "hard" theories understand psychopathology largely from unconscious conflicts, the "soft" object-relations theories understand pathology more from the child's environmental conditions. These theories posit that better environmental conditions inside and outside psychotherapy can also lead to relevant changes. Lemma, Target, and Fonagy, the leading theorists in the mentalization concept, place themselves somewhere between these extremes (Lemma et al., 2011, p. 37).

Figure 5.7 provides a general idea of the formation of an interpersonal focus related to the patient's central problem. The treatment focus incorporates object-relations theories that emphasize the affective parts. Depending on the state of the patient's structural limitations, the severity of the personality disorder, or the situational circumstances (e.g., current stress), the disorder may have the character of a defense mechanism or a mentalization deficit (see Section 5.5).

Examples of the Parts of the Interpersonal Focus

- A self-representation developing in the child: "I am helplessly at the mercy of my father as a significant other."
- Developing object representation in the child: "My father is unpredictable, sometimes hostile, sometimes friendly."
- Affect: "I'm scared, I'm confused, I don't trust anyone."

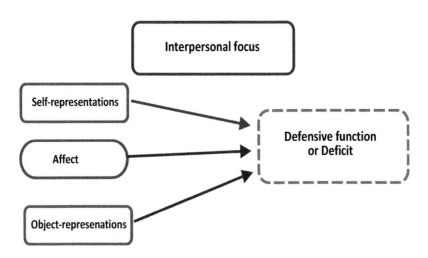

Figure 5.7 The interpersonal focus.

- Defense in adulthood, e.g., the defense mechanism of splitting: Experiencing and evaluating another as completely good and then as completely bad, alternating according to one's inner emotional state, without experiencing this as contradictory. Or the defense mechanism of rationalization: "Everything is half as bad!"
- Deficit in adulthood: Loss or limitations in the ability to mentalize one's affects, rapid switching to equivalence mode, or early switching to struggle mode.

This model is supported through its coherence with the mentalization concept. Yet, it is just a model and not reality: Too rigid adherence to a model can be misleading, sometimes even harmful.[1] We should also understand in this sense a remark of Kächele (a German psychoanalyst and well-known international therapy researcher): "Beware of therapists who know only one therapy method" (personal communication).

For treatment to proceed in a coherent context, the interpretations occurring in the mentalization-promoting process should have the following character (Lemma et al., 2011):

- relate primarily (but not exclusively) to the preconscious and less to the deep unconscious;
- encourage the development of a different perspective (challenging);
- focus on fear in connection with defenses and defensiveness (see Triangle of Conflict, Chapter 5.5);
- point to the self- and object-representations for visualizing positive and negative parts;
- point out what is unclear, confusing, or contradictory.

Hypotheses should be considered the therapist's hypotheses, i.e., as a possible way of understanding relationships. Thus, at the end of the statement, the therapist says, for example, "Does this make sense to you? What do you think?"

Interpretations of conscious and unconscious patterns should take reference to a focus. One can understand longer-lasting psychotherapy that follows this model as a succession of different procedural and content foci (Thomä & Kächele, 2011). The therapist works out the focus formulations together with the patient, which recognizably take the form of hypotheses, because their truth content is intersubjective and provisional. The focus lies largely on the here and now, and the affective parts are in the foreground.

The interpersonal focus should (1) include a formulation of the problem or difficulty, (2) consider the connection to the context of the problem (e.g., the current life situation), (3) formulate a link between the interpersonal representations and the patient's problem or difficulty, and (4) identify the defensive nature of the interpersonal representations.

In the process section (see Section 5.6), we already proposed how to formulate a treatment focus. The process and content foci overlap in their content, and it can be enriching to consider both approaches when formulating a common focus. However, it also remains a subjective decision on the therapist's part regarding which focus they wish to apply at any given stage of treatment. There is little difference in the treatment technique if the therapist uses the content focus rather sparingly during the therapeutic interaction to transform the hypotheses derived from the psychoanalytic model into interpretations directed toward the patient. The therapeutic attitude of the MBT therapist lets the patient participate in their thoughts to an appropriate degree, also regarding thoughts originating from their therapeutic model. Such a therapist does not exclude interpretations and comments. Two factors determine to what extent either the process aspect (the promotion of mentalization) or the content aspect is in the foreground: The structural, general, or situational limitations in the mentalizing abilities determine the focus, and the therapist's beliefs (which therapy model fits the therapist's personal development) justifies the process aspect. Future results of psychotherapy research will show where we go from here.

Note

1 Physics also successfully works with multiple models. For example, for a long time the wave–particle dualism was used to explain the phenomenon of "light." Although it was later superseded by quantum mechanics, it is still considered a good and necessary explanatory model in physics today.

Case Studies

This chapter demonstrates the mentalization-based therapy (MBT) treatment technique as incorporated into psychodynamic or psychoanalytic treatments. A concluding commentary interprets each episode and addresses the similarities and differences between MBT and traditional psychodynamic or psychoanalytic approaches. The case presentations are thematically oriented to central aspects of mentalization theory and its practical application.

From the point of view of the mentalization concept, traumatic experiences are considered a "transdiagnostic phenomenon" (Luyten & Fonagy, 2019). Traumatic experiences are associated with many diagnoses and are often difficult to distinguish from subsequent experiences leading to epistemic mistrust. For example, severe, prolonged childhood neglect is one of the most severe traumatic experiences that may surface in various symptoms. The mentalization concept is related to the transdiagnostic treatment approach and refers to processes relevant to the development and maintenance of various mental disorders. We thus find trauma-specific parts and aspects in all four case studies.

The focus of our proposed model is twofold:

(a) *Process focus:* The promotion of mentalization with typical MBT interventions: identifying feelings, providing assistance with affect regulation, differentiating feelings from actions, and identifying new connections between feelings and actions.
(b) *Content focus:* The therapist explores and interprets interpersonal, conscious, and unconscious patterns, especially their affective parts. The focus lies largely on the here and now.

Remember that the following descriptions and episodes are not "model examples" from an MBT treatment program but case examples from psychoanalytic or psychodynamic long-term treatments (see Chapter 5.7).

The therapeutic interventions largely follow the process focus during the episodes; only in the concluding remarks do we discuss the content focus. Our decision to consider the two aspects separately has somewhat didactic reasons: According to our experience from training sessions, psychodynamic thinking and its translation

DOI: 10.4324/9781032674117-7

into content interpretations are very familiar to most therapists. Thus, we prefer to focus here especially on the process focus and mentalization.

We examine the case studies under different headings and perspectives that more or less represent the patient's current issue. Of course, other issues are also addressed because they are real episodes and not artificial teaching lessons. For example, the theme of epistemic trust is present in several case studies.

The patients, their personal data, and places have been changed to make it impossible to identify them, while preserving essential elements. In the process, we linguistically smoothed and shortened the dialogs in the individual episodes to ensure readability. At some points in the reproduced dialogs, we inserted commentaries that characterize the interventions according to the MBT model.

6.1   Mentalized Affectivity

In Brief

According to the mentalization concept, a central therapeutic goal of MBT is "mentalized affectivity," which is understood as a form of affect regulation involving the reappraisal and modulation of affect (Fonagy et al., 2002) and should ultimately lead to better control of behavior. In mentalized affectivity, affect and mentalization are perceived and viewed. Experience shows that mentalization is not easy in the presence of strong affects. The classical view of affect regulation (for example, in CBT) focuses on controlling cognitions over affects, using cognitive distancing from affects. The goal of mentalized affectivity, on the other hand, is to enable a person to experience affects consciously and to give those affects meaning, both in the here and now and regarding past experiences. The person thereby gains a more mature psychodynamic regulation, control over the acting out of affects, and control functions regarding behavior.

Greenberg et al. (2017) distinguish three phases of the therapeutic process:

1. the identification of affects;
2. the processing of affects (modulation and differentiation);
3. internal and external communication.

The authors differentiate between the identification of affects, i.e., the naming of affects, and the communication of affects, which includes the interpretation of affects in the social context. That is often the core problem in some patients, e.g., borderline patients (see also Chapter 5.1).

The promotion of mentalized affectivity is also the focus in more highly structured patients who lose their mentalizing abilities only because of conflict and in specific situations. If mentalization succeeds, then it is more about conflict and content; if it breaks down, it is about restoring mentalization and affect regulation. This can be understood figuratively as a foreground phenomenon (conflicts) or as a background phenomenon (mentalizing).

Affect elaboration assumes a special significance in long-term psychotherapy, where there is sufficient time for tracing, verbalizing, and processing affects. In that case, affect elaboration can become a focus and path of treatment.

Initially, we distinguish two different directions for promoting the mentalization of affects: A patient can be too "cognition-heavy" or too "affect-heavy" in the therapeutic process. An impulse breakthrough, for example, may result from being too cognition-heavy; affects may not be accessible or available to the patient, swooping in "like a UFO" without notice. For example, the patient reports: "It just happens to me. All of a sudden—it was there. The feelings come out of nowhere!" Here, we need to allow the implicitly occurring process to become an explicit process through microlevel observations.

However, an impulse breakthrough may also result from long-lasting and hard-to-control affects that cause control over affects to vanish in a moment. The promotion of mentalization in the therapeutic process should go in the respective direction of the pole that is too little present in the current process. The case studies below exhibit these differences.

Sven A.

Sven (34) is an economist in a renowned management consultancy. He is very performance-oriented. Regarding the polarities of mentalization (see Chapter 5.4), Sven is more cognitive and oriented toward others, more focused on the perception of external signals and less on internal signals, which he should be perceiving or tapping into in both himself and the other person. Sven has impulse breakthroughs, especially in his relationship with his partner, who is from South America and works as an airline manager. He has not committed to a steady relationship for a long time. He also has anxiety about meetings where more than ten people are present. He frequently takes his anxiety-reducing medication prescribed for emergencies. The anxiety has lessened over the course of two years of psychotherapy, so he can now (almost always) do without the medication.

His mother suffered from failing to be successful professionally after graduating as a sociologist. She had had high hopes for her career. As far back as Sven can remember, his mother was in severe pain, which she numbed with medication, and eventually became addicted to drugs. Her thoughts revolved solely around herself and her failed career. His father was a highly decorated and widely traveled law professor, publishing works on ethics and law co-authored with his wife. The father is remembered at home as lovable but passive and weak, living a secluded life and stoically enduring his wife. He was supportive of Sven but showed little presence.

Sven's treatment took place as long-term psychoanalytic therapy. According to the psychotherapy guidelines of the German healthcare system, his therapist put in a request for analytical psychotherapy.

In Sven's case, structural disturbance components in impulse control/affect regulation and self-perception/object perception (OPD Task Force, 2008) were considered central. On the symptom level, depressive components and social anxiety were diagnosed. At the same time, Sven maintained a rather high general psychosocial functioning level, which could be drawn upon in psychotherapy; it facilitated the establishment of a stable working alliance from the beginning. Psychodynamically, it was assumed that the parents related strongly to each other, and that the mother was caught in a narcissistic affront and made seductive insinuations. For example, she erotically related her own body to her adolescent son's rapturous statements toward a coveted classmate. The father lived in another world. The feeling of being left alone led Sven to adopt a rather avoidant attachment style in intensive relationships. We can assume that Sven experienced little coherent affect mirroring and affect resonance in the described constellation. A mild positive father transference characterized the transference and countertransference. It obviously did Sven good to be perceived in a friendly way by an older man who, in his eyes, was an authority.

The therapist discussed the common treatment goals with the patient during the first session. The first common goal was to expand impulse and affect control; another goal was to reduce the constant self-doubt and fear of other people, especially in larger groups.

During the first sessions, the therapist and Sven jointly created a "personal map" to assist in formulating the focus. Such a personal map attempts to describe interpersonal behavior using the two axes of attachment anxiety and attachment avoidance (see Chapter 5.6). A common assessment Y was found between the therapist and Sven, as shown by the respective marker in Figure 6.1. Sven and the therapist jointly assessed him as rather dismissive and socially anxious, with a strong factual and high achievement orientation.

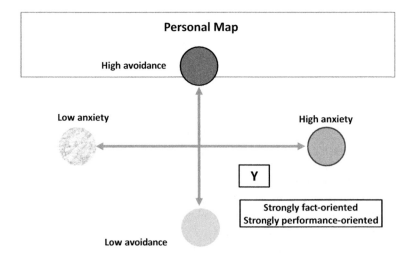

Figure 6.1 The interpersonal circle model as part of the formulation of focus. Adapted from Bateman et al. (2019, p. 107).

First Episode

The following conversation took place after about a year of long-term psychoanalytic psychotherapy.

Patient (resignedly):	I had another fuss with my girlfriend in the last few days.
Therapist:	What happened?
Patient:	Out of the blue, I attacked her.
Therapist:	Out of the blue?
Patient:	I can usually handle it better than that, but then I couldn't.
Therapist:	Wait, can you describe it in more detail first?
	This is a suggestion to report the event concretely, to develop a detailed narrative. The therapist slows down the interaction by intervening with "stop and stand," moving toward the explicit pole and thereby encouraging explicit mentalization: "What really happened?" marks the beginning of the "mentalization loop" (see below). The therapist also does this to later identify any apparent limitations in mentalization.
Patient:	I came home late. I had met with a good friend, an old friend. On the way home, I felt the dissatisfaction with my girlfriend already bubbling up in me, constantly working and always being tired!
Therapist:	So, how was the evening with your friend?
Patient:	It was okay. He was in a pretty good mood. He talked about his new girlfriend. And that it's pretty exciting with her. We were in a pretty good mood together that evening.
Therapist:	And, then, on the way home, this dissatisfaction came over you. What happened next?
	Suggestion to explore the specific event further.
Patient:	I laid down in bed with my girlfriend. She was already asleep, so I just said "Hello." Then I lay awake while she slept. I couldn't fall asleep. That upset me even more. I said to myself: "Stop it!" But I ended up freaking out. I started yelling at her.
Therapist (incredulous):	Out of the blue, just like that?
Patient:	No, I tried to talk to her first.
Therapist:	And then?
Patient (excitedly):	And then I yelled at her!
Therapist (in a calm voice):	Slow down, slow down. Let's go back again: How did she react when you tried to talk to her?
	The therapist reverts somewhat, trying to soften the rising affect, and follows the point of view of not-knowing. The technique of "stop, rewind, and explore" allows aspects to be mentalized that were previously unmentalized.

Patient:	She didn't, she just turned away.
Therapist:	That must have been hard for you. Then what?
	The therapist assumes an empathic standpoint, contributing to arousal management and promoting mentalizing.
Patient:	I tried to continue talking to her.
Therapist:	So you hadn't given up yet. Was that working?
Patient:	She said, "Sven, stop it! I have to be fit again tomorrow morning!" or something like that.
Therapist:	And how did that go over?
Patient:	I told her I couldn't stand having such little sex in the long run. Always being put off. "In three months, things will be better, I just need less stress" she said. I shouldn't always put her under pressure. At that moment, I'd had enough! I said we'd better just split up. I know I shouldn't have done that. I had made up my mind not to say it again.
Therapist:	Okay, okay. So, at what point did you lose control?
	The therapist continues to slow down the process by suggesting a contrary move from the implicit pole to the explicit pole and from the affective pole to the cognitive pole.
Patient:	She was asleep, and I was lying there and couldn't sleep.
Therapist:	And how was that feeling?
	Only now does the therapist focus on affect, as the patient shows less arousal.
Patient:	I don't know …
Therapist:	Okay, okay. That's a tough one. Put yourself in the scene once again. What kind of feeling was it? Give it a try, take your time.
Patient:	Anger? Yes, probably anger.
Therapist (searching):	You felt anger. Anger about what?
	The therapist tries to keep the patient attentive to the affect. When the patient resists exploration, the therapist encourages him to identify affect via empathic validation.
Patient:	Like I said. She said, "Be reasonable, you'll be sorry for this again tomorrow!"
Therapist:	And how did you respond to that?
Patient:	I screamed.
Therapist:	What was going on inside you?
	A further attempt by the therapist to stimulate the patient's introspection by reflecting on his experience during the interaction with the partner.
Patient:	It happens so suddenly. I lose control in such crucial situations.
	The patient's reaction is the typical "UFO phenomenon": the event comes "out of the blue."
Therapist:	Stay in the situation for a moment.
Patient:	I can't remember it anymore. It's gone.

Therapist:	What is the last thing you remember?
	It was first important for the therapist to clarify the facts to further assess where and what distortions happened because of limited mentalizing. Therefore, the therapist first continues to ask for specific and detailed facts. Only then does the therapist start elaborating the affects.
Patient:	She cornered me. I got so angry at her.
Therapist:	Let's go back one more time. What feelings did you have when you laid down in bed with her?
	The therapist now goes into the affects present in the situation ("stop, rewind, and explore"). But again, starting from the beginning of the incident.
Patient:	I wanted to have sex with her.
Therapist:	You were—horny?
Patient:	Yes... I... I guess I was.
Therapist (irritated, unsure):	You guess?

Patient:	Well, actually, not so much—I just wanted her to pay more attention to me.
	Affect differentiation.
Therapist:	And?
Patient:	Nothing but frustration. I thought: She's letting me down—again, "You're so unattractive—you're such a victim!"
Therapist:	Which of the two was the strongest emotion?
	Looking for the central affect.
Patient:	"You're a victim!"
Therapist:	An unattractive, ridiculous figure?
Patient:	I was so angry, I just let it rip.
Therapist:	Can you be more specific?
Patient:	I felt dependent on her, and she doesn't make the cut!
Therapist:	So you're dependent, and she's a loser? But what's the core thing?
	An attempt to further differentiate the affect.
Patient:	I don't know.
Therapist:	If you are dependent, you are weak. If she is a loser, it means she is weak, and you are strong. Does that interpretation go too far?
Patient:	Dependence is not my thing.
Therapist:	Describe it in that situation.
Patient:	She's so reasonable! But I didn't give a shit!
Therapist:	You didn't give a shit about that.
Patient:	I thought it would be different with another woman!
Therapist:	What made you so angry?
Patient:	Her fucking rationality! Jesus!
Therapist:	Her fucking rationality!
	The therapist validates the emotion.

Patient:	I need more life, more excitement. She's always putting me off!
	The affects are elaborated:
Therapist:	What do you think was going on in your girlfriend, at that moment in the night, when she turned away? What was *she* thinking?
	The therapist stimulates a change of perspective. It's a contrary movement from the pole of "self" to the pole of "others."
Patient:	I don't know.
Therapist:	But maybe it would be interesting to know it.
Patient:	I'm sure she was thinking, "Leave me alone!"
Therapist:	Aha. And then?
Patient:	Probably, "You're a victim!"
Therapist:	What would you have preferred?
Patient:	I would have liked her to be more loving and empathetic.
Therapist:	So, be there more for you.
	In this sequence, the therapist tries to encourage Sven to mentalize his girlfriend: to move away from himself and toward his girlfriend, since Sven is initially strongly centered on himself.
Therapist:	What is going on in you now when we discuss this event?
Patient:	She was right. The next morning, I felt lousy, small, and guilty. I had lost control.
	The therapist tries to focus the affect on the here and now.
Therapist:	And how are you feeling now?
Patient:	I'm a little ashamed of it all. But it relieves me to talk about it here. I need to get it out.
Therapist:	Okay. It did not go well. But now, how to get out of things and better represent your own needs. That's the next task. Right?

Final Comment

The therapist tries to induce a "mentalization loop" (see Chapter 3.7) as well as consider the polarities cognitive vs. affective, implicit vs. explicit, internal vs. external, self vs. other (see Chapter 5.4), i.e., to bring the neglected pole into the patient's consciousness and into the dialog.

In Sven's case, mentalization is severely limited: He cannot tell a coherent story. His level of emotional arousal is high. The therapist helps to develop a narrative and the associated affects through validation and exploration. The "stop and rewind" intervention is often helpful in this regard. Sven is initially very cognitively oriented and distances himself from any emotional intensity. He experiences strong affects, leading to loss of control. The therapist prompts Sven recall his feelings in the moments before he lost control and to identify and name his feelings.

It is not entirely atypical that feelings change during the search for identification. In this episode, we observe how difficult Sven finds it to tolerate the feelings of being rejected, lonely, and dependent during close social contacts. They do not fit his self-image, but they do fit his biography and central hypotheses of the psychoanalyst about psychodynamics. Because Sven is so strongly centered on himself, in the end, the therapist tries to initiate a change of perspective, to put Sven in his girlfriend's place.

Similarities and Differences to the Psychoanalytic Approach

The therapist largely refrains from interpretations. In classical psychoanalytic treatment, in addition to introducing clarification, the therapist would have addressed a connection to biography (repetition) and transference earlier, for example, when the passive father does not help the child to get out of the disappointing, close relationship with the mother.

Classical psychoanalysis would have underlined the elaboration of affects with interpretations, e.g., Sven's desires not to be alone and for sex, his disappointment, anger, and feelings of dependence. The analyst would have referred more to the considerations of psychodynamics and paid attention to the defenses of the negative affects (e.g., being alone and enduring disappointments). The analyst would have encouraged reference to childhood and addressed, emphasized, and interpreted repetitive patterns of experience. However, in doing so, the therapy would likely have become centered more on cognitions and stayed less in the here and now. It would have been more content-oriented and less concerned with experience and thought patterns found in MBT. This approach might even have led to the structural disorder exhibited here being understood by the psychoanalyst as a conflict dynamic. The differing views are closely related to whether Sven's mentalization breakdown represents a defense mechanism or a structural weakness.

Regarding the different priorities in the various forms of treatment, we can summarize that classical psychoanalytic therapy would probably have preferred more resistance interpretations or transference interpretations and less arousal management. In depth-psychology-based therapy, the focus would probably have been oriented more toward the therapy goal and included suggestions regarding behavioral alternatives. In MBT, as in classical psychoanalytic therapy, the process aspect would take center stage by working in the transference (not shown here). However, in classical psychoanalytic therapy, the process aspect would be more closely linked to content.

Second Episode

This session occurred after a year of long-term psychoanalytic psychotherapy.

Patient:	I've been tense all the time the last few days. I have to tell you something.
Therapist (friendly, interested):	Okay. What's up?
Patient:	I was walking across the street the other day to the cafeteria, when I passed two colleagues, a woman I know from the hiring interview and an older colleague, whom I know superficially. I had the impression they were talking about me. She said to him, "That's the guy I hired. He's not really cutting it." And he said, "Yeah, I know him." Though I didn't hear it exactly that way.
Therapist:	Are you saying you're unsure whether you heard it that way?
Patient:	Well, they just looked at me and said "Hello."

Therapist:	So, what exactly do you remember about that situation?
Patient:	Not so much. It was noon, and the sun was shining. I saw the two of them coming. They said "Hello" to me. And I was alone.
Therapist:	And then?
Patient:	The woman was actually okay in the interview. If she hadn't supported me, I'm sure I wouldn't have made it to the next round of the selection process.
	The therapist tries to get the facts straight.
Therapist:	Let's go back now. What mood were you in when walking down the street like that? It was lunchtime.
Patient:	The sun was shining.
Therapist:	And your mood?
Patient:	Nothing special.
Therapist:	Nothing special. But what was it like?
	The therapist tries to encourage Sven to explore the situation that preceded the disturbing perception.
Patient:	The usual tension. Oh yes, just before, I had pleasantly registered how the gaze of an attractive woman had lingered on me—while they were coming toward me.
Therapist:	And then?
Patient:	Then I saw the two of them.
Therapist:	And what was your feeling?
	Further centering on the affect.
Patient:	I became slightly scared.
Therapist:	And, in the situation as you remember it, what was it like? Emotionally, I mean?
	The therapist elaborates on the affect in the "then" and not yet in the "here and now."
Patient:	It was actually quite normal.
Therapist:	Can you be more specific? What does "quite normal" mean?
Patient:	It was a little uncomfortable for me that they saw that attractive woman looking at me and observed me looking back at her.
Therapist:	What does uncomfortable mean?
Patient:	That they might judge me negatively because of that. (*Pause*)
Therapist:	How do you feel now, talking about it?
Patient:	I was pretty sure that's what they were saying.
Therapist:	That's not a feeling; that's what's going on in your mind. How are you feeling now?
	The therapist tries to refocus on the affect, now not in the "then," but trying to access the affect in the "here and now."
Patient:	I don't know. There's no feeling there.
Therapist:	I notice you're bobbing your leg violently back and forth.
Patient:	Maybe. I often do that, and it makes me feel uncomfortable.
Therapist:	I'm sorry if I offended you—I didn't mean to criticize you. Sometimes, I just blurt things out carelessly.

Patient:	No, no. It's okay that you said something. Yes, people notice that something is not okay with me. I feel very uncomfortable about it, but I don't have access to my feelings in situations like now—or when I met the woman who hired me and the colleague.
Therapist:	What is it like to have no feel for your own feelings?
Patient:	I feel kind of cut off, I guess.
Therapist:	Tell more about what it's like to be cut off from your feelings.
Patient:	I feel kind of... helpless... It makes me feel insecure.
Therapist:	... insecure... helpless...
Patient:	Yeah... what...
Therapist:	Let's just stick with that... insecure... helpless....
Patient (more uneasy):	The whole thing is kind of scary.
Therapist:	Can you say more about it?
Patient:	I'm afraid of falling apart, of not understanding things, like back in my wild hashish and drug days.
Therapist:	So, it's a fear you're losing yourself or losing your grip?
Patient:	It reminds me of the situation I experienced in the prestigious office in the United States. I felt increasingly under pressure, as did everyone else there. I felt like all kinds of people were talking about me.
Therapist:	You told me about it a few sessions ago, about the extraordinary pressure. Absolute commitment for 12–14 hours, flying from abroad back to the office the same day. Terrible thing. How did you endure that?
Patient:	But the fantasies didn't stop. I was glad to leave. I was almost psychotic or close to it or... I don't know.
Therapist:	The fear and the pressure. Let's go back to the situation when you met the two supervisors and almost simultaneously met eyes with an attractive woman. What do you feel about that now?
	Moving the focus again to the central situation in the here and now.
Patient:	I felt ashamed—somehow.
	The patient reverts once again to the "then."
Therapist:	It's an awful situation. You're being observed and feel yourself caught, didn't you?
	Validation.
Patient:	Yeah, so... when I think about it... yeah, it's like I'm anxious... also because... they might think badly of me because of the woman.
Therapist:	How are you doing now?
	Focusing on the here and now.
Patient:	Oh, it's okay now. I'm not going to get worked up about it now. Talking to you about it now calms me down.
Therapist:	What's reassuring about that?
Patient:	I felt caught, and then I got scared that they were talking about me.
	Sven mentalized!
Therapist:	Yes, good. I can understand that.

Patient (affect has subsided):	I actually haven't had any unpleasant experiences now at G & K (i.e., at his job in the current company), not like when I was in the United States.
Therapist:	Let's go back to the situation you described. You were, after all, completely preoccupied with fear, shame, and the fantasies of others in that situation. How do you see it now: If you put yourself in the shoes of the two colleagues who came toward you, what do you think was going on in them?

This is an attempt by the therapist to encourage Sven to look at the reported situation with less affect and in the here and now.

Patient (*more relaxed*): I was probably only marginally important to them. They were talking about something completely different at first. It wasn't that important to them. And they're probably not that prudish, either.

Therapist:	Yes, that sounds quite reasonable.

Final Comment

In this episode, the therapist also tries to follow the "mentalization loop" (see Chapter 3.7). Likewise, the therapist considers the polarities cognitive vs. affective, implicit vs. explicit, internal vs. external, self vs. other (see Chapter 5.4), bringing the neglected pole into consciousness and the respective dialog. The focus of the episode lies on Sven's social anxiety, which manifests itself in the professional environment.

Sven is caught in a state of tension, combined with subliminal feelings of fear and shame. As a result, he experiences the world outside as threatening. This may be understood as a result of projections/externalization of strange self-parts. In reality, however, the world has not become more threatening because of his feeling this way.

The patient is in the mode of mental equivalence: "I feel anxious and ashamed; the world has become threatening." His mentalization is severely impaired at this point. In the mentalization loop, the therapist first addresses the facts to see what conditions led to his restricted mentalization, enabling the patient to develop a new perspective.

Possible Similarities and Differences to the Psychoanalytic Approach

The MBT therapist concentrates on affects, stimulates intense exploration, and focuses on the "how," the process in the here and now. The therapist also hopes that the mirrored affects can help the patient develop a coherent picture of the situation.

Traditional psychoanalytic or psychodynamic interventions might have focused more on content and defenses. The therapist would have interpreted the projection of performance demands or considered the activation of an otherwise averted shame to thwart his libidinal desire. Since Sven's strong social anxiety occurs almost exclusively in the work environment, the psychoanalyst would possibly ask himself and Sven to what extent the anxieties go back to the maternal (and paternal) performance demands Sven had internalized, becoming an unconscious ego ideal projected onto his work colleagues.

In the transference, the therapist might wonder whether the patient is now seeking paternal support from the analyst in his emotional insecurity toward seductive and desirable women. He doesn't want the therapist to abandon him in the therapeutic relationship with his feelings toward the seductive and demanding mother, like the passive father used to do. The encounter on the street repeats his fear of condemnation of his curiosity; he even expects it from the colleagues he encounters. The transference is thus an unconscious reenactment, characterized by performance fears and averted shame. Now, we can understand the paranoid parts if we assume that more mature structural parts are being addressed here. Assuming a relatively low structural integration also makes the fears understandable in light of a threat to his self-coherence. The feelings triggered in the therapist can help differentiate the situation. In this episode, however, the anxieties did not feel that way to the therapist.

To summarize: These episodes and the analyst's interventions clearly show an active therapeutic attitude, oriented to the here and now and to experiences and thoughts rather than to contents and conflicts. Against the background of a fixation on some poles of multidimensional mentalization, according to the MBT model, the therapist intervenes in the opposite direction. However, this also means largely renouncing interpretations and instead projecting an interested, questioning attitude. The therapist does not initially address insight into inner conflicts but rather stimulates the patient to control mentalization by learning to differentiate his own "psychic inner space," i.e., above all, to better perceive and differentiate affects and emotions and thus to develop new perspectives—that may well also contain insight into patterns or interpretive templates. An analogous hypothesis is that these interventions stimulate reflection and support the correction of secondary, symbolized representations.

The mentalization approach encourages the patient to develop curiosity toward themselves and others, to take the meaning of their affects more seriously, and to become aware of what latent bias might lie in the interpretations of their social experience. If, as a result, they can be more sympathetic to themselves and others, their self-worth increases and their social anxiety attenuates. The psychological equivalence mode also decreases, which can sometimes contribute to the patient's threatening perceptions. As a result, the patient becomes more flexible in social relationships. A mentalization-oriented patient works on own insights, whereas in classical psychodynamic and psychoanalytic therapy, the therapist works more on the content. The assumption is that MBT is more effective than a treatment methodology that focuses on the etiopathogenetic context discovered through interpretations. Of course, this claim needs to be discussed further. The question is: To what extent is mentalized affectivity more effective in promoting insight and psychological flexibility than interpretations?

6.2   Epistemic Trust

In Brief

"Trust comes from a sense of feeling one's self understood by another mind" (interview with Peter Fonagy, in Duschinsky et al., 2019, p. 224). Epistemic trust in psychotherapy is a willingness to regard communication that conveys the knowledge of a trustworthy person as generalizable and relevant to the individual (Fonagy & Luyten, 2016).

From the perspective of the MBT, epistemic trust initially develops in early safe relational experiences. Yet, it can change as a result of the relational experiences a person has later in life (e.g., a traumatic experience). Epistemic trust develops in the social context and is later influenced by the person's interpersonal skills. In the therapeutic relationship, epistemic trust develops through the "epistemic match"—the epistemic fit between patient and therapist (see Chapter 5.2).

Cornelia L.

Cornelia L. was a 40-year-old who worked at a large institution in the Human Relations Department. She functioned perfectly at work, which kept her deep depressive affect in check; she could largely overplay it in her social contacts.

Her childhood was shaped by a mother she experienced as massively hostile and violent. The mother was impulsive and little empathetic—if ever at all. She sometimes violently physically attacked Cornelia. The patient recalls the mother saying, "It would be better if you didn't exist!" Cornelia was a gifted child who read a lot before starting school, escaping into her own world and thus arousing the aggressive incomprehension of her poorly educated mother. The father was a journalist and devoted to her. He was secretly pleased to have a clever child who did not put up with anything, though he failed to openly protect her from her mother's aggressions. Later, since puberty, he lost interest in her. At school, a teacher recognized her abilities. Eventually, Cornelia went to the Youth-Welfare Office and asked to get transferred into a home. She struggled off and on with anorexia. At 16, she moved into a therapeutic residential group and lived a successful life. At the beginning of therapy, Cornelia's relationships with men were characterized by intellectual and cultural issues. This changed during the long-term psychotherapeutic treatment.

Cornelia was strongly cognitively oriented and very autonomous in her work and friendships. In a love relationship initiated during treatment, Cornelia often experienced strong emotions. At times, she was relieved, at other times she felt deep abandonment and loneliness. She became strongly oriented toward the other person and felt the threat that comes from the possibility of losing an intense relationship.

Regarding Cornelia's attachment experiences, the therapist initially assumed an avoidant attachment pattern. However, during the more extended experience in psychotherapy, it became clear that Cornelia had established general protection from intense emotional relationship experiences, which masked an underlying ambivalent attachment pattern. Whereas the initial treatment focused on autonomous behavior, in the second part of treatment, she experienced great anxiety about trust-ing someone in an intensifying attachment. When she did exhibit trust, she had fears of being ridiculed.

Professionally, her mentalizing skills were at a high level. This was evident in her success and popularity at work. By banishing all strong affects—while main-taining empathy and sensitivity toward others—she could keep her stress levels low, which, in turn, stabilized her mentalizing skills.

However, in the first session, Cornelia reported, "Sometimes I have violent anxi-ety that overtakes me in critical professional negotiations. I don't really understand this fear." She said that inexplicability makes the anxiety all the more threatening because she never knows when it will crop up. She also did not want to get in-volved in a love relationship: "Then I can no longer function properly. Then eve-rything goes wrong. I can't have relationships, because then I endanger myself and others, professionally as well. That's why I live alone, but spending my whole life that way is a terrible thought." In her symptomatology, social anxiety first became conscious as a strong affect and was confirmed by her high global psychological functioning level.

Treatment took place as long-term psychoanalytic therapy with a frequency of one to two hours per week in sitting. The psychoanalyst and Cornelia agreed that the treatment should not be done lying down, and that eye contact would better create safety and trust. According to the German psychotherapy guidelines, the treatment applied for was analytical psychotherapy.

The treatment focused on the self- and interpersonal functioning deficits. The focus was the patient's self-coherence and resilient self, object representations, and the related affect control. Regarding attachment relationships, epistemic mistrust was expected to be reflected in the therapeutic relationship (transference). The defi-cits resulted from the early traumatic relationship with the mother, which explained a deep epistemic mistrust not expressed in the patient's professional contacts but influenced by her life in other regards. This became evident both during therapy (first episode) and in her description of a love relationship (second episode). The anxiety attacks that came "out of the blue" for Cornelia also resulted from past traumatic experiences and were understandable. Against this background, the ther-apist focused on the aspects of affect regulation and attachment.

First Episode

This took place after about one and a half years of long-term psychoanalytic psychotherapy.

Start of session:

Therapist:	How are you doing?
Patient:	And how are you doing?
	Therapist (*a little uncertain, but this is not the first time the patient has asked this*): Well—okay, so far, so good today. I am reasonably well rested—and you?

	The therapist does not deflect the question. He doesn't really know Cornelia's motives for asking this question today. Is she worried about him? Does she want to distract? Does she want to provoke? The therapist decides to answer the question authentically but not too deeply.
Patient:	Lately, when I come here, I feel bad. It starts the night before and doesn't get any better over time.
Therapist:	It has to do with coming here?
	The therapist encourages Cornelia to describe the situation in more detail.
Patient:	I don't really know.
Therapist:	Can you describe in more detail what's happening to you?
Patient:	I don't know, it's diffuse. I feel restless, bad, diffuse, somehow threatened.
Therapist (empathically interested):	Okay, tell more about it. *Not-knowing stance.*
Patient:	I'm scared, it's like a panic attack.
Therapist:	Anxiety? That sounds terrible. What kind of anxiety is it?
Patient:	Yeah, maybe anxiety. When I'm here for a while, it subsides.
Therapist:	It subsides. Do you have any idea what is subsiding?
Patient:	No, I don't know.
Therapist:	How are you feeling right now?
Patient:	Some restlessness.
	The therapist stays in the here and now and maintains the not-knowing stance.
Therapist:	Can I do something to make this restlessness recede? *The therapist searches for something to reduce the affect. Expressing such care could already be reassuring, but here it remains unsuccessful.*
Patient:	You don't really understand me.
Therapist:	Okay. Ah... Why don't I understand you?
Patient (rather desperately):	I've told you before. It's always the same thing.
Therapist:	Can you please tell me again?
Patient:	You find me difficult.
Therapist:	You're afraid that I find you difficult?
Patient:	That you don't like me—that I'm a burden to you.
Therapist (confused):	I don't understand. What have I said or done to make you come to these conclusions? *The therapist maintains the not-knowing stance and tries to tie the more diffuse feelings to something concrete. This means working on affect focus and mentalizing the relationship between therapist and patient.*

	Silence.
Patient:	Are you angry with me?
Therapist (confused):	I don't understand that either. What do you mean? What would make me angry?
Patient:	I don't know.
Therapist:	What is it, then?
	Maintains the not-knowing stance.
Patient:	I feel alone and somehow threatened.
Therapist:	"Somehow threatened" is a rather vague feeling for me. Do you feel threatened right now?
Patient:	Right now, it's weaker than it was before today's session.
Silence.	
Therapist:	What is threatening you here? Is it something in the room? Is it something about me or something else?
	Another attempt by the therapist to connect the affects to concrete triggers in the therapeutic relationship.
Patient:	After the session, I always remember what I had wanted to tell you. Afterward, it occurs to me. Now, it doesn't occur to me.
Silence.	
Therapist:	I'm still wondering whether you can determine what you're interpreting as a sign that you are being threatened here.
	The therapist encourages the patient to look further for what is triggering these affects in the relationship.
Patient:	Sometimes you are not very empathic when I tell you something.
	The patient addresses a rupture in the therapeutic relationship.
Therapist:	What do you mean by "not very empathic"? Can you be more specific?
Patient:	I don't feel like you're taking my suffering seriously. You see it too superficially.
Therapist (hesitating):	Aha... Is that so?... Okay. What are you basing that on?
Patient:	You don't really listen.
Therapist:	Yes, it may be because sometimes I am unfocused. I'm sorry. Sometimes I'm too detached, too. I may be protecting myself.
	The therapist shares their own mental processes and works on the "rupture" in the real relationship, taking responsibility for how the patient feels, in the sense that she has perceived something important in the relationship.
Patient (smiling):	At least now you're honest!
Therapist (smiling):	Okay... But how can my being unfocused and unsympathetic make you feel threatened? Disappointed, yes, that I understand. But threatened?
	Attempt at clarification. However, the therapist misses the opportunity to understand the lack of empathy. Is it because of the nature of the narrative? Of being forced into psychological equivalence?

Patient: It does, though.

Therapist: Tell more about it.

Patient: I don't feel anything at the moment.

Therapist: How is that "I don't feel anything" now?

Patient (*after prolonged silence and hesitation*): I feel abandoned.

Therapist: You feel abandoned—even by me?

Silence.

Patient: I told you, some things you just don't understand. Maybe it's my fault after all. I may not be expressing it properly.

Silence.

Therapist: I'm just thinking: I'll leave you alone—I really don't understand you.

The therapist lets the patient recede into her inner world, her thoughts. Trust comes from the feeling that the other person understands you. It is an admission by the therapist that he is participating in the patient's created mistrust in the here and now. The therapist also interrupts the silence here, which could threaten the patient.

Silence.

Patient (emotional):   You know, my mother always wanted to break my will. She was very violent. It was awful! I can't do that anymore. You don't believe it.

Therapist (irritated): Yes, I do... You're suspicious... that I don't believe it... okay...

Patient: That's part of feeling threatened—I was abandoned.

Therapist: Also by your father, when your mother was violent.

Patient: But I didn't let her get away with it. I had my own way.

Therapist (relieved): You felt threatened, abandoned, but didn't let her break your will!

Patient: I provoked her with that. I wanted to provoke her, too.

Therapist: To show her: "You won't break my will? You won't break me!"

Patient: I don't understand how anyone can put up with that!

Therapist: You definitely didn't put up with it. And that's a good thing.

Patient: Yes. I feel the same way in negotiations today!

Therapist (relieved): Yes, that's true!

Silence.

Patient: I'm alone and lonely, so what's the use? It's so exhausting. The loneliness never ends.

Therapist: You are alone and lonely.

The therapist tries to be empathetic.

Patient: I looked again at the video recording of the session before last you gave me. During the last session, I felt you were being hostile or reserved toward me at various points. But all these things, the hostility and the reserved attitude I remembered there, they didn't apply at all when I watched the video.

The therapist makes video recordings with the patient's consent. Cornelia had expressed the wish to watch the sessions at home. The therapist agreed. Mentally, the patient has returned to her feelings of mistrust but can now also accept another point of view.

Therapist
(relieved): That's really good. How do you feel about that?

The therapist hopes that the patient can connect these experiences with her affects.

Patient: Yes, I was relieved, too.

Therapist: What does it relieve you of?

Patient: My fears that you were rejecting me during the session were allayed.

Therapist: And now, how do you feel now?

The difference between memory and video would have been worth further exploration: What was different? What did you experience in the situation? What did you remember, and what are you observing now? The therapist's creativity and curiosity were unfortunately limited.

Patient: I feel lonely. It's always like that. It never stops. It's not going to change. It's been like that all my life.

Therapist: Why are you so sure it won't stop?

Patient: You're just here because you're here professionally. You're not a real friend.

The patient returns to the topic of distrust in relationships.

Therapist: Yes, that still seems difficult for you?

Patient: It's not that I don't trust them, and that I can tell you all this means something. I didn't think that therapy would engage me so much.

Final Comment

Gaining epistemic trust is a struggle. Affects change. The therapist supports Cornelia in trying to attach her affects to something. She initially starts to mentalize, which the therapist supports. The topic of epistemic trust is attacked head-on, it is encircled.

Similarities and Differences to the Psychoanalytic Approach

The traditional psychoanalyst also sees the therapeutic relationship as one in which old attachment patterns are revived and significant biographical experiences are refracted in the "here and now." The patient's affects and vagaries are important in this process. In this regard, epistemic trust is closely related to transference, both being aspects of the therapeutic relationship. Epistemic trust brings the communicative aspects to the fore. These are two perspectives that can be complementary and enriching; the difference lies in the treatment technique. The difference between the classical psychoanalytic and the MBT approach is that the latter works out this understanding from the relationship and does not interpret it. The therapist shoulders the entire dynamics ("unfocused," "distanced"). Of course, the therapist could have taken another step by asking Cornelia how to understand the therapist's lack of empathy; that would have represented an attempt to understand the "rupture" from within the relationship.

Psychoanalytically speaking, aspects of transference (distortion) and negative transference are in the foreground. In this excerpt, the therapist does not go into the transference/reflection of the relationship interpretively but sticks with exploring the transference triggers and the affects. He leaves the patient alone by not offering any enriching interpretations.

The psychoanalyst might have processed the transference and countertransference in the here and now. He could have supported the expectation in the patient that, by carefully interpreting the unconscious or preconscious, some insight would emerge. However, from an MBT therapist's point of view, there lies a danger, especially with patients with severe impairment, that the therapist's "views" are not perceived by the patient as neutral but as the opinions of a psychoanalytic authority. This is certainly true even if an analyst formulates their interpretation cautiously and questioningly. Therefore, the MBT therapist largely refrains from interpretations, including interpretations related to childhood or unconscious/preconscious strivings. The analyst is more concerned with the perception of the feelings involved and discussing the distortion in the here and now.

Second Episode

This took place after two and a half years of long-term psychoanalytic psychotherapy. One year later, Cornelia L. has fallen in love.

Patient:	When I live alone, I have my life under control. Then everything is okay. I am stable and have good, friendly relationships. But when I fall in love, everything always goes wrong. I get totally... Now it's like this. I can't bring myself not to constantly call him and wait on his answer.
Therapist:	What does "constantly" mean in this context?
Patient:	If I haven't heard from him, like every few hours. But once I've contacted him via WhatsApp and he doesn't answer promptly, it gets real bad. Sometimes, I can't stand it for even an hour.
Therapist:	Not even an hour... And then what happens?
	Request to explore.
Patient:	I almost go crazy.
Therapist:	After an hour?
Patient:	Well, because we were arguing again.
Therapist:	Tell me more about that.
Patient:	I then needed an emergency number. Like a medical emergency number.

Therapist:	I don't understand that now. Can you explain it to me from the beginning?
Patient (agitation rising):	But then, why doesn't he answer the phone or write back? There's got to be a reason for that, right?
Therapist:	Slow down. Are you talking about a specific situation from the last few days?
	Mentalization has broken down. The therapist tries to steer the situation back to the concrete to understand the triggers for the intensive affect and the cognitive distortions. At the same time, the therapist tries to calm the situation.
Patient:	Yes, my friend went to a seminar in Berlin. At first, he didn't answer.
Therapist:	How was that for you?
	The situation is broken down into small steps. The therapist slows down the process by asking for details. This deceleration promotes the shift from implicit to explicit mentalization.
Patient:	By the time he answered, I was already annoyed. At first, he sounded quite friendly when I reached him.
Therapist:	And then?
Patient:	I was annoyed and blamed him for not getting back to me. He then became very irritated.
Therapist:	And how did you feel then?
Patient:	I'm embarrassed, but in a moment like that, I seriously doubted whether he was really in Berlin, whether I could believe him, or whether he was actually deceiving me. I'm the naive one.
Therapist:	How did you feel on the inside? Can you describe it?
	Suggestion to focus on the inner world, since Cornelia was totally focused on her boyfriend (self vs. other pole).
Patient:	I became more and more distrustful.
Therapist:	Did the distrust attach itself to anything else?
Patient:	It's my experience. Because of such quarrels, after all, relationships often break up.
Therapist:	If I understand you correctly, you have fantasies about what he is doing, and you can no longer be sure he is standing by you.
Patient:	He gets angry. Why is he getting angry? He's trying to hide something.
Therapist:	You are very upset. You need quick and concrete proof, right?
Patient:	Yes, I do.
Therapist:	Why is that?
Patient:	I know I'm suspicious, but I can't help it.
Therapist:	It bears down on you. It's like a tunnel—there's only this way. Is it like that?
	Validation by the therapist.
Patient:	Because he's not there.

> *Teleological mode: The patient searches for concrete proof to con-*
> *clude from the behavior to the inner state. The patient feels the pres-*
> *sure to act (to call).*

Therapist: What could you do differently to escape the tunnel?

Patient: I would have to somehow learn to endure stress and uncertainties. I
don't always know what's going on with the other person.

Therapist: That sounds good to me.

Closing Comment

In this sequence, the therapist and Cornelia attempt to evaluate affect and connect her distrust to triggers. One trigger is that the patient is trapped in a teleological mode: "He is no longer there. Only when he is there does he love me." The high arousal, along with high activation of the attachment system, leads to a breakdown of mentalization. At the same time, it activates disappointing object experiences, which in turn affects epistemic trust. The epistemic trust that would be necessary to restabilize her mentalizing abilities is absent—a vicious cycle described in Chapter 2.4. This scene is all about epistemic trust (learning from social relationships), though it also concerns general trust in oneself (self-worth) and fear of abandonment.

Possible Similarities and Differences with the Psychoanalytic Approach

Traditional psychoanalysts may not be familiar with all the modes of mentalizing disorders (here: the teleological mode), but they would probably sense disconnected communication. They would see the behavior as acting out and possibly attempt symbolization—which is very close to the mentalization approach. The traditional psychoanalyst would likewise first clarify and then focus on the defense mechanisms and the averted, trying to understand the anxiety regarding the activation of inner object relations, i.e., as a distortion of present experience from the patient's past unconscious. The analyst interprets this cautiously, expecting that the patient's insight into these relationships will resolve their anxiety in the long run and in light of the transference experience. The approach of the MBT therapist, though, is different here: They first address the teleological mode and then stimulate attempts to mentalize and symbolize. This is a more structured means of controlling the process.

The MBT therapist is alerted by the teleological mode not to follow Cornelia down the teleological rabbit hole. The MBT therapist does not expect real insights to arise in the patient from interpretations as long as they remain in this mode. Recognizing nonmentalization invites the attempt to return to mentalization with the patient. The psychoanalyst would focus more on the preconscious and unconscious dynamics that prevent new experiences: The revived early object relationship (the mother) prevents Cornelia from developing stable, secure internal images of people and thus maintaining independence from their external/factual presence. Structurally, we can understand this as the internalization of attachment experiences: Current anxiety and insecurity revive early attachment experiences, and anxiety triggers early traumatic experiences. By applying understanding, the traditional psychoanalyst may succeed in empathically "containing" the patient's experiences and bringing the patient a little closer to their understanding of the situation. That is, one can understand Cornelia's affects and cognitions from the "there and then," that is, from a time when they made sense. The MBT therapist intervenes in a rather similar way, albeit by reverting more to communicative aspects and the here and now.

6.3   The Alien Self

In Brief

The alien self represents parts of the self that are foreign to a person's own self. The person experiences them as largely not belonging to them. These parts may be poorly symbolized, preconscious, or unconscious. They crop up in affects or actions experienced by the person as being in a different state—as not belonging to the self. Extraneous parts of the self are often at odds with the conscious parts of the self that are accessible to reflection. This incoherence creates unbearable feelings of tension, emptiness, and anxiety.

Everyone has extraneous self parts, parts that have arisen, partly through prolonged failed or faulty affect reflections with attachment figures in childhood or through traumatic experiences that have burrowed deeply into the self-structure and are experienced as incoherent with other self parts (see Chapter 2.6).

Claudius D.

The 35-year-old Claudius D. is currently unemployed, having previously worked for several years in trade fair construction and for airlines. His family lived (and still lives) in deplorable conditions in a southern European country. Sometimes, the family did not have enough to eat. During his childhood, Claudius was a victim of massive psychological and physical violence, neglect, and sexual abuse. His father threatened and tortured him, as he did his mother. Sometimes, Claudius was afraid that his father would actually kill his mother. The fear was not unfounded: He was his mother's favorite child, though she was just as sexually abusive toward him.

Claudius had been in and out of clinics several times over the past ten years, triggered by crises following the loss of a trusted person or a job. His history revealed no suicide attempts, no drug abuse, but there was some self-harm. Thanks to his friendly nature and communication skills, however, he was always able to quickly find good working conditions in expanding sectors of the economy.

In social experiences involving strong criticism or restrictions to his autonomy, he was in danger of being flooded with fantasies and losing himself. A partnership in the past had caused many painful experiences. Once he had become totally dependent on a man who mistreated him as well as exploited him sexually and financially. Separating from him brought no inner relief. On the contrary, the separation plunged Claudius into a severe crisis, leading to a stay in the hospital. He has already been in therapy for longer (once a week). Despite his long-term experience, he remains extremely ambivalent toward low-frequency psychoanalytic therapy. He presently lives with a man in a shared apartment in a friendly relationship but with no shared sexuality.

Claudius' general and structural level of psychological functioning is severely impaired. The early, severe traumatizations make his symptomatology understandable. At the beginning of treatment, his panic attacks were very distressing and also occurred during the therapy sessions. But, in the course of treatment, these declined significantly, and there were no further self-injurious acts. His professional life was (and still is) difficult because of the psychological stress he experiences, especially because of the recurring interpersonal conflicts and his social anxieties.

The treatment requested was low-frequency psychoanalytic treatment. In the following two episodes, Claudius is strongly self-referential. The strange self and the largely healthy parts of his self are separated from each other; the strange self parts influence or threaten the domination of his interpersonal experiences at different stages.

First Episode

This took place after about one year of long-term psychoanalytic psychotherapy.

Patient (irritated):	I don't feel well.
Therapist:	Oh... What's wrong?
	Silence.
Patient (annoyed):	I'm keeping quiet here because you don't believe me anyway. I've said it several times: You always defend everyone else.
Therapist:	I think I remember that, a week ago, in the last session, we communicated very well.
Patient:	We only talked about superficial topics then.
Therapist (irritated):	Really? I don't remember it like that at all.... But okay.... But what's going on now?
Patient:	I've already told you.
Therapist:	Can you explain it to me a little more?
Patient (still angry and insistent):	You said that I might have criticized Lukas harshly at work, which is why he reacted the way he did.
Therapist:	Yes, that's what I said.
Patient:	You believe others more than you believe me!
Therapist (irritated and somewhat guilty):	I apparently caused a misunderstanding. I didn't mean it that way. Sorry.
Patient (ironically, smiling):	The road to hell is paved with good intentions.

	The patient is on a confrontational course, and the therapist is very irritated.
Therapist:	Okay... My job is to help you. I don't care about the others you mentioned. Honestly.
Patient:	Lukas hit the table with his fist during the argument. Only a couple of inches from my head. You understood that, right? So why did you say: "Poor Lukas!!!"
Therapist (irritated, looking for a clear path):	I don't remember saying it like that. I didn't experience the scene so dramatically at the time... I don't remember it that way. But maybe you experienced it that way?
Patient (ironically and angrily):	Didn't experience it like that? But that's the way it was!
Therapist:	Okay, it was like that, maybe. *The therapist is still irritated but hesitantly accepts the patient's view of "That's the way it was." It is a means of validating.*
Patient:	You always don't remember things then!
Therapist:	Maybe. You are very angry with me, and I am a little surprised by this reaction.
Patient:	Once, in a similar situation, you said I react like my mother. I'm always the aggressive one. It just comes out of me.
Therapist (rather guiltily):	Yes, I said something like that at the time. I shouldn't have said it. It was not good. Sorry. *The patient here addresses a "rupture" in the therapeutic relationship. The therapist takes responsibility for the relationship and the rupture in mentalization.*
Patient:	Yes... no. I don't believe you really think that!!
Therapist:	You think I'm on their side and not on yours. Is that how it is?
Patient (offensively):	You're wrong. My mother was much worse to me than I was to you.
Therapist (somewhat relieved):	Yes, you're absolutely right. No question about it. And you were a child, whereas we are both adults. *The therapist now tries to authentically and empathically validate Claudius' experience.*
Patient:	There it is again. You qualify everything. Therapist (*trying to bring calmness into the situation*): Okay... But you're giving too much weight to my words. You're angry with me, aren't you? Maybe you can try to take a step back from these strong feelings? Otherwise, it's hard for me to think about them. *The therapist addresses the patient's high arousal.*
Patient (ironically, laughing slightly):	There it is again! You think you're such a great therapist!

Therapist:	Well, as you say—and there's something to that—I do forget things, side with others, fail to understand you.
	The therapist validates the patient's experience.
Patient:	Yes, you do!
Therapist:	Okay. But I don't agree with what you're saying, because I don't want to fall out of your favor because of my perceptions.
	A self-revelation of the therapist.
Patient (a little softer, calmer, more empathetic):	You shouldn't. You're right—that's why I have such difficulties. The others are usually right.
Therapist:	Okay... though I don't know if it's really true that the others are mostly right.
	The therapist tries to address the split between "good" and "bad."
Patient (the mood shifts):	I'm a failure. The person I hate most is myself.
Therapist (emotional):	Such self-hatred is hard to bear.
	The therapist validates.
	Silence.
	A very emotional situation.
Patient (agitated, angry, desperate?):	I am attacking myself, hurting myself, banging my head like an idiot against the wall. It's all so meaningless here.
	An attack on himself and then an attack on therapy.
Therapist (rather matter-of-factly):	Yes, it's terrible.... Let's see how you can get the hatred and the self-hatred under control. That part damages and threatens your life.
	The therapist challenges the patient to move from the affective pole to the cognitive pole. The intervention contains an interpretive component, albeit one that relates to aspects near to consciousness.
Patient (composed):	Yes, but I can't stand your being so kind to me.
Therapist (sympathetically):	I understand, that's hard to bear. But it's important to recognize it and say it out loud.
	The therapist tries to empathically validate the patient's affect and cognition.
Patient:	It's strange—I'm always different here than when I'm outside. Outside, I can talk normally. Outside, I feel sorry for the way I was here. Outside, very different conversations are possible. I feel so ashamed of how I am here.
Therapist:	But you can express that here. That's good. Both things are possible: the aggression, the hate, the destructive and self-destructive tendencies—and the friendly and affectionate aspects.
	The therapist's intervention serves to clarify and also as a means of interpretation to overcome the schism. The interpretation refers to parts close to consciousness.

Patient: I'm going to go now.

Therapist: If you can't stand it anymore, of course, you can leave, but let me suggest staying for just a moment, if you can stand it.

The therapist understands that the patient wants to be alone now, to distance himself from the therapeutic relationship and downregulate his affects. But maybe, by giving permission, the patient can stay.

Patient: You are not wrong. Everything looks so bad on the inside. I often feel ashamed after our sessions that I behaved like I did. Outside of therapy, I am completely different. Then I feel ashamed... I don't want to take it anymore.

Therapist: It's okay the way you are, and it's good that you can express it. I'm sure it's hard to bear.

The therapist empathically validates the patient's experience. The solution lies in "radical acceptance," meaning "it is what it is."

Patient: Sometimes I want to email you that I'm not coming anymore, and I write down all the reasons why. It's just difficult, and I feel ashamed of myself. It gets me down. Then I don't send it. I read it again after a couple of hours and delete everything because I'm convinced it's not true, so I check back with you if the next appointment is set.

Therapist: Okay, so there are also friendly parts. I have experienced those with you as well. And, at the same time, you then feel ashamed about how you are here. We should talk about that some more.

Claudius can communicate that he is ashamed of how he sometimes acts. Apparently, he is not in control of that portion; it is foreign to him, and he is ashamed of it.

Concluding Comment

In this session, Claudius experiences his various parts (self vs. alien). In this phase of the therapy, he initially perceives these parts only indirectly and dimly as foreign and destructive, whereas he projects the strange, more evil, and hostile parts onto the therapist, i.e., the therapist is experienced as hostile and evil. This represents his attempt to externalize the strange self parts onto the therapist, the goal being to establish self-coherence. Then, the scene shifts: He experiences this part emerging from the coherent part of the self as alien and beyond his control. Claudius now becomes the object of his hatred. Contact with the therapist is now determined more by the coherent self.

Strong affects prevail in this scene and take center court. In contrast to transference-focused psychotherapy TFP (Yeomans et al., 2015), the focus lies not on confrontation and interpretation but on validating experience. According to the mentalization approach, the therapeutic goal is to pursue a better strategy in dealing with other-self parts in the sense of: "These are parts of me, but I also have other parts, so I can stand it."

Possible Similarities and Differences from the Psychoanalytic Approach

The therapist addresses the patient's parts in the here and now, regulating the intensity of the affects. Therapists too wrestle with their own mentalizing ability and involve the patient in this process. Epistemic distrust leads to a negative transference in which the therapist comes to be perceived as the perpetrator. Projections play a significant role in this process and can be understood against the background of an alien self, which creates an unbearable tension and needs to be externalized. Empathic validation and help in regulating emotional arousal bring the parts closer together, allowing them to be better symbolized or mentalized. This reduces the pressure to act out. In psychoanalytic terminology, the effort of both persons is considered work within transference not work *on (about)* transference: the mentalization of the relationship (see Chapter 5.2).

The procedure according to Bion's container–contained model or Klein's model of the paranoid-schizoid and the depressive position shows certain similarities to the process described above. However, the differences between the approach of an MBT therapist and traditional psychoanalysis lie in the realm of interpretations (e.g., generic or biographical), how defense mechanisms and the averted are handled, and finally how the transference and the processing thereof are understood. Psychoanalysts recognize in transference the activation of different object representations (both good and bad) the patient is projecting onto them. One can incorporate this understanding into the interpretations intended to render the patient's aggressive impulses understandable: Through projection, the patient experiences the therapist as hostile, uninterested, and unsympathetic. The traditional psychoanalyst (like the transference-focused therapist) interprets the aggression in the transference in this manner. At the same time, however, patients cannot escape dealing with the therapist, having projected parts of their self onto the therapist (projective identification). The object parts projected onto the therapist influence the therapist's reaction—whether real or in the patient's imagination—because the therapist is now identified with them. This is what the psychoanalyst would consider when reflecting on own countertransference.

MBT avoids the terms transference and countertransference; current publications speak of the "therapeutic relationship" to avoid misunderstandings regarding the traditional psychoanalytic concept of transference (see also Chapter 5.2). The psychoanalytic view is not alien to the MBT therapist with its concepts of self, other–self, and projective identification, but the MBT therapist would not formulate an interpretation using this approach but would prefer to remain in the here and now of cognitive and affective experiences—experiences that are different for the patient and the therapist. The MBT therapist would see themselves as an equal player and validate the patient's perception (see Chapter 5.4).

Many psychoanalysts understand aggression against the background of some original drive event. In contrast, in MBT, the patient's aggression largely results from negative experiences (e.g., experiences of violence or misunderstandings) that may reactivate deep layers of the unconscious (Fonagy & Allison, 2017). It is legitimate to wonder whether the MBT therapist, with their noninterpretive approach and resolute acceptance of the patient's aggression, is defusing the issue of aggression.

Second Episode

This took place after about three years of psychoanalytic treatment.

Patient:	I feel uncomfortable telling it. I feel ashamed. But my sister said to me, "You are very harsh sometimes." Actually, it's worse than that. I came into the kitchen yesterday morning. I had slept badly all night, had nightmares. I was pretty beat. My friend John was making himself breakfast. And the kitchen was dirty. I don't like things being dirty. I don't care about anything else. I just need it to be clean. I know why: He had dropped something and not picked it up. I yelled at him, "You dirty bastard!"
Therapist (surprised):	Oh... What was going on there?
Patient:	I felt hurt. Actually, I don't want to attack anyone.
Therapist (not really in the situation yet):	You felt offended? *Attempt to center on the affect. The therapist mentions an affect, though it would have been better to have asked openly.*
Patient:	I was feeling hostile.
Therapist:	Can you describe it in more detail?
Patient:	I was hostile, and the dirt was my enemy—and John.
Therapist:	A "hostile feeling," what do you mean by that?
Patient:	It takes one more drop for the dam to just burst out of me.
Therapist:	Let's go back for a moment to the situation in which that happened. Was there something already brewing? *Attempt to center on the specific event and its triggering conditions (stop and rewind to the moment before things shifted (mentalizing vs. fight/flight).*
Patient:	Actually, no.
Therapist:	Think about it again. What was going on? *The therapist tries to have the patient return to the situation before the mentalization collapsed.*
Patient:	Yes, I had slept badly that night. Again, these nightmares. I was in a really bad mood when I came into the kitchen, already irritated.
Therapist:	And then you saw the dirty kitchen, just like that?
Patient (agitated):	Something hostile bubbled up in me. It hurt me.
Therapist:	Hostile and hurt, you said. Why hurt? *An attempt to differentiate the affect.*
Patient:	Yes, it hurt me.
Therapist:	What images or thoughts are associated with that?
Patient:	I don't know. Sometimes I get a feeling of disgust when people get too close to me. *Further affect differentiation by Claudius.*
Therapist:	A feeling of disgust? Tell me more about that?

Patient:	I don't know, disgust. I feel it often.
Therapist:	Disgust is an intense physical feeling. The body reacts to something toxic that needs to get out or shouldn't get in.
	Stimulating further exploration. This involves an interpretation that relates to states close to consciousness.
Patient:	When people get too close to me. For example, yesterday the sub way didn't come. More and more people were standing on the plat-form. Then, three trains came in a row. Everyone got on the first subway. Thank God the other two subways came so I could get on!
Therapist:	You said people disgust you when they get too close. Let's go back to the situation with your friend.
	The therapist doesn't let this thread continue but focuses on what the patient has brought to the session as a problem.
Patient:	Sometimes, I then become abusive... rage gets the best of me.
Therapist:	In that situation, the dirty kitchen disgusted you, but sometimes a person disgusts you. Is that correct?
	The attempt to stimulate differentiation, curiosity, and an attitude of not-knowing.
Patient:	It was more than the dirty kitchen.
Therapist:	But it's also not something you can differentiate?
	The further attempt to elaborate affect.
Patient:	No, it just boils up in me like that. I said, "Thank God you're leaving!"
Therapist:	Were you directing your anger or your disgust at John? Or both?
Patient:	By then, it was just anger.
Therapist:	And what happened next?
Patient:	I sat in the kitchen. Tried to be normal again.
	Silence.
Therapist:	How do you think your friend was feeling?
	Suggestion to take the perspective of the other, since the patient is very much involved with their own inner world.
Patient:	Not good. He felt unfairly and poorly treated... He is my friend... He is good-natured and patient with me.
Therapist:	That moves you now, too.
	The therapist validates empathically and concentrates on the here and now.
Patient:	He was getting too close to me. But what I did went too far.
Therapist:	What do you mean by "too far"?
	The therapist maintains the not-knowing stance.
Patient (upset):	It's something—you know, my father was always a stranger to me. I never felt close to him. To me, he was... he was a disgusting person. He attacked me and my mother. And that feeling, I know I got that from him. It's something I learned, in my opinion... I don't know, maybe it's learned.
	This is an authentic elaboration of affects regarding autobiographical experiences and memories. A good attempt at mentalizing.

Therapist:	You got it from him unwillingly? Is that what you mean? *Suggestion for further exploration.* *Silence.*
Therapist:	How do you feel now, thinking about everything? *Centering on the here and now.*
Patient:	It makes me tired.
Therapist:	What makes you so tired?
Patient:	It wears me out... It's a part of me, and I'm so mean.
Therapist:	It's hard to bear. Is that what you mean?
Patient:	Yes.
Therapist:	There are two sides to your friend John: the kind and patient John and the hurting, the hostile, the offensive. *"The hurting, the hostile, the offensive" goes in two directions: The patient feels hurt and under attack, while at the same time hurting and reacting with hostility.*
Patient:	I put my hand in a wasps' nest and got stung.
Therapist (surprised by this statement):	That's a good description. So, what is this wasps' nest?
Patient:	The people around me.

Final Comment

In the situation reported above (i.e., in the kitchen), regarding the mentalization dimensions, Claudius is strongly related to the poles: "+ implicit + external + self-oriented + strongly affective." The therapist tries to move him toward the other poles in the scene (see Figure 6.2).

Mentalization dimensions

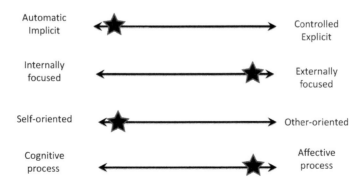

Figure 6.2 Mentalization dimensions in the example of Claudius D.

The patient's experiences become understandable through the concept of the alien self. Deep affects experienced as not belonging to him are explored and connected to early events, providing the chance to connect affects with autobiographical experiences. In retrospect, one can assume that the dirty kitchen triggers Claudius to dig up old experiences from his parental home and precipitate hostility, pain, and disgust. He connects these feelings with traumatic events experienced with and through his father. He feels threatened and defends himself aggressively. The past and the here and now dissolve into one (experiencing in the psychic equivalence mode).

Possible Similarities and Differences to the Psychoanalytic Approach

The concept of the alien self is a theoretical concept closely related to developmental psychology and psychoanalysis: Such parts may be largely removed or withdrawn from consciousness. The notion of projecting foreign parts onto one's partner is closely related to the notion of defense mechanisms. In MBT, the foreign parts of the self create unbearable feelings of anxiety, emptiness, and tension, which lead to defending against such foreign self parts with the help of projective identification. Psychoanalytically speaking, there are many reasons why such defense mechanisms ensue, depending on the respective psychoanalytic school.

The differences in treatment techniques result partly from theoretical presuppositions. Whereas traditional psychoanalysis deems drive-theoretical assumptions as the causes behind defense mechanisms, MBT pursues more strongly social experiences—as do many other psychoanalytic directions (e.g., largely object-relations theory and self-psychology). According to the mentalization concept, these experiences—primarily massive fear/threat/neglect, especially in significant attachment relationships, as well as violent contrasting experiences and affects (e.g., giving protection and threat)—cannot be processed mentally in a coherent manner.

The classical psychoanalyst may attempt to bring the split-off parts closer together by interpreting the transference, thereby providing the patient with cognitive and affective insights. The MBT therapist, on the other hand, focuses on evaluating affects and cognitions to build a more coherent (symbolized) representational system. The latter requires creating a structured and safe space (see also Chapter 5).

6.4   Severe Impairment of Mentalizing Abilities in the Presence of High Psychosocial Functioning

In Brief

Patients with a mild personality disorder are not infrequently persons with a high level of psychosocial functioning who are successful in various social fields (e.g., culture, science). As in the case described here, their problem may be limited to one or two specific areas, e.g., love relationships (attachment), though the limitations of their mentalizing abilities may be very severe in these areas. They can be characterized by the prementalizing modes, by extreme persistence on the poles in the four polarities (see Chapter 5.4), by high epistemic distrust (see Chapter 2.4), and by the projection of alien parts of their self (see Chapter 2.6). Severe impairments of mentalizing abilities are characteristic of various personality disorders. The mentalization approach assumes the coexistence of different self-states that cannot be integrated into a coherent self-image because of the limitations of mentalization.

Carola U.

Carola U. came to us on the advice of a psychiatrist. She had turned to him in a severe crisis. Diagnostically, the criteria for a borderline personality disorder (BPD) according to DSM-5 were not met (hybrid model of assessment of a borderline disorder (American Psychiatric Association, 2013; Calvo et al., 2016). Since Carola's problem was related mainly to love relationships, only a moderate impairment in the area of closeness had been diagnosed. The personality traits separation anxiety, impulsivity, hostility, and fearfulness were noted, but again the assessments related largely to love relationships. Severe symptomatology referred primarily to partnerships in which attachment desires had been activated. Other relationships were only slightly affected.

During the initial interview, Carola said: "I am at wits' end. I work in a large accounting firm in a senior position. I am in a secure position, although because of the current situation in this industry, you never know what tomorrow will bring. My main problem is my relationship with men. Past relationships often escalated and ended in break-ups. Sexually, I am very capable of love and suffering. I am currently together with Gabriel. I'll soon be 34 years old and would like to have a stable relationship and children. Emotionally, I always trust men more than women, which is why I am here with you now."

Carola is the child of successful parents; her father was initially a pilot and later moved up in the corporate world. Her mother works as a publicist, had a lover, but could not separate from her husband. The parents expressed little care for the child. There was much quarreling, which often degenerated into violence. The father had an intense and strong emotional relationship with his adolescent daughter at the end of his life.

Carola was a bright child who was interested in boys and sexuality from an early age. She adored her father and recalls exciting moments flying with him in the cockpit. School was easy for her. She was achievement-oriented and effortlessly managed her studies. Her relationship with men and fears of failing professionally became a problem, but she got them under control.

Her love relationships revive her intense early attachment patterns, which largely reflect an ambivalent pattern. Her love relationships quickly become very intense and quickly become very erotically heated, severely limiting her mentalization abilities. The prementalizing mode of mental equivalence then often prevails.

The mentalization dimensions provide further orientation. Polarization in the dimensions is evident everywhere in high affect and heated conflicts (see Figure 6.3).

Whenever the patient refers to others too much, the therapist tries to bring the respective neglected pole, i.e., the self-orientation, into focus at various points during the therapy sequence by inquiring about her cognitions when affects take too great a control over Carola. The therapist encourages Carola to mentalize more explicitly (reflectively, more slowly) when she starts mentalizing implicitly (automatically, too quickly).

Mentalization dimensions

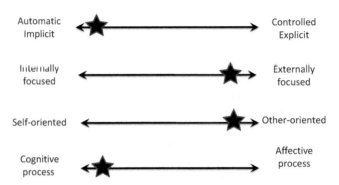

Figure 6.3 Mentalization dimensions in the example of Carola U.

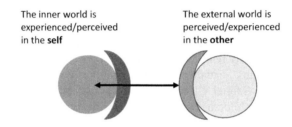

Figure 6.4 The inner world is experienced/perceived in the self.

The mentalization dimensions internal/self–external/other require some differentiation (see Figure 6.4).

In the following episode, we can observe how Carola tends to perceive the external signals of her partner and the internal signals in herself. She is strongly oriented toward the other, albeit externally; that is, she is externally oriented, for example, to Gabriel's actions ("Does he call her on time?"). She perceives Gabriel's inner world only very weakly. And when she does perceive Gabriel's inner world, it is often highly distorted. On the other hand, Carola's inner perception is her main focus. How she acts and appears to others is largely not conscious during a crisis mood, or she doesn't truly care in such moments.

First Episode

This took place after about six months of long-term psychoanalytic therapy.

Patient: Last week was Gabriel's birthday. We hadn't had any significant contact lately. I gave him a party with me for his birthday, and it was wonderful. I believed he was the right man for me.
The patient starts with a specific episode. She already knows the structure of the treatment.

Therapist:	It's new to me that you were having contact with him again.
Patient:	Who'd have thought! I didn't either. Yes, he contacted me again. I wouldn't have dared.
Therapist:	Why?
Patient:	Because I didn't think I deserved Gabriel. He's the one who's serious about me, and he's reliable.
Therapist:	Yes, you said as much. But then you suddenly broke up with him.
Patient:	I've talked to my girlfriends in the meantime, and they had said that I made a huge mistake with Gabriel. But now I'm relieved.
Therapist (irritated):	You're separated?
Patient:	Gabriel doesn't commit entirely to the relationship. I don't need someone who is always hesitant.
Therapist (irritated):	He was hesitant. What happened? *To get a first impression of the extent to which mentalization could be maintained in the situation, the therapist first asks about what the patient specifically experienced.*
Patient:	On his birthday, I was completely happy again. I told him during that evening that I wanted to marry him and have a child with him. A little daughter of our own. He thought that was a great idea.
Therapist (irritated):	Yes, go on.
Patient:	And then he didn't get in touch for a whole day.
Therapist:	The following day?
Patient:	Yes. He backed out again. He said he needed time to readjust to everything. That would take some time with him. He repeated some old accusations. He said if I hadn't acted like that before, we would be much further along in our relationship. We could be living together now. *Restriction of mentalization, teleological mode: Gabriel hesitates = He doesn't really want me!*
Therapist:	Wait a moment, there must have been something in between. I have the impression that you are skipping something, that things are going too fast, right? *The therapist tries to slow down the process, to reduce the rising affects, and to get more details of the process. He does not succeed. Carola is carried away by the whirlpool of events.*
Patient:	Last night, he called at 10 pm. He was stalking me. I threatened to inform the police.
Therapist:	Why was that? What was going on inside you? *The patient is focused completely on Gabriel. The therapist tries to get her to focus on herself.*
Patient:	I felt threatened by him.
Therapist:	You felt threatened. Last night. Why is that? *Exploring Carola's rapidly changing affects.*
Patient:	I didn't want him anymore, and he approached me! You don't understand that again.

Therapist (irritated again):	That is correct. I don't understand it, at least not so quickly. Let me repeat it slowly again: At that point, you didn't want him anymore. But he nevertheless approached you... Was that the case?
Patient:	I didn't want to have anything more to do with him!
Therapist:	You must have felt very threatened to react so violently.
Patient:	You don't understand.
Therapist:	Yes, it's quite difficult for me, so quickly. So it was like this: You felt threatened and reacted clearly.
Patient:	I feel relieved now.
Therapist (irritated):	Oh, I see. Really? Can we go back one more time? Do you remember the specific situation?
	The therapist tries once again to go back to the triggering situation. This time, it works a little better.
Patient:	When Gabriel didn't get in touch the next evening after our meeting.
Therapist:	Yes, what was your emotional reaction?
Patient:	I thought it was disrespectful!
Therapist:	Disrespectful? What do you mean by that? I don't understand.
	The therapist encourages Carola to look at her feelings in a more differentiated way. He asks from the position of not-knowing.
Patient:	I've decided I can't stand this anymore, such degradation. It's high time to break up!
Therapist:	What is it that you can't stand? What do you mean by degradation?
	It would have been better to ask just one question. Usually, patients then evade by answering the easier question.
Patient:	Just a ton of anger. Sometimes, I feel like I have to take my revenge on him or bang my head against the wall.
Therapist:	Let's go back again: What did you mean by degradation?
Patient:	The disgraceful waiting!
Therapist:	Disgraceful waiting and then anger. Where does this anger come from?
Patient:	From inside me.
	Carola answers concretely.
Therapist:	Of course. I phrased that wrong. I mean where from in you?
Patient:	I don't know.
Therapist:	Not so fast—try to feel it once again: What's going on inside you?
	Silence.
Patient:	It just bursts out of me. I don't want him. He's not fully committed to me. He doesn't want me. He's depressed, too. I don't need that kind of thing.
Therapist:	Let's go back a little bit to what you said earlier, please. I'm confused there. First, you were completely convinced, and then things turned around quite suddenly. Is that correct?
	The therapist again encourages the patient to go back to her experiences, to slow down the process, to recall what she experienced in more detail, to explore her inner world, and to try to combine the parts that were kept separate.

Patient:	I was wrong.
	The therapist was unsuccessful.
Therapist:	Okay. It's like you were initially exploding with fireworks. And then they burned down, and what remains is ashes. Is it like that?
	The therapist attempts to focus the conversation.
Patient (excitedly):	Oh, yeah. I love fireworks! The last time we had fireworks, there were these environmentalists who were demonstrating. I'll tell you honestly, they just want to ruin all the fun for everyone else.
Therapist:	Could it be that your emotions were driving you, as you are now?
Patient:	That's what really counts, isn't it?
	Insisting on the view that only the affects/feelings count.
Therapist:	Why is that, actually?
	The therapist challenges her.
Patient:	You must mean reason now. I've known you for quite a while!
Therapist:	For example, yes, you're not wrong...
Patient:	But that's not how sex works.
Therapist:	What do you mean by that? How does sex work?
Patient:	Sex and fireworks.
Therapist:	How does sex work for you?
Patient:	... When we have sex, the emptiness and despair disappear.
Therapist:	Yes, I understand that now. Tell me more about that?
Patient:	At that moment, we are completely present. I look deep into his eyes during sex and see his excitement. That excites me. He only wants me. All I want to do is to satisfy him. That excites me. I only want him. This is pure love. We merge.
Therapist:	Okay, I don't know if arousal and desire always have to have something to do with love, but with you, it does. It's nearly limitless, the intense desire and wild fantasies, is that it?
Patient:	It's total arousal; we unite. I arouse him, he is mine, and he arouses me, I am his.
Therapist:	Is that what you mean when you say love is pure, what I would cautiously call desire and arousal for now?
	This comprises a careful challenge, a careful questioning of the equation of love and sex (Fonagy, 2008; Laplanche, 1995).
Patient:	When I totally let myself fall. It goes back and forth.
Therapist (irritated):	What goes back and forth?
Patient:	The arousal. It's exciting and without boundaries.
Therapist:	So sexuality means dissolving boundaries. You in him, he in you. Is it like that?
	Empathic validation.
Patient:	Yes, that's how it is.
Therapist:	It's confusing. But why does that always refer to love? You said you loved Gabriel deeply at that moment?
Patient:	Yes.

Therapist:	And now you're separated again. How is that for you?
Patient:	He disappoints me completely. Gabriel is not really there for me.
Therapist:	How is that for you?
Patient:	He totally withdraws. It's like a withdrawal. Like an addiction.
Therapist:	Ah yes, a violent withdrawal. Experiencing that is very, very painful for you. Isn't it?

The therapist is empathic because he understands: Her projective identification is associated with high sexual arousal, and the separation is experienced as unbearable.

Patient:	I don't know. Yes, that's the problem. I can't rely on anything there, with him.
Therapist (irritated, doesn't know what to do at first):	Yes, of course, but what's the use. Hold on for a moment. Don't answer right away... How are you doing now? *Silence.*
Patient (hesitating):	A little misunderstood... alone and empty.
Therapist:	Misunderstood—alone. I can understand that. But why empty?
Patient:	I don't know—I feel more lonely when nothing happens. Somehow unbearable. *Silence.*

The mentalizing becomes more effective.

Patient:	It's unbearable, and then I made up my mind. There was no other way.
Therapist:	And now, when you try to look at it from a distance?
Patient:	Maybe I shouldn't have acted so quickly. Maybe I should have endured the fireworks extinguishing a little longer.
Therapist:	Yes, that sounds good. How are you feeling now?
Patient:	I'm just reacting from a feeling. A feeling is only a feeling, you once said.

Now Carola reactivates the cognitive pole.

Therapist:	Okay. Yes, that's what I said. Let's go back a little bit. You said you shouldn't have acted so quickly. Is that the case?
Patient:	It would have been better.
Therapist:	But how can you do that, not act so quickly?
Patient:	I have to stay with my feelings. I mean, Gabriel could be little more empathetic.
	Therapist (*relieved, with some humor*): Yes, you're right. But, unfortunately, he is not.
Patient:	Yes, unfortunately.
Therapist:	Can you now try to put yourself in Gabriel's shoes again, to understand him. How did he feel during these situations?

The therapist challenges Carola to change her point of view, to take Gabriel's perspective.

Patient:	On his birthday, he was happy, but then he felt overwhelmed. I cornered him… Just like I did a few days later when I threatened to go to the police …
Therapist:	Yes, that could be.
Patient:	I should have stuck it out. Emotionally, I should not have reacted like that.
Therapist (somewhat relieved):	What might that look like, sticking it out?
Patient:	Not making decisions right away. And telling myself: Every feeling can be endured.
	Carola partially regains her mentalizing ability and is supported by the therapist.
Therapist:	Yes, good. How would that work in this situation?
Patient:	I should make a drawing: a red circle for "alarm" and a green circle for "stop" and write: "Press here!" And hang it on my wall in the kitchen.
Therapist (humorously):	Okay. Such a concrete measure can also be useful.

Final Comment

Carola is often in a teleological mode. Gabriel's action is proof for Carola, and only his hesitation counts. Only Gabriel's action shows Carola whether she is being rejected or whether he is (still) connected to her. Her past experiences with him no longer count. Carola cannot change her perspective. Here, positive inner experiences with Gabriel, the fact that he loves her, stands by her, and appreciates her, are kept separate from the current, external, disappointing experiences. Thus, she experiences in the here and now only those external, disappointing parts, which are kept separate (see Figure 6.4). Characteristically, a shift also occurs into the equivalence mode, associated here with paranoid feelings: "It is how I feel it is!" or "I felt threatened = He was stalking me." A mentalizing connection with the other person's world is more difficult in this situation. The reason lies in the high affective charge. Carola seeks this out and defends it via sexuality: Only the affective proof counts! She fails to imagine different perspectives or mentalize feelings by connecting them with her cognitions. The therapist remains somewhat emotionally distant to facilitate mentalizing. He validates and stimulates her exploring her feelings. He tries to move Carola first away from the other person to herself and then later, once mentalization has been restored to some extent, to put herself in Gabriel's place. The therapist brings the cognitive pole into play to facilitate her taking a different perspective. The patient can follow him.

The mentalization problems also become apparent in the external form of the narrative. Carola initially narrates in a very unstructured way, as if everything is clear. Initially, the therapist is therefore concerned with structuring the narrative, finding a focus, and sticking with it. The therapist addresses the psychic equivalence through validation. This allows a new perspective to develop almost by itself. The therapist manages the process but does not prescribe content.

Possible Similarities and Differences to the Psychoanalytic Approach

The therapeutic relationship is a central mediator for change for both the traditional psychoanalyst and the MBT therapist. A relatively stable positive transference characterizes the therapeutic relationship between Carola and the therapist. Prolonged therapeutic work has fostered a trusting relationship that tolerates idealization, disillusionment, and aggression.

This episode contains interpretations by the therapist regarding the topic of sexual experience, linking the understanding of sexual arousal and its interpersonal meaning to the mentalization concept by Fonagy as well as drawing on Laplanche (Fonagy, 2008; Laplanche, 1995; see also Chapter 4.2): The boundaries between self and object are momentarily suspended. High sexual arousal with a partner contains elements of projective identification: I arouse the other, and in turn the identification with the other arouses me. Separation from Gabriel after sex becomes unbearable for Carola in the long run, triggered feelings of emptiness and loneliness, associated with the painful return to oneself.

The traditional psychoanalytic and psychodynamic therapist likely would have tried to achieve insight into Carola's affective dynamics, distorted cognitions, and resulting actions through actualgenetic and genetic interpretations (see Chapter 5.3). Yet, that approach reaches its limits in the treatment of personality disorders. Personality disorders, in contrast to neurotic conflicts, were long considered very difficult or impossible to treat with psychoanalysis. That led to the development of new forms of treatment. Starting with treating BPD, the indication for treating other severe personality disorders has expanded, and the new forms of treatment include dialectical behavior therapy (DBT), TFP, and MBT. They share several common structural features, including active intervention by the therapist to protect the therapeutic relationship, a clear structural framework, limitation of regression, joint determination of treatment focus, and a cooperative agreement on the task and goals of therapy. Commonalities also include psychoeducation, the validation and normalization of feelings by the therapist, and the improvement of affect-regulation strategies.

Of the three forms of treatment, TFP ranks closest to the traditional psychoanalytic treatment concept, since it refers to the classical defense mechanisms and the drive concept. Early defense mechanisms such as splitting, which are interpreted in the transference relationship, stand out in the object relations.

6.5   Summary

The case reports depicted above illustrate the concrete mentalization-oriented procedure, how it can become the leading methodological procedure in psychoanalytic and psychodynamic psychotherapy, and how to integrate it. There are clearly overlaps with classical psychoanalytic approaches, such as the deeper understanding of the treatment process. But there are also differences surrounding the therapist's actions, the structuring of the therapeutic process, the handling of regression, and the particular nature of the interventions. We summarize this again in Chapter 7.

7

Take-Home Message

The following presents and condenses the core ideas of mentalization-oriented work within psychoanalytic therapies. The final chapter (see Chapter 8) refers to the demands that integrating this modified approach makes on the therapist.

The concept of psychotherapy as a threefold communication system (Fonagy et al., 2019) generally involves the following three aspects:

1. the therapist's theory of therapy;
2. improving mentalization;
3. restoring social learning (epistemic trust).

The change model is grounded in therapy research findings (Fonagy et al., 2019) and heralds a paradigm shift. One can apply the model to psychoanalytic therapies, MBT, and all other psychotherapy approaches by positing psychotherapy as a coherent frame of reference that promotes epistemic trust. Social learning reflects the readiness to open up to new, socially mediated experiences and enables cycles of positive interpersonal experiences—even outside the therapeutic relationship.

Epistemic Trust

Epistemic trust is closely related to the development of mentalizing ability. In psychotherapy, it means the patient's willingness to understand the information conveyed by a trustworthy person as relevant and generalizable. Epistemic trust represents a basic trust in information derived from interpersonal communication. It has two parts: First, the information must be relevant to the addressee; second, it must come from a sender who considers the addressee's perspective. In the therapeutic relationship, epistemic trust emerges from the "epistemic match," the fit between patient and therapist.

Mentalized Affectivity

Mentalized affectivity is the central focus of MBT and a central element of any psychoanalytic treatment. Mentalized affectivity creates a psychological buffer

DOI: 10.4324/9781032674117-8

between experience and action. It is an affective understanding gained through experience and cognitions. This process is fraught with defense or resistance mechanisms directed not only against the affective experiences; it is also associated with deficits and inhibitions related to mentalization itself (according to Fonagy & Target, 2003).

The Influence of the Mentalization Concept on Psychoanalytic Theory

The mentalization concept is rooted in psychoanalysis and is compatible with psychoanalytic models of symbolization, representation, and affect regulation. Yet, it modifies the classic view of the unconscious and consciousness by incorporating recent findings from developmental psychology, theory of mind, attachment theory, and anthropological findings. The perspective of mentalization theory has changed the role of sexuality and drive.

Fundamental Changes in Psychodynamic and Psychoanalytic Psychotherapy Because of the Mentalization Concept

The use of mentalization in psychodynamic and psychoanalytic psychotherapy has changed treatment approaches because of the differences in therapeutic attitude, therapeutic framework, and treatment technique. The differences are especially marked regarding treatment technique.

The mentalization concept is strongly related to research. Including psychotherapy research has led to the realization that treatment modification is necessary for structural disorders. This includes limiting regression, allowing a more active attitude on the therapist's part, including psychoeducation, and structuring treatment by the patient and therapist jointly formulating a focus.

Mentalizing in Psychodynamic and Psychoanalytic Psychotherapy – an Integrative Model

The proposed integrative model has a twofold focus:

(1) *the process focus,* characterized by the promotion of mentalization with typical MBT interventions, with attempts to identify feelings, separate feelings from actions, and make new connections between feelings and actions;
(2) *the content focus,* characterized by the therapist's formulations and interpretations of interpersonal conscious and unconscious patterns, especially their affective parts—the focus remains largely on the here and now and is oriented toward psychoanalytic object-relations theories.

According to the integrative model, the therapist's central interventions are no longer interpretations but rather explorations based on an attitude of not-knowing, thereby recognizing mentalizing deficits and promoting effective mentalization. Interpretations of conscious and unconscious patterns represent only the therapist's hypotheses, used sparingly and reflected in the dialog with the patient.

Treatments with a mentalizing focus aim at further developing or building secondary representations and less at making unconscious conflicts conscious.

Nevertheless, regardless of the diagnosis, a mentalizing focus is indicated in psychodynamic and psychoanalytic therapy:

(a) for patients who have structural limitations or severe functional limitations;
(b) for patients with difficulties in affect regulation related to mentalization problems. These difficulties in affect regulation or mentalization may be structural, but they also may be specific to the issue or relationship. This is the case for many patients who enter psychotherapy.

Whereas classical psychoanalysis conceived of insight as the central mechanism of change, MBT emphasizes the promotion of the *capacity for insight* and the promotion of *interest in insightful processes*. Mary Target (2016) provides a single-case account of how to use the mentalization approach to create conditions at the beginning of long-term psychoanalytic therapy so that the patient can benefit from more work focused on inner conflict and transference. Similarly, Vermote et al. (2012) and Lemma et al. (2011) propose models for combining psychoanalytic therapy approaches with the mentalization model.

Practical Implementation

MBT provides a theoretically grounded approach that is more emphatically aligned with psychotherapy research than traditional psychoanalytic treatment approaches. But it also increasingly seeks to make the treatment technique transparent through clinical demonstrations, video recordings, and role-playing. That is why case studies occupy such a large space in this book (see Chapters 3 and 6).

The episodes reported above illustrate a small part of clinical practice. They have a process character, highlighted by the meticulous reporting, and show typical mentalization-based interventions and patient reactions.

8

Instead of a Conclusion

The Mentalizing Skills of Therapists: Consequences for Education and Training

According to the results of psychotherapy research, the effectiveness of psycho-therapy is determined largely by factors shared by all evidence-based treatments, the so-called "common factors" (Laska et al., 2014). Among the common factors, the therapeutic relationship plays a prominent role (Norcross & Wampold, 2011): It directly affects the therapeutic process and is presumably shaped largely by the therapists themselves. That is why therapist variables—such as empathy and "responsiveness," i.e., how much therapists personalize therapies—play such a major role in recent publications. Last but not least, the mentalizing ability of the therapists themselves is crucial (Caspar et al., 2021).

Mentalization-oriented work demands of the therapist an active attitude and the ability to maintain an empathic, validating, and mentalization-challenging stance even in the face of massive failures in the mentalization of one's counterpart. Further, one must be willing to use coregulatory interventions and selective openness to disclose one's own mental processes. Here, neutrality and abstinence refer not to one's own mental processes of communicating and explaining what the patient discloses or how the therapist understands them and the role feelings play in the therapeutic relationship. Therapists are challenged to think about themselves in the interpersonal process and to reflect on their own contribution when cracks occur in the working alliance, to repair them if necessary, and to recognize their own gaps in empathy and mentalization. Thus, MBT therapists must repeatedly leave their comfort zone and work more intensively in the real relationship than the traditional psychoanalyst. In our opinion, this presumes that the therapist can fearlessly (or at least courageously) disclose and explore their own mental processes in the presence of another person. This assumes a certain spontaneity and the ability to repeatedly question oneself, in the sense of constructive professional doubt.

The mentalization concept and MBT are closely related to attachment research. Bowlby (1988, pp. 139–151), the founder of attachment theory, expressed disappointment that his theory had been intensively received in developmental psychology (where much research is still being done) but hardly reflected in

DOI: 10.4324/9781032674117-9

psychotherapy—at least during his lifetime. He assumed that therapists must become a safe haven for their patients before they can use therapy to explore their inner world. This approach leads to the hypothesis that therapists with secure attachment patterns will most likely succeed in becoming such safe havens. Indeed, there is evidence that securely attached therapists generally have a better therapeutic alliance and respond more competently in interpersonally challenging situations. The latter are considered particularly common in treating personality disorders (Dinger et al., 2009; Steel et al., 2018).

In a research project, Talia et al. (2019, 2020) showed that therapists' attachment representations influence how they approach the therapeutic relationship, the additional quality of their interventions, and how they can subtly promote or inhibit epistemic trust. But what distinguishes the interactions of securely attached therapists from those of insecurely attached therapists? In their study of 50 psychodynamically working therapists, Thalia et al. showed that specific communication patterns are associated with attachment representations. They started by observing the moment-to-moment process of the therapists' attunement to their patients' narratives, which in the psychoanalytic literature is also called containment. The focus lay solely on the verbal utterances, though the nonverbal attunement would have also been significant.

a) Securely attached therapists showed three different forms of communication: First, their hypothesis about the patient's experience was open to correction. Second, they made more empathic validations. And third, they openly expressed how they experienced the patients. This coincides with the intervention recommendations according to the mentalization approach. They were developed in the study independently from the mentalization approach and have since been validated for other therapy approaches (Talia et al., 2019).

b) Insecurely avoidant therapists, on the other hand, did not provide their own perspective on their counterpart's experience. Rather, they tended to repeat what was said by the patients and tended to downplay any feelings expressed (e.g., Patient: "I was *pretty* sad that day." Therapist: "So you were *a little* sad.").

c) Insecure ambivalent therapists did demonstrate validating interventions but appeared too certain in their interpretations of the mental states of patients and their significant others (e.g., Patient: "My dad scares me when he gets angry"; Therapist: "Oh, her father is just pretending, he's not really angry at all.").

Regarding communicating how we comprehend ("having mind in mind") and talk about the other person's mental state, attachment-secure communication may best promote epistemic trust because we communicate that we trust the speaker's subjective mode of experience. The attachment-unsafe form of communication, on the other hand, provides feedback to the other person that questions either subjective self-experience (avoidant communication, e.g., trivializing emotions and emphasizing factual content) or the other person's view of their central caregivers (enmeshed communication, e.g., when affect is high, so is the danger of self-object confusion).

This serves to derive recommendations for further training and supervision of therapists (Talia et al., 2019, 2020). That does not mean that attachment-secure therapists are per se the better therapists or even that a change in attachment styles among some therapists is desirable. Individual findings from attachment research cannot be applied in such a one-dimensional way to the personal relationships of all therapists. Nevertheless, it could become an important task to discover and practice attachment-safe forms of communication in one's own communication and reduce attachment-unsafe communication forms. Regardless, what is indispensable is tracing and evaluating the microprocesses of one's own work by recording one's own sessions. Last but not least, it can be helpful for one's self-experience, teaching therapy, and teaching analysis to deal with and become aware of one's attachment representations.

Only future studies can determine to what extent these considerations are also significant regarding therapists' mentalizing skills. In one study (Klasen et al., 2019), therapists had, on average, significantly above-average reflective competence; only in a few individual cases did they display a limited ability to mentalize. This study of psychodynamic and behavioral therapy trainees revealed correlations between limitations in mentalizing and own aversive experiences in their biographies. However, this could be balanced out by adopting intensive self-awareness or therapies before beginning training. We can use the findings of the mentalization-oriented approach to improve psychotherapeutic processes as well as to establish more process-sensitive further training and clarify the importance of self-awareness processes that depend on the respective biographical preconditions.

References

Ainsworth, M. D. S., Blehar, M. C., Waters, E., & Wall, S. (1978). *Patterns of Attachment: A Psychological Study of the Strange Situation*. Hillsdale, NJ: Erlbaum.

Allen J. G. & Fonagy P. (2006). *Handbook of Mentalization-Based Treatment*. Chichester: J. Wiley & Sons.

Allen, J. G., Fonagy, P., & Bateman, A. W. (2008). *Mentalizing in Clinical Practice*. Washington, DC: American Psychiatric Publishing.

Altmeyer, M. & Thomä, H. (Eds.) (2016). *Die vernetzte Seele: Die intersubjektive Wende in der Psychoanalyse*. 3rd ed. Stuttgart: Klett-Cotta.

American Psychiatric Association. (2013). *Diagnostic and Statistical Manual of Mental Disorders*. 5th ed. https://doi.org/10.1176/appi.books.9780890425596.

Bales, D. & Bateman, A. W. (2012). Partial hospitalization settings. In A. Bateman & P. Fonagy (Eds.) *Handbook of Mentalizing in Mental Health Practice*. Washington, DC: American Psychiatric Association Publishing, pp. 197–226.

Balint, M. (1968). *The Basic Fault: Therapeutic Aspects of Regression*. London: Tavistock.

Bartholomew, K. & Horowitz, L. M. (1991). Attachment styles among young adults: A test of four-category model. *Journal of Personality and Social Psychology* 61(2), 226–244.

Bateman A. W. (2011). Commentary on 'Minding the difficult patient': Mentalizing and the use of formulation in patients with borderline personality disorder comorbid with antisocial personality disorder. *Personality & Mental Health* 5(1), 85–90

Bateman, A. W. (2020). Mentalization-based treatment: Training workshop. https://www.annafreud.org/media/12141/basic-training-theory-and-clinical-january-2020-no-video.pdf.

Bateman, A. W. & Fonagy, P. (2004). *Psychotherapy for Borderline Personality Disorder: Mentalization-Based Treatment*. Oxford: Oxford University Press.

Bateman, A. & Fonagy, P. (Eds.) (2012). *Handbook of Mentalizing in Mental Health Practice*. Washington, DC: American Psychiatric Association Publishing.

Bateman, A. & Fonagy, P. (2016). *Mentalization-Based Treatment for Personality Disorders –A Practical Guide*. Oxford: Oxford University Press.

Bateman, A. & Fonagy, P. (Eds.) (2019). *Handbook of Mentalizing in Mental Health Practice*. 2nd ed. Washington, DC: American Psychiatric Association Publishing.

Bateman, A., Unruh, B., & Fonagy, P. (2019). Individual therapy techniques. In A. Bateman, & P. Fonagy (Eds.) *Handbook of Mentalizing in Mental Health Practice*. 2nd ed. Washington, DC: American Psychiatric Association Publishing, pp. 103–115.

Bender, D. S., Morey, L. C., & Skodol, A. E. (2011). Toward a model for assessing level of personality functioning in DSM-5, part I: A review of theory and methods. *Journal of Personality Assessment.* https://doi.org/10.1080/00223891.2011.583808.

Benjamin, J. (2009). A relational psychoanalysis perspective on the necessity of acknowledging failure in order to restore the facilitating and containing features of the intersubjective relationship (The Shared Third). *International Journal of PsychoAnalysis* 90, 441–450.

Bernfeld, S. (1973). *Sisyphus or the Limits of Education.* Berkeley, CA: University of California Press.

Bion, W. R. (1962). *Learning from Experience.* London: Heinemann

Bion, W. R. (1970). *Attention and Interpretation.* London: Tavistock.

Böckler-Raettig, A. (2019). *Theory of Mind.* Munich: Ernst Reinhardt

Bohart, A. & Wade, A. (2013). The client in psychotherapy. In M. Lambert (Ed.) *Handbook of Psychotherapy and Behavior Change.* 6th ed. Hoboken, NJ: John Wiley & Sons, pp. 219–257.

Bordin, E. S. (1979). The generalizability of the psychoanalytic concept of the working alliance. *Psychotherapy: Theory, Research, Practice, Training* 16(3), 252–260. https://doi.org/10.1037/h0085885.

Bowlby, J. (1969). *Attachment and Loss*, Vol. 1 *Attachment.* New York: Basic Books.

Bowlby, J. (1973) *Attachment and Loss*, Vol. 2 *Separation, Anxiety and Anger.* New York: Basic Books.

Bowlby, J. (1981). Psychoanalysis as natural science. *The International Review of Psycho-Analysis* 8, 243–255.

Bowlby J. (1982) *Loss Sadness and Separation.* New York: Basic Books.

Bowlby, J. (1984). Violence in the family as a disorder of the attachment and caregiving systems. *Journal of the American Psychoanalytic Association* 44(1), 9–27, 29–31

Bowlby, J. (1988). *A Secure Base: Clinical Application of Attachment Theory.* London: Routledge.

Bram, A. & Gabbard, G. (2001). Potential space and reflective functioning. *The International Journal of Psycho-Analysis* 82, 685–746.

Brand, T., Hecke, D., Rietz, C., & Schultz-Venrath, U. (2016). Therapieeffekte mentalisie-rungsbasierter und psychodynamischer Gruppenpsychotherapie in einer randomisierten Tagesklinik-Studie. *Gruppenpsychotherapie und Gruppendynamik* 52(2), 156–174. https://doi.org/10.13109/grup.2016.52.2.156.

Brauner, F. (2018). *Mentalisieren und Fremdenfeindlichkeit.* Gießen: Psychosozial-Verlag.

Breuer J. & Freud S. (2004 [1895]). *Studies in Hysteria.* Translated by Nicola Luckhurst. London: Penguin Books. German: (1895). *Studien zur Hysterie.* Leipzig/Wien: Franz Deuticke.

Brink, K. A., Lane J. D., & Wellmann H. M. (2015). Developmental pathways for social understanding: Linking social cognition to social contexts. *Frontiers in Psychology* 6, 719.

Britton, R. (1998). *Belief and Imagination: Explorations in Psychoanalysis.* London: Routledge.

Britton R (2000). The Nettle. Paper presented at the Annual Research Lecture of the British Psychoanalytical Society on March 1.

Brockman, J. (1995). *The Third Culture: Beyond the Scientific Revolution.* New York: Simon & Schuster.

Brockmann, J., Kirsch, H., Dembler, K., König, D., de Vries, I., Wancke, C. U., & Zabolitzki, M. (2017). "Mr K" – A successful case of analytic oriented therapy documented empirically:

The role of the therapeutic relationship and reflexive self-awareness. *Psychoanalytic Psychotherapy.* http://dx.doi.org/10.1080/02668734.2016.1264454.

Brockmann, J., Kirsch, H., Hatcher, R., Andreas, S., Benz, S., & Sammet, I. (2011). [Dimensions of the therapeutic alliance from patients' view-development of the "Skala Therapeutische Allianz-Revised STA-R"]. *Psychotherapie, Psychosomatik, Medizinische Psychologie* 61(5), 208–215. doi:10.1055/s-0030–1263142.

Buchholz, M. B. (2006). Konversation, erzählung, metapher. In M. Altmeyer & H. Thomä (Eds.) *Die vernetzte Seele.* Stuttgart: Klett-Cotta, pp. 282–313.

Buchholz, M. B. (2014). Peter Fonagy und die Mentalisierung. In G. Gödde & J. Zirfas (Eds.) *Lebenskunst im 20. Jahrhundert. Stimmen von Philosophen, Künstlern und Therapeuten.* Paderborn: Wilhelm Fink, pp. 353–372.

Calkins, S. D. & Hill, A. (2007). Caregiver influences on emerging emotion regulation: Biological and environmental transactions in early development. In J. J. Gross (Ed.) *Handbook of Emotion Regulation.* New York: Guilford Press, pp. 229–248

Calvo, N., Valero, S., Sáez-Francàs, N., Gutiérrez, F., Casas, M., & Ferrer, M. (2016). Borderline Personality Disorder and Personality Inventory for DSM-5 (PID-5): Dimensional personality assessment with DSM-5. *Comprehensive Psychiatry* 70: 105–111. doi:10.1016/j.comppsych.2016.07.002. Epub 2016 Jul 5. PMID: 27624429.

Campagna, R. L., Dirks, K. T., Knight, A. P., Crossley, C., & Robinson, S. L. (2019). On the relation between felt trust and actual trust: Examining pathways to and implications of leader trust meta-accuracy. *Journal of Applied Psychology.* Advance online publication. https://doi.org/10.1037/apl0000474.

Carcione, A., Dimaggio, G., Fiore, D., Nicolo, G., Procacci, M., Semerari. A., & Pedone, R. (2008). An intensive case analysis of client metacognition in a good-outcome psycho- therapy: Lisa's case. *Psychotherapy Research* 18, 667–676. doi:10.1080/10503300802 2 20132.

Carroll, L. (1865 [2015]). *Alice's Adventures in Wonderland.* London: Walker Books.

Caspar, F., Deisenhofer, A. K., Evers, O., Laireiter, A. R., Lutz, W., Prinz, J., Rief, W., Strauß, B., & Taubner, S. (2021). Psychotherapeutische Kompetenzen. In W. Rief, E. Schramm, & B. Strauß (Eds.) *Psychotherapie – Ein kompetenzorientiertes Lehrbuch.* Munich: Elsevier, pp. 3–30.

Caspi, A., Houts, R. M., Belsky, D. W., Goldman-Mellor, S. J., Harrington, H., Salomon, I., [...] & Moffitt, T. E. (2014). The p factor: One general psychopathology factor in the structure of psychiatric disorders? *Clinical Psychological Science* 2, 119–137.

Castonguay, L. G. & Beutler, L. E. (2005). *Principles of Therapeutic Change That Work.* Oxford: Oxford University Press. https://doi.org/10.1093/med:psych/9780195156843.001.0001.

Castonguay, L. G., Eubanks, C. F., Goldfried, M. R., Muran, J. C., & Lutz, W. (2015). Research on psychotherapy integration: Building on the past, looking to the future. *Psychotherapy Research* 25(3), 365–382. https://doi.org/10.1080/10503307.2015.1014010.

Chambless, D. L. & Hollon, S. D. (1998). Defining empirically supported therapies. *Journal of Consulting and Clinical Psychology* 66(1), 7–18. https://doi.org/10.1037/0022–006X.66.1.7.

Choi-Kain, L. W. & Gunderson, J. G. (2008). Mentalization: Ontogeny, assessment, and application in the treatment of borderline personality disorder. *American Journal of Psychiatry* 165(9), 1127–1135.

Collyer, H., Eisler, I., & Woolgar, M. (2020). Systematic literature review and meta-analysis of the relationship between adherence, competence and outcome in psychotherapy for children and adolescents. *European Child & Adolescent Psychiatry* 29(4), 417–431. https://doi.org/10.1007/s00787-018-1265-2.

Csibra, G. & Gergely. G. (1998). The teleological origins of mentalistic action explanations: A developmental hypothesis. *Development Science* 1, 255–259

Csibra, G. & Gergely, G. (2009). Natural pedagogy. *Trends in Cognitive Sciences* 13, 148–153

Csibra, G. & Gergely, G. (2011). Natural pedagogy as an evolutionary adaptation. *Philosophical Transactions of the Royal Society of London*. Series B, Biological Sciences 366(1567), 1149–1157. doi:10.1098/rstb.2010.031.

Cuijpers, P., Geraedts, A. S., van Oppen, P., Andersson, G., Markowitz, J. C., & van Straten, A. (2011). Interpersonal psychotherapy for depression: A meta-analysis. *The American Journal of Psychiatry* 168(6), 581–592. https://doi.org/10.1176/appi. ajp.2010.10101411.

Cuijpers, P., Reijnders, M., & Huibers, M. J. H. (2019). The role of common factors in psychotherapy outcomes. *Annual Review of Clinical Psychology* 15, 207–231. https://doi. org/10.1146/annurev-clinpsy-050718-095424.

Dennett, D. (1987). *The Intentional Stance*. Cambridge, MA: MIT Press

DeRubeis, R. J., Brotman, M. A., & Gibbons, C. J. (2005). A conceptual and methodological analysis of the nonspecifics argument. *Clinical Psychology: Science and Practice* 12(2), 174–183. https://doi.org/10.1093/clipsy.bpi022.

Devine, R. T. & Hughes, C. (2018). Family correlates of false belief understanding in early childhood: A meta-analysis. *Child Development* 89(3), 971–987.

Dinger, U., Strack, M., Sachsse, T., & Schauenburg, H. (2009). Therapists' attachment, patients' interpersonal problems and alliance development over time in inpatient psychotherapy. *Psychotherapy: Theory, Research, Practice, Training* 46(3), 277.

Dornes, M. (1992). *Der kompetente Säugling: Die präverbale Entwicklung des Menschen*. Frankfurt am Main: Fischer TB.

Dornes, M. (1997). *Die frühe Kindheit*. Frankfurt am Main: Fischer TB.

Dornes, M. (2000). *Die emotionale Welt des Kindes*. Frankfurt am Main: Fischer TB.

Duschinsky, R., Collver, J., & Carel, H. (2019). "Trust comes from a sense of feeling one's self understood by another mind": An interview with Peter Fonagy. *Psychoanalytic Psychology* 36(3), 224–227. https://doi.org/10.1037/pap000024.

Ekeblad, A., Falkenström, F., & Holmqvist, R. (2016). Reflective functioning as predictor of working alliance and outcome in the treatment of depression. *Journal of Consulting and Clinical Psychology* 84(1), 67–78. https://doi.org/10.1037/ccp0000055.

Fain, M. & David, C. (1963). Aspects fonctionnels de la vie oririque. *Revue Française de Psychoanalyse* 27, 241–243.

Fain, M. & Marty, P. (1964). Perspective psychosomatique sur la function des fantasmes. *Revue Française de Psychoanalyse* 28, 609–622.

Fairbairn, W. (1952). *Psychoanalytical Studies of the Personality*. London: Routledge.

Fearon, P., Target, M., Fonagy, P., Williams, L. L., Mc Gregor, J., Sargent, J., & Bleiberg, E. (2006). Short-Term Mentalization and Relational Therapy (SMART). In J. G. Allen & P. Fonagy (Eds.) *Handbook of Mentalization-Based Treatment*. Chichester: J. Wiley & Sons.

Fonagy, P. (1988). Psychodynamic theory. In A. S. Bellak & M. Hersen (Eds.) *Comprehensive Clinical Psychology*, Vol. 1, pp. 423–447. doi.org/10.1016/ B0080–4270(73)00182-6.

Fonagy, P. (1989). On tolerating mental states: Theory of mind in borderline patients. *Bulletin of the Anna Freud Center* 12, 91–115.

Fonagy, P. (1991). Thinking about thinking: Some clinical and theoretical considerations in the treatment of a borderline patient. *The International Journal of Psychoanalysis* 72, 639–656.

Fonagy, P. (1995). Playing with reality: The development of psychic reality and its malfunction in borderline patients. *The International Journal of Psychoanalysis* 72, 1–18.

Fonagy, P. (1999a). Memory and therapeutic action. *The International Journal of Psychoanalysis* 80(2), 215–223.

Fonagy, P. (1999b). The relation of theory and practice in psychodynamic therapy. *Journal of Clinical Child Psychology* 28, 513–520.

Fonagy, P. (2001). *Attachment Theory and Psychoanalysis* (1st ed.). London: Routledge. https://doi.org/10.4324/9780429472060.

Fonagy P. (2008). A genuinely developmental theory of sexual enjoyment and its implications for psychoanalytic technique. *Journal of the American Psychoanalytic Association* 56(1), 11–36.

Fonagy, P. (2015) Psychotherapy for emerging borderline personality disorder. https://www.escap.eu/uploads/Events/Madrid%202015/peter-fonagy-escap-presentation.pdf.

Fonagy, P. & Allison, E. (2014). The role of mentalizing and epistemic trust in the therapeutic relationship. *Psychotherapy* 51(3), 372–380.

Fonagy, P. & Allison, E. (2015). A scientific theory of homosexuality for psychoanalysis. In A. Lemma & P. E. Lynch (Eds.) *Sexualities: Contemporary Psychoanalytic Perspectives.* London: Routledge.

Fonagy, P. & Allison, E. (2016). Psychic reality and the nature of consciousness. *International Journal of Psychoanalysis* 97, 5–24. doi:10.1111/1745-8315.12403.

Fonagy, P., Campbell, C., & Allison, E. (2019). Therapeutic Models. In A. Bateman & P. Fonagy (Eds.) *Handbook of Mentalizing in Mental Health Practice.* 2nd ed. Washington, DC: American Psychiatric Association Publishing, pp. 169–180.

Fonagy, P., Campbell, S., & Bateman, A. (2017). Mentalizing, attachment, and epistemic trust in group therapy. *International Journal of Group Psychotherapy* 67, 176–201. doi:10.180/00207284.2016. 1263156.

Fonagy, P. & Cooper, A. (1999). Joseph Sandler's intellectual contributions to theoretical and clinical psychoanalysis. In P. Fonagy, A. Cooper, & R. Wallerstein (Eds.) *Psychoanalysis on the Move: The Work of Joseph Sandler.* London: Routledge, pp. 1–29.

Fonagy, P., Gergely, G., Jurist, E., & Target, M. (2002). *Affect Regulation, Mentalization, and the Development of the Self.* New York: Other Press.

Fonagy, P. & Luyten, P. (2009). A developmental, mentalization-based approach to the understanding and treatment of borderline personality disorder. *Development and Psychopathology* 21(4), 1355–1381.

Fonagy, P. & Luyten, P. (2016). A multilevel perspective on the development of borderline personality disorder. In D. Cicchetti (Ed.) *Developmental psychopathology: Maladaptation and Psychopathology.* 3rd ed. Hoboken, NJ: John Wiley & Sons, pp. 726–792.

Fonagy, P., Luyten, P., & Allison, E. (2015). Epistemic petrification and the restoration of epistemic trust: A new conceptualization of borderline personality disorder and its psychosocial treatment. *Journal of Personality Disorders* 29(5), 575–609. 10.1521/pedi.2015.29.5.575.

Fonagy, P., Luyten, P., Allison, E., & Campbell, C. (2017a). What we have changed our minds about: Part 1. Borderline personality disorder as a limitation of resilience. *Borderline Personality Disorder and Emotion Dysregulation* 4(11). https://doi.org/10.1186/s40479-017-0061-9.

Fonagy, P., Luyten, P., Allison, E., & Campbell, C. (2017b). What we have changed our minds about: Part 2. Borderline personality disorder, epistemic trust and the developmental significance of social communication. *Borderline Personality Disorder and Emotion Dysregulation* 4(9). https://doi.org/10.1186/s40479-017-0062-8.

Fonagy, P., Moran, G. S., Steele, H., & Higgit, A. (1993). Measuring the Ghost in the nursery. *Journal of the American Psychoanalytic Association* 41, 957–989.

Fonagy, P., Moran, G. S., Steele, H., & Steele, M. (1992). The integration of psychoanalytic theory and work on attachment. In D. Stern & M. Ammaniti (Eds.) *Attacamento e Psiconais*. Bari: Laterza.

Fonagy, P., Steele, M., Moran, G. S., Steele, H., & Higgit, A. (1991). Maternal representations of attachment during pregnancy predict the organization of infant–mother attachment at one year of age. *Child Development* 62, 891–905.

Fonagy, P. & Target, M. (1995). Understanding the violent patient: The use of the body and the role of the father. *International Journal of Psycho-Analysis* 76, 487–501.

Fonagy, P. & Target, M. (1996a). Playing with reality I: Theory of mind and the normal development of psychic reality. *International Journal of Psycho-Analysis* 77, 217–233.

Fonagy, P. & Target, M. (1996b). Playing with reality II: The development of psychic reality from a theoretical perspective. *International Journal of Psycho-Analysis* 77, 459–479.

Fonagy, P. & Target, M. (1997). Attachment and reflective function: Their role in self-organization. *Development and Psychopathology* 9, 679–700.

Fonagy, P. & Target, M. (2000). Playing with reality: III. The persistence of dual psychic reality in borderline patients. *International Journal of Psycho-Analysis* 81(5), 853–874.

Fonagy, P. & Target, M. (2002) Early interventions and the development of self-regulation. *Psychoanalytic Inquiry* 22(3) 307–335. doi:10.1080/07351692209348990.

Fonagy, P. & Target, M. (2003) *Psychoanalytic Theories – Perspectives from Development and Psychopathology*. London: Whurr.

Fonagy, P. & Target, M. (2007a). Playing with reality: IV. A theory of external reality rooted in intersubjectivity. *The International Journal of Psycho-Analysis* 88(4), 917–937.

Fonagy, P. & Target, M. (2007b). The rooting of the mind in the body: New links between attachment theory and psychoanalytic thought. *Journal of the American Psychoanalytic Association* 55(2), 411–456.

Fonagy, P., Target, M., Steele, H., & Steele, M. (1998). *Reflective Functioning Manual: Version 5.0 for Application to Adult Attachment Interviews*. London: University College

Förstl, H. (Ed.) (2012). *Theory of Mind*. 2nd ed. Heidelberg: Springer.

Freud, S. (1910). *"Wild" Psycho-analysis. The Standard Edition of the Complete Psychological Works of Sigmund Freud*, Volume XI: *Five Lectures on Psycho-Analysis, Leonardo da Vinci and Other Works*. London: Hogarth Press.

Freud, S. (1912). The dynamics of transference. *The Standard Edition of the Complete Psychological Works of Sigmund Freud*, Volume XII: *The Case of Schreber, Papers on Technique and Other Works*. London: Hogarth Press, pp. 97–108.

Freud, S. (1925). Formulations on the two principles of mental functioning. *The Standard Edition of the Complete Psychological Works of Sigmund Freud*, Volume XII: *The Case of Schreber, Papers on Technique and Other Works*. London: Hogarth Press, pp. 218–226.

Freud, S. (1926). Inhibitions, symptoms and anxiety. *The Standard Edition of the Complete Psychological Works of Sigmund Freud*, Volume XX: *An Autobiographical Study, Inhibitions, Symptoms and Anxiety, The Question of Lay Analysis and Other Works*. London: Hogarth Press, pp. 77–175.

Frith, U. (1989). *Autism: Explaining the Enigma*. Oxford: Blackwell.

Gilead, M. & Ochsner, K. N. (Eds.) (2021). *The Neural Basis of Mentalizing*. Cham: Springer Nature.

Gödde, G. (2018). *Mit dem Unbewussten arbeiten*. Göttingen: Vandenhoeck & Ruprecht.

Gödde, G. & Buchholz, M. B. (2011). *Unbewusstes*. Gießen: Psychosozial-Verlag.

Goethe, J. W. (1985). *Sämtliche Werke. Briefe. Tagebücher und Gespräche.* Frankfurter Ausgabe. Deutscher Klassiker, Frankfurt am Main.

Goldfried, M. R. & Davila, J. (2005). The role of relationship and technique in therapeutic change. *Psychotherapy: Theory, Research, Practice, Training*, 42(4), 421–430. https://doi. org/10.1037/0033–3204.42.4.421.

Green, A. (1998). Primordial mind and the work of the negative. *International Journal of Psychoanalysis* 79(4), 649–665.

Greenberg, D. M., Kolasi, J., Hegsted, C. P., Berkowitz. Y., & Jurist, E. L. (2017). Mentalized affectivity: A new model and assessment of emotion regulation. *PLoS ONE* 12(10): e0185264. https://doi.org/10.1371/journal.pone.0185264.

Gross, J. J. & Jazaieri, H. (2014). Emotion, emotion regulation, and psychopathology: An affective science perspective. *Clinical Psychological Science* 214, 387–401

Grove, P. & Smith, E. (2022). A framework for MBT formulations: The narrative formulation and MBT passport. *Journal of Contemporary Psychotherapy*. https://doi.org/10.1007/s10879-022-09531-0.

Habermas, J. (1984). *The Theory of Communicative Actions*. Boston: Beacon Press.

Habermas, J. (2009). Es beginnt mit dem Zeigefinger. (It started with the index finger.) *Die Zeit*, December 10.

Haslam-Hopwood, G. T. G., Allen, J. G., Stein, A., & Bleiberg, E. (2006). Enhancing mentalizing through psycho-education. In J. G. Allen & P. Fonagy (Eds.) *Handbook of Mentalization-Based Treatment*. Chichester: J. Wiley & Sons, pp. 249–269.

Herzog, D. (2015). What happened to psychoanalysis in the wake of the sexual revolution?

In A. Lemma & P. E. Lynch (Eds.) *Sexualities: Contemporary Psychoanalytic Perspectives*. London: Routledge.

Hoffman, I. Z. (2004). Miss A – Commentary 2. *The International Journal of Psychoanalysis* 85, 817–822.

Hoffman, I. Z. (2009). Doublethinking our way to "scientific" legitimacy: The desiccation of human experience. *Journal of the American Psychoanalytic Association* 57(5), 1043–1069.

Honneth, A. (2012). *The I in the We: Studies in the Theory of Recognition*. Cambridge: Polity.

Imuta, K., Henry, J. D., Slaughter, V., Selcuk, B., & Ruffman, T. (2016). Theory of mind and prosocial behavior in childhood: A meta-analytic review. *Developmental Psychology* 52(8), 1192–1205.

Jennissen, S., Huber, J., Ehrenthal, J. C., Schauenburg, H., & Dinger, U. (2018). Association between insight and outcome of psychotherapy: Systematic review and meta-analysis. *American Journal of Psychiatry* 175, 961–969. doi:10.1176/appi.ajp.2018.17080847.

Jørgensen, M. S., Bo, S., Vestergaard, M., Storebø, O. J., Sharp, C., & Simonsen, E. (2021). Predictors of dropout among adolescents with borderline personality disorder attending mentalization-based group treatment. *Psychotherapy Research*, 1–12. https://doi.org/10.1080/10503307.2020.1871525.

Jurist, E. (2018). *Minding Emotions – Cultivating Mentalization in Psychotherapy*. New York: Guilford Press.

Katznelson, H. (2014). Reflective functioning: A review. *Clinical Psychology Review* 34(2), 107–117. https://doi.org/10.1016/j.cpr.2013.12.003.

Katznelson, H., Falkenström, F., Daniel, S. I. F., Lunn, S., Folke, S., Pedersen, S. H., & Poulsen, S. (2020). Reflective functioning, psychotherapeutic alliance, and outcome in two psychotherapies for bulimia nervosa. *Psychotherapy: Theory, Research, Practice, Training*, 57(2), 129–140. https://doi.org/10.1037/pst0000245.

Keller, H. (2022). *The Myth of Attachment Theory: A Critical Understanding for Multicultural Societies*. London: Routledge.

Kernberg, O. (1980). *Internal World and External Reality: Object Relations Theory Applied*. New York: Jason Aronson.

Kernberg, O. (2006). The pressing need to increase research in and on psychoanalysis. *The International Journal of Psychoanalysis* 87(4), 919–926. doi:10.1516/46N7-ULAM-DQKR-VGRT.

Kernberg, O. F. (2012). Suicide prevention for psychoanalytic institutes and societies. *Journal of the American Psychoanalytic Association* 60(4): 707–719. doi:10.1177/0003065112449861.

Kinsey, A., Pomeroy, W., & Martin, C. (1948). *Sexual Behavior in the Human Male*. Philadelphia: Saunders.

Kinsey, A., Pomeroy, W., Martin, C., & Gebhard, P. (1953). *Sexual Behavior in the Human Female*. Philadelphia: Saunders.

Kirsch, H. (2019) Der Zeigefinger oder die Entwicklung sozialer Kognitionen. Zschr. Individualpsychol 44: 286-198.

Kivity, Y., Levy, K. N., Wasserman, R. H., Beeney, J. E., Meehan, K. B., & Clarkin, J. F. (2019). Conformity to prototypical therapeutic principles and its relation with change in reflective functioning in three treatments for borderline personality disorder. *Journal of Consulting and Clinical Psychology* 87(11), 975–988. https://doi.org/10.1037/ccp0000445.

Klasen, J., Nolte, T., Möller, H., & Taubner, S. (2019). Aversive Kindheitserfahrungen, Bindungsrepräsentationen und Mentalisierungsfähigkeit von Psychotherapeuten in Ausbildung. *Zeitschrift für Psychosomatische Medizin und Psychotherapie* 65(4), 353–371. doi:10.13109/zptm.2019.65.4.353.

Klein, M. (1952). *Some Theoretical Conclusions Regarding the Emotional Life of the Infant. Envy and Gratitude and Other Works 1946–1963*. London: Hogarth Press and the Institute of Psycho-Analysis (published 1975).

Klüwer, R. (1995). *Studien zur Fokaltherapie*. Frankfurt am Main: Suhrkamp.

Klüwer, R. (2004). Das Konzept Fokus im Psychoanalytischen Denken. In R. Klüwer & R. Lachauer (Eds.) *Der Fokus: Perspektiven für die Zukunft*. Göttingen: Vandenhoeck & Ruprecht, pp. 20–37.

Kohut, H. (1971). *The Analysis of the Self*. New York: International Universities.

Kohut, H. (1984). *How Does Analysis Cure?* Chicago: University of Chicago Press.

Körner, J. (1989). Arbeit an der Übertragung? Arbeit in der Übertragung! *Forum der Psychoanalyse* 5, 209–223.

Kosugi, M. & Yamagishi, T. (1998). General trust and judgments of trustworthiness. *The Japanese Journal of Psychology*, 69, 349–357.

Kuipers, G. S., Hollander, S. den, van der Ark, L. A., & Bekker, M. H. J. (2017). Recovery from eating disorder 1 year after start of treatment is related to better mentalization and strong reduction of sensitivity to others. *Eating and Weight Disorders* 22(3), 535–547. https://doi.org/10.1007/s40519-017-0405-x.

Lambert, M. J. (2013). The efficacy and effectiveness of psychotherapy. In M. J. Lambert, (Ed.). *Bergin and Garfield's Handbook of Psychotherapy and Behavior Change*. Hoboken, NJ: John Wiley & Sons, pp. 169–218.

Laplanche, J. (1995). Seduction, persecution, revelation. *The International Journal of Psychoanalysis* 76, 663–682.

Laplanche J. (1997). The theory of seduction and the problem of the other. *The International Journal of Psychoanalysis* 78(4), 653–666.

Laplanche, J. & Pontalis, J.-B. (1967). *The Language of Psychoanalysis*. 1st ed. London: Routledge. https://doi.org/10.4324/9780429482243.

Laplanche, J. & Pontalis, J.-B. (1968). Fantasy and the origins of sexuality. *The International Journal of Psychoanalysis* 49, 1–19.

Laska, K., Gurman, A., & Wampold, B. (2014). Expanding the lens of evidence-based practice in psychotherapy: A common factors perspective. *Psychotherapy* 51, 467–481. doi:10.1037/a0034332.

Lebovici, S. (1967). Intervention du Dr S. Lebovici: Prononcée à la séance plénière du XXIVe Congrès international de Psychanalyse, Amsterdam, 1965, après les interventions des discutants et les rapports des discussions dans les groupes linguistiques. *Revue Française de Psychoanalyse* 30, 569–572.

Lecours, S. & Bouchard, M.-A. (1997). Dimensions of Mentalisation: Outlining levels of psychic transformation. *The International Journal of Psychoanalysis* 78, 855–875.

Lemma, A. & Johnson, J. (2010). Editorial. *Psychoanalytic Psychotherapy: Applications, Theory, and Research* 24(3), 179–182.

Lemma, A. & Lynch, P. E. (Eds.) (2015) *Sexualities: Contemporary Psychoanalytic Perspectives*. London: Routledge.

Lemma, A., Target, M., & Fonagy, P. (2011). *Brief Dynamic Interpersonal Therapy. A Clinican's Guide*. New York: Oxford University Press.

Loewald, H. W. (1973). On internalization. In *Papers on Psychoanalysis*. New Haven, CT: Yale University Press, pp. 69–86

Luquet, P. (1981). Le changement dans la mentalisation. *Revue française de psychanalyse* 45, 1023–1028.

Luquet, P. (1987). *Langage, pensée et structure psychique. Première Partie: De la pensée au langage*. Paris: Société Psychanalytique de Paris.

Luyten, P. & Fonagy, P. (2019) Mentalizing and Trauma. In A. Bateman & P. Fonagy (Eds.) *Handbook of Mentalizing in Mental Health Practice*. 2nd ed. Washington, DC: American Psychiatric Association Publishing, pp. 79–102

Luyten, P., Fonagy, P., Lowyck, B., & Vermote, R. (2012). Assessment of mentalization. In A. W. Bateman & P. Fonagy (Ed.) *Handbook of Mentalizing in Mental Health Practice*. Washington, DC: American Psychiatric Publishing, pp. 43–65.

Luyten, P., Meulemeester, C. De, & Fonagy, P. (2021). The self-other distinction in psycho- pathology: Recent developments from a mentalizing perspective. In M. Gilead & K. N. Ochsner (Eds.) *The Neural Bases of Mentalizing*. Cham: Springer International Publishing.

Main, M. (1991). Metacognitive knowledge, metacognitive monitoring, and singular (coherent) vs. multiple (incoherent) model of attachment: findings and directions for future research. In C. M. Parkes, J. Stevenson-Hinde, & P. Marris (Eds.) *Attachment Across the Life Cycle*. London: Routledge

Main, M. & Goldwyn, R. (1996). *Adult Attachment Classification System*. Berkeley, CA: University of California, Department of Psychology.

Marty, P. (1990). *La psychosomatique der l'adulte*. Paris: Presses Universitaires France.

Masters, W. H. & Johnson, V. E. (1966). *Human Sexual Response*. Boston: Little Brown.

Mayes, L. C. (2000). A developmental perspective on regulation of arousal states. *Seminars in Perinatology* 24, 267–279.

Mayes, L. C. (2006). Arousal regulation, emotional flexibility, medial amygdala function, and the impact of early experience: Comments on the paper of Lewis et al. *Annals of the New York Academy of Sciences* 1094(1), 178–192.

MBT Adherence and Competence Scale (2019). https://www.annafreud.org/media/12348/acs-scoring-template-rating-mbt-group-or-individual-session.pdf.

McDermott, V. A. (2003). Is free association still fundamental? *Journal of the American Psychoanalytic Association* 51, 1349–1356.

Menninger, K. A. & Holzman, P. S. (1958). *Theory of Psychoanalytic Technique*. New York: Basic Books.

Mentzos, S. (2017). *Lehrbuch der Psychodynamik*. 8. unveränderte Aufl. Göttingen: Vandenhoeck & Ruprecht.

Mertens, W. (2012). *Psychoanalytische Schulen im Gespräch, Bd. 3: Psychoanalytische Bindungstheorie und moderne Kleinkindforschung*. Bern: Huber.

Mertens, W. (2015). *Psychoanalytische Behandlungstechnik – Konzepte und Themen psychoanalytisch begründeter Behandlungsverfahren*. Stuttgart: Kohlhammer.

Meulemeester, C. de, Vansteelandt, K., Luyten, P., & Lowyck, B. (2018). Mentalizing as a mechanism of change in the treatment of patients with borderline personality disorder: A parallel process growth modeling approach. *Personality Disorders*, 9(1), 22–29. https://doi.org/10.1037/per0000256

Mitchell, S. (1988). *Relational Concepts in Psychoanalysis: An Integration*. Cambridge, MA: Harvard University Press.

Mitchell, S (2000). *Relationality: From Attachment to Intersubjectivity*. New York: Routledge.

Michell, S. & Black, M. (1995). *Freud and Beyond: A History of Modern Psychoanalytic Thought*. New York: Basic Books.

Mitmansgruber, H. (2020). Die "neue" Borderline-Persönlichkeitsstörung: Dimensionale Klassifikation im DSM-5 und ICD-11. *Psychotherapie Forum* 24, 89–99. https://doi.org/10.1007/s00729-020-00151-4.

Möller, C., Karlgren, L., Sandell, A., Falkenström, F., & Philips, B. (2017). Mentalization-based therapy adherence and competence stimulates in-session mentalization in psychotherapy for borderline personality disorder with co-morbid substance dependence. *Psychotherapy Research*, 27(6), 749–765. https://doi.org/10.1080/10503307.2016.1158433.

Norcross, J. C. (2010). The therapeutic relationship. In B. L. Duncan, S. D. Miller, B. E. Wampold, & M. A. Hubble (Ed.) *The Heart and Soul of Change: Delivering What Works in Therapy*. 2nd ed. Washington, DC: American Psychological Association, pp. 113–141.

Norcross, J. C. & Lambert, M. J. (Ed.). (2019a). *Psychotherapy Relationships that Work*. Oxford: Oxford University Press.

Norcross, J. C. & Lambert, M. J. (2019b). What works in the psychotherapy relationship: Results, conclusions, and practices. In J. C. Norcross & M. J. Lambert (Eds.) *Psychotherapy Relationships that Work*. Oxford: Oxford University Press, pp. 631–646. https://doi.org/10.1093/med-psych/9780190843953.003.0018.

Norcross, J. C. & Wampold, B. E. (2011). Evidence-based therapy relationships: Research conclusions and clinical practices. *Psychotherapy* 48(1), 98–102. doi:10.1037/ a0022161.

Norcross, J. C. & Wampold, B. E. (Ed.) (2019). *Psychotherapy Relationships That Work*. Vol. 2: *Evidence Based Therapist Responsiveness*. 3rd ed. Oxford: Oxford University Press.

OPD Task Force. (2008). Operationalized Psychodynamic Diagnosis OPD-2. Manual of Diagnosis and Treatment Planning. Kirkland: Hogrefe and Huber.

Orange, D. M., Atwood, G. E., & Stolorow, R. D. (1997). *Working Intersubjectively: Contextualism in Psychoanalytic Practice.* Hillsdale, NJ: The Analytic Press.

Orlinsky, D. E., Rønnestad, M. H., & Willutzki, U. (2004). Fifty years of psychotherapy process-outcome research: Continuity and change. In M. J. Lambert (Ed.) *Handbook of Psychotherapy Research and Behavior Change.* Hoboken, NJ: John Wiley & Sons, pp. 307–389.

Otto, H. & Keller, H. (Ed.) (2014). *Different Faces of Attachment.* Cambridge: Cambridge University Press.

Oud, M., Arntz, A., Hermens, M. L., Verhoef, R., & Kendall, T. (2018). Specialized psychotherapies for adults with borderline personality disorder: A systematic review and meta-analysis. *The Australian and New Zealand Journal of Psychiatry* 52(10), 949–961. https://doi.org/10.1177/0004867418791257.

Park, B. K., Kim, M., & Young, L. (2021). An examination of accurate versus "biased" mentalizing in moral economic decision-making. In M. Gilead & K. Ochsner (Eds.) *The Neural Basis of Mentalizing.* Cham: Springer, pp. 537–553.

Premack, D. & Woodruff, G. (1978). Does the chimpanzee have a theory of mind? *The Behavioural and Brain Sciences* 1, 515–526

Rossouw, T. I. & Fonagy, P. (2012). Mentalization-based treatment for self-harm in adolescents: A randomized controlled trial. *Journal of the American Academy of Child and Adolescent Psychiatry*, 51(12), 1304–1313. https://doi.org/10.1016/j.jaac.2012.09.018.

Sandler, J. (1960). On the concept of superego. *The Psychoanalytic Study of the Child* 15, 128–162.

Sandler, J. (1962). The Hampstead Index as an instrument of psychoanalytic research. The *International Journal of Psychoanalysis* 43, 287–291.

Sandler, J. (1987). *From Safety to the Superego: Selected Papers of Joseph Sandler.* New York: Guilford Press.

Sandler, J. & Joffe, W. G. (1969). Towards a basic psychoanalytic model. *The International Journal of Psychoanalysis* 50(1), 79–90.

Sandler, J. & Rosenblatt, B. (1962). The concept of the representational world. *The Psychoanalytic Study of the Child* 17(1), 128–145

Schlicht, T. (2022). *Philosophy of Social Cognition.* Basingstoke: Palgrave Macmillan.

Schröder-Pfeifer, P., Georg, A., Zettl, M., & Taubner, S. (2020). Prozess des Mentalisierens in einer mentalisierungsbasierten Langzeittherapie für Borderline-Persönlichkeitsstörungen. *Psychotherapeut* 65, 357–365.

Schultz-Venrath, U. (2024). *Mentalizing the Body.* London: Routledge.

Semerari, A., Carcione, A., Dimaggio, G., Falcone, M., Nicolò, G., Procacci, M., & Alleva, G. (2003). How to evaluate metacognitive functioning in psychotherapy? The metacognition assessment scale and its applications. *Clinical Psychology & Psychotherapy* 10, 238–261. doi:10.1002/cpp.362.

Sharp, C., Ha, C., Carbone, C., Kim, S., Perry, K., Williams, L., & Fonagy, P. (2013). Hypermentalizing in adolescent inpatients: Treatment effects and association with borderline traits. *Journal of Personality Disorders* 27(1), 3–18. doi:10.1521/pedi.2013.27.1.3.

Sharp, C., Wright, A. G. C., Fowler, J. C., Frueh, B. C., Allen, J. G., Oldham, J., & Clark, L. A. (2015). The structure of personality pathology: Both general ($\rangle$g$\langle$) and specific ($\rangle$s$\langle$) factors? *Journal of Abnormal Psychology* 124(2), 387–398.

Simonsen, S., Bateman, A., Bohus, M., Dalewijk, H. J., Doering, S., Kaera, A., Moran, P., Renneberg, B., Ribaudi, J. S., Taubner, S., Wilberg, T., & Mehlum, L. (2019). European guidelines for personality disorders: Past, present and future. *Borderline Personality Disorder and Emotion Dysregulation* 6(9). https://doi.org/10.1186/s40479-019-0106-3.

Sperber, D., Clement, F., Heintz, C., Mascaro, O., Mercier, H., Origgi, G., & Wilson, D. (2010). Epistemic vigilance. *Mind & Language* 25(4), 359–393.

Sperber, D. & Wilson, D. (1995). *Relevance: Communication and Cognition.* Oxford: Blackwell.

Spitz, R. & Wolf, M. K. (1946). Anaclitic depression: An inquiry into the genesis of psychiatric conditions in early childhood. *Psychoanalytical Study of the Child* 2, 313–342.

Steel, C., MacDonald, J., & Schroder, T. (2018). A systematic review of the effect of therapists' internalized models of relationships on the quality of the therapeutic relationship. *Journal of Clinical Psychology* 74(1), 5–42.

Stern, D. (1985). *The Interpersonal World of the Infant: A View from Psychoanalysis and Development Psychology.* New York: Basic Books.

Stolorow, R. D., Brandchaft, B., & Atwood, G. E. (1987). *Psychoanalytic Treatment: An Intersubjective Approach.* Hillsdale, NJ: The Analytic Press.

Storebø, O. J., Stoffers-Winterling, J. M., Völlm, B. A., Kongerslev, M. T., Mattivi, J. T., Jørgensen, M. S., Faltinsen, E., Todorovac, A., Sales, C. P., Callesen, H. E., Lieb, K., & Simonsen, E. (2020). Psychological therapies for people with borderline personality disorder. *The Cochrane Database of Systematic Reviews* 5, CD012955. https://doi.org/10.1002/14651858.CD012955.pub2

Talia, A., Muzi, L., Linigiardi, V., & Taubner, S. (2020). How to be a secure base: Therapists' attachment representations and their link to attunement in psychotherapy. *Attachment & Human Development* 22(2), 189–206. doi:10.1080/14616734.2018.1534247.

Talia, A., Taubner, S., & Miller-Bottome, M. (2019). Advances in research on attachment-related psychotherapy processes: Seven teaching points for trainees and supervisors. *Research in Psychotherapy: Psychopathology, Process and Outcome* 22(3), 359–368. doi:10.4081/ripppo.2019.405.

Target, M. (2013). Ist unsere Sexualität unsere eigene? Ein Entwicklungsmodell der Sexualität auf der Basis früher Affektspiegelung. *Zeitschrift für Individualpsychologie* 38, 125–141

Target, M. (2015). A developmental model of sexual excitement, desire and alienation. In A. Lemma & P. E. Lynch (Eds.) *Sexualities: Contemporary Psychoanalytic Perspectives.* London: Routledge.

Target, M. (2016). Mentalization within intensive analysis with a borderline patient British. *Journal of Psychotherapy* 32(2), 202–214. doi:10.1111/bjp.12211.

Target, M. & Fonagy, P. (1996). Playing with reality: II. The development of psychic reality from a theoretical perspective. *The International Journal of Psychoanalysis* 77(3), 459–479.

Taubner, S., Curth, C., Unger, A., & Kotte, S. (2014). Die Mentalisierende Berufsausbildung –Praxisbericht aus einer Pilotstudie an einem Berufsbildungswerk für lernbehinderte Adoleszente. *Praxis der Kinderpsychologie und Kinderpsychiatrie* 63, 738–760.

Taubner, S., Fonagy, P., & Bateman, A. W. (2019). *Mentalisierungsbasierte Therapie.* (Fortschritte der Psychotherapie, Bd. 75.) Göttingen: Hogrefe. https://doi.org/10.1026/02834-000.

Taubner, S., Hauschild, S., Korhas, L., Kaess, M., Sobanski, E., Gablonski, T.-C., Schröder-Pfeifer, P., & Volkert, J. (2020). Mentalization-Based Treatment for Adolescents with Conduct Disorder (MBT-CD): Protocol of a Feasibility and Pilot Study. https://doi.org/ 10.21203/rs.3.rs-63999/v1.

Taubner, S., Hörz, S., Fischer-Kern, M., Doering, S., Buchheim, A., & Zimmermann, J. (2013). Internal structure of the Reflective Functioning Scale. *Psychological Assessment* 25(1), 127–135. https://doi.org/10.1037/a0029138.

Taubner, S., Klasen, J., & Munder, T. (2014). Why do psychotherapists participate in psychotherapy research and why not? Results of the Attitudes to Psychotherapy Research Questionnaire with a sample of experienced German psychotherapists. *Psychotherapy Research* 26(3), 318–331. https://doi.org/10.1080/10503307.2014.938256.

Taubner, S. & Sevecke, K. (2015). Kernmodell der Mentalisierungsbasierten Therapie. *Psychotherapeut* 60, 169–184.

Taylor, J. B. (2008). *My Stroke of Insight: A Brain Scientist's Personal Journey*. London: Hodder & Stoughton.

Thomä, H. & Kächele, H. (2011). *Psychoanalytic Practice*, Vol. 1 *Principles*. Cham: Springer.

Tomasello, M. (2014). *A Natural History of Human Thinking*. Cambridge, MA: Harvard University Press.

Tyrer, P., Mulder, R., Kim, Y.-R., & Crawford, M. J. (2019). The Development of the ICD-11 Classification of Personality Disorders: An amalgam of science, pragmatism, and politics. *Annual Review of Clinical Psychology* 15, 481–502. https://doi.org/10.1146/annurev-clinpsy-050718-095736.

Vermote, R., Lowyck, B., Vandeneede, B., Bateman, A., & Luyten, P. (2012). Psychodynamically Oriented Therapeutic Settings. In A. Bateman & P. Fonagy (Eds.) *Handbook of Mentalizing in Mental Health Practice*. Washington, DC: American Psychiatric Publishing, pp. 247–273.

Volkert, J., Hauschild, S., & Taubner, S. (2019). Mentalization-Based Treatment for Personality Disorders: Efficacy, Effectiveness, and New Developments. *Current Psychiatry Reports*, 21(4), 25. https://doi.org/10.1007/s11920-019-1012-5.

Wampold, B. E. (2015). How important are the common factors in psychotherapy? An update. *World Psychiatry* 14(3), 270–277. dos: 10.1002/ wps.20238.

Wampold, B. E. & Imel, Z. E. (2015). *The Great Psychotherapy Debate: The Evidence for What Makes Psychotherapy Work*. 2nd ed. London: Routledge.

Wampold, B. E., Imel, Z. E., Laska, K. M., Benish, S., Miller, S. D., Flückiger, C., Del Re, A. C., Baardseth, T. P., & Budge, S. (2010). Determining what works in the treatment of PTSD. *Clinical Psychology Review* 30(8), 923–933. doi:10.1016/j.cpr.2010.06.005.

Webb, C. A., DeRubeis, R. J., & Barber, J. P. (2010). Therapist adherence/competence and treatment outcome: A meta-analytic review. *Journal of Consulting and Clinical Psychology*, 78(2), 200–211. https://doi.org/10.1037/a0018912.

Wellman, H. M., Cross, D., & Watson, J. (2001). Meta-analysis of theory-of-mind development: The truth about false belief. *Child Development* 72(3), 655–684.

White, K. (2019). Rezension von Mary Target (2016): Mentalisation within intensive analysis. *British Journal of Psychotherapy* 32(2), 202–214.

Wilson, D. & Sperber, D. (2012). *Meaning and Relevance*. Cambridge: Cambridge University Press.

Wimmer, H. & Perner, J. (1983). Beliefs about beliefs: Representation and constraining function of wrong beliefs in young children's understanding of deception. *Cognition* 13, 103–128.

Wininger, M., Datler, W., & Dörr, M. (2013). Psychoanalyse in der Pädagogik der frühen Kindheit. In M. Wininger, W. Datler & M. Dörr (Eds.). *Psychoanalytische Pädagogik der frühen Kindheit*. Opladen: Barbara Budrich, pp. 7–22.

Winnicott, D. W. (1962a). Ego integration and child development. In D. W. Winnicott (Ed.) *The Maturational Processes and the Facilitating Environment: Studies in the Theory of Emotional Development*. London: Karnac Books, pp. 56–63.

Winnicott, D. W. (Ed.) (1962b). *The Maturational Processes and the Facilitating Environment: Studies in the Theory of Emotional Development*. London: Karnac Books.

World Health Organization. (2020). International statistical classification of diseases and related health problems. 11th ed. https://icd.who.int/en.

Yamagishi, T. (2001). Trust as a form of social intelligence. In K. Cook (Ed.) *Trust in Society*. New York: Russel Sage Foundation, pp. 121–147.

Yamagishi, T. (2011). Trust and Social Intelligence. In I. Wakeman, E. Gudes, C. D. Jensen, & J. Crampton (Ed.) *Trust Management V. IFIPTM 2011*. (IFIP Advances in Information and Communication Technology, Bd. 358.) Berlin/Heidelberg: Springer.

Yamagishi, T., Kikuchi, M. & Kosugi, M. (1999). Trust, gullibility, and social intelligence. *Asian Journal of Social Psychology* 2(1), 145–161.

Yeomans, F. E., Clarkin, J. F., & Kernberg, O. F. (2015). Transference-focused psychotherapy for borderline personality disorder: A clinical guide. Washington, DC: APA. doi:10.1176/appi.books.9781615371006.

Zettl, M., Volkert, J., Vögele, C., Herpertz, S. C., Kubera, K. M., & Taubner, S. (2020). Mentalization and criterion of the alternative model for personality disorders: Results from a clinical and nonclinical sample. *Personality Disorders* 11(3), 191–201. https://doi.org/10.1037/per0000356.

Index